AUSTRIAN STUDIES is a new annual volume reflecting a growing interest in the distinctive cultural traditions of the Habsburg Empire and the Austrian Republic. By publishing a wide range of articles and book reviews in English, it aims to make recent research accessible to a broadly based international readership.

THE FOCUS is on Austrian culture from 1750 to the present and treats literature in relation to psychology, philosophy, political theory, music, theatre and the visual arts. 'Austrian' includes the German-language culture of former areas of the Habsburg Empire, such as Prague and the Bukovina, as well as the work of people of Austrian origin living abroad. Austrian interactions with other linguistic and ethnic groups (for example the Jewish communities of Austria-Hungary) are also taken into account.

LITERARY CRITICS & CULTURAL HISTORIANS will find Austrian Studies a useful forum for their work. The editors and contributors believe that literary texts and intellectual theories need to be securely situated in their historic context if they are to reveal their true significance. The emphasis in the first volume is on literary studies, while future numbers will include an extended range of contextual investigations.

THE EDITORS are both well-known proponents of this multi-disciplinary approach. Edward Timms (University of Cambridge) is author of *Karl Kraus: Apocalyptic Satirist - Culture and Catastrophe in Habsburg Vienna*. Ritchie Robertson (University of Oxford) is author of *Kafka: Judaism, Politics and Literature*.

Vienna 1900
From Altenberg to Wittgenstein

Edited by Edward Timms and Ritchie Robertson
AUSTRIAN STUDIES 1

Vienna 1900
From Altenberg to Wittgenstein

Edited by Edward Timms and Ritchie Robertson

AUSTRIAN STUDIES 1

EDINBURGH UNIVERSITY PRESS

© Edinburgh University Press 1990
22 George Square, Edinburgh

Set in Linotron Ehrhardt by
Koinonia, Bury, and
printed in Great Britain by
The Alden Press, Oxford

British Library Cataloguing
  in Publication Data
Vienna 1900: from Altenberg to
  Wittgenstein. – (Austrian studies).
1. Austria. Vienna. Intellectual life,
  1815-1919
I. Timms, Edward II. Robertson,
  Ritchie III. Series
  943.61304

ISBN 0 7486 0169 4
ISBN 0 7486 0175 9 pbk

Contents

Contents

PART THREE: REVIEWS

Contents

List of illustrations

Notes on contributors

HARRIET ANDERSON wrote her doctoral dissertation at University College London on the Austrian feminist Rosa Mayreder. Her edition of Mayreder's diaries, *Tagebücher 1873–1937*, was published by Insel Verlag in 1988. She is now giving courses on women's history at Vienna University and writing a more detailed account of the Austrian women's movement.

NEAL ASCHERSON writes for the London *Observer* and *Sunday Independent*, and has a special interest in Central European affairs. His most recent book is a collection of essays, *Games with Shadows* (Radius, 1988).

ANDREW BARKER is Senior Lecturer in German at the University of Edinburgh. He is working on a book on Peter Altenberg.

DAGMAR BARNOUW is Professor of German at the University of Southern California. Her most recent book is *Weimar Intellectuals and the Threat of Modernity* (Indiana University Press, 1988).

STEVEN BELLER, formerly Fellow in History at Peterhouse, Cambridge, is the author of *Vienna and the Jews, 1867–1938: A Cultural History* (Cambridge University Press, 1989).

LESLIE BODI is Emeritus Professor of German at Monash University, Melbourne, and the author of *Tauwetter in Wien: Zur Prosa der österreichischen Aufklärung 1781–1795* (S. Fischer Verlag, 1977).

PETER BRANSCOMBE is Professor of Austrian Studies at the University of St Andrews. He edited (with E. Badura-Skoda) *Schubert Studies: Problems of Style and Chronology* (Cambridge University Press, 1982).

GEOFFREY BUTLER, who has a special interest in English translations of German fiction, has just retired from the Chair of German at the University of Bath.

PAUL CONNERTON is author of *The Tragedy of Enlightenment: An Essay on the Frankfurt School* (Cambridge University Press, 1980) and *How Societies Remember* (Cambridge University Press, 1989).

IAN FOSTER is Lektor in English at Zürich University. He has just completed a Cambridge Ph.D. thesis on the literary representation of the army in turn-of-the-century Austrian fiction.

SANDER L. GILMAN is Goldwin Smith Professor of Humane Studies at Cornell University. Besides teaching in the Departments of German and Near Eastern

Studies there, he is Professor of the History of Psychiatry at Cornell Medical College in New York. The most recent of his numerous books are *Jewish Self-Hatred: Anti-Semitism and the Hidden Language of the Jews* (Johns Hopkins University Press, 1986) and *Disease and Representation: Images of Illness from Madness to AIDS* (Cornell University Press, 1988).

MARGARET JACOBS is a Fellow of St Hugh's College, Oxford. She has published numerous articles on the German and Austrian theatre.

LEO A. LENSING is Professor of German at Wesleyan University, Middletown, Connecticut, and author of a study of Wilhelm Raabe. He is at work on a biography of Karl Kraus.

JACQUES LE RIDER (University of Paris XII — Val de Marne) is the author of *Le cas Otto Weininger: Racines de l'antiféminisme et de l'antisémitisme* (Paris, 1982; German translation published by Löcker Verlag, 1985). His contribution to this volume is a condensed version of the central argument of his dissertation, *Modernité viennoise et crises d'identité (thèse de doctorat d'État)* presented at the Sorbonne on 9 May 1989 and scheduled for publication in 1990 by Presses Universitaires de France.

RALPH MANHEIM's career as a translator began in the early 1940s with his English version of Konrad Heiden's *Der Führer*. Since then he has translated over a hundred volumes, including works by Brecht, Canetti, Céline, Grass, Handke, Heidegger, and Proust. He now lives in Cambridge, England, and is working on a study of Günter Grass.

DAVID MIDGLEY is Fellow in German at St John's College, Cambridge, and author of *Arnold Zweig: Eine Einführung in Leben und Werk* (Athenäum Verlag, 1987).

RITCHIE ROBERTSON is Fellow and Tutor in German at St John's College, Oxford, and author of *Kafka: Judaism, Politics, and Literature* (Oxford University Press, 1985; German translation published by Metzler, 1988). He is now working on a study of Elias Canetti.

W. G. SEBALD is Professor in the School of Modern Languages and European History at the University of East Anglia, and author of *Die Beschreibung des Unglücks: Zur österreichischen Literatur von Stifter bis Handke* (Residenz Verlag, 1985).

J. P. STERN is Emeritus Professor of German at University College London. His many books include *Re-interpretations: Seven Studies in Nineteenth-Century German Literature* (1964; reprinted by Cambridge University Press, 1981) and *Hitler: The Führer and the People* (Fontana, 1975). He is now at work on a study of German and Austrian literature in the early twentieth century, to be entitled *The Dear Purchase*.

EDWARD TIMMS is Fellow in German at Gonville and Caius College, Cambridge, and the author of *Karl Kraus, Apocalyptic Satirist* (Yale University Press, 1986). He is now working on a sequel dealing with Austrian literature and politics in the 1920s and 1930s, and would be glad to hear from anyone with memories of that period.

REINHARD URBACH, formerly *Dramaturg* at the Burgtheater, is now Director of the *Theater der Jugend* in Vienna, and has published widely on Austrian literature, particularly Schnitzler.

ANDREW WEBBER is a lecturer in German at Queen Mary College London, and is the author of *Sexuality and the Sense of Self in the Works of Georg Trakl and Robert Musil*, No. 15 in the Bithell Series of Dissertations (Modern Humanities Research Association, 1990)

EWAN WEST is Research Fellow in Music at Mansfield College, Oxford. He is working on a study of the Viennese *Lied*.

ROBERT WISTRICH is Professor of History at the Hebrew University of Jerusalem. His most recent book is *The Jews of Vienna in the Age of Franz Joseph* (Oxford University Press, 1989).

W. E. YATES is Professor of German at the University of Exeter. His books include *Grillparzer* and *Nestroy* (both published by Cambridge University Press in 1972), and he is one of the editors of the new edition of Nestroy.

HARRY ZOHN is Chairman of the Department of Germanic and Slavic Languages at Brandeis University, Waltham, Massachusetts. His most recent book is '*ich bin ein Sohn der deutschen Sprache nur. . .': Jüdisches Erbe in der österreichischen Literatur* (Amalthea Verlag, 1986). His many translations include selections from Karl Kraus.

Preface

The launching of a new yearbook under the general title *Austrian Studies* reflects a growing interest in the distinctive cultural traditions of the Habsburg Empire and the Austrian Republic. The aim is to make the findings of recent research accessible to a broadly based international readership by publishing in English a wide range of articles and book reviews.

The focus will be on Austrian culture from 1750 to the present (including literature, psychology, philosophy, political theory, music, theatre and the visual arts). The term 'Austrian' is used in an extended sense to include the German-language culture of former areas of the Habsburg Empire, like Prague or the Bukovina, as well as the work of people of Austrian origin living abroad. Interactions with other linguistic and ethnic groups will also be taken into account, not least with the Jewish communities of Austria–Hungary.

It is hoped to attract contributions from many different countries and disciplines. The emphasis in this first volume is on literary studies. However, the assumption shared by all our contributors is that literary texts and intellectual theories need to be firmly situated in their historical context if they are to acquire their full significance. The aim in future numbers will be to extend the range of these contextual investigations, so that *Austrian Studies* provides a forum for both literary critics and cultural historians.

The focus on Vienna 1900 in this first number reflects the inherent appeal of Viennese modernism, which – as Jacques Le Rider suggests in the opening article – anticipates some of the dilemmas of contemporary postmodernism. Subsequent articles draw on new archival and biographical sources in order to reassess the achievements of key figures like Altenberg, Kraus, Schnitzler, Freud, and Wittgenstein, as well as neglected authors like Gustav Sieber, Fritz Wittels, and the early Austrian feminists. The theme of 'femininity', which links the debates about racial and sexual 'difference', forms a leitmotif which is also reflected in our cover design.

The second number of *Austrian Studies*, for which articles have already been commissioned, will focus on the Enlightenment and its aftermath. Subsequent numbers will be devoted to the origins of psychoanalysis (No.3), the performing arts (No.4), and the problem of defining national identity in a multinational context (No.5).

Preface

The editors welcome comments on this first number and suggestions for the future. Books for review should be sent to Dr Ritchie Robertson, St John's College, Oxford. Proposals for articles for possible inclusion in future numbers of *Austrian Studies* should be addressed to Dr Edward Timms, Gonville and Caius College, Cambridge. Further details, including guidelines for the submission of typescripts, are given on our final page.

Part One

Between Modernism and Postmodernism

The Viennese Identity Crisis

Jacques Le Rider

(translated by Ralph Manheim)

Certain aspects of Viennese modernism (*die Wiener Moderne*), which flourished between 1890 and 1910, can be explained by the socio-economic backwardness of Vienna as compared with London, Paris or Berlin. A similar backwardness (often a source of fruitful originality) can also be observed in the cultural field. The persistence of specifically Austrian traditions excluded Austria from the major currents of German thought. Austrian philosophers stood aloof from the post-Kantian movement, while Naturalism in art as well as literature never took root in Vienna. In the late 1880s Viennese intellectuals looked to Berlin with a certain envy. Hermann Bahr wrote in his memoirs: 'Up there they've had Sedan, Bismarck and Wagner. What have we had?'[1]

The reaction of Vienna's artists and thinkers to German preponderance, to the apparent solidity of the Reich, and to the prestige of German *Kultur* was to withdraw into themselves. While the Naturalists were preoccupied with physical realities, the Viennese explored the psyche. In other words, the individual and his inner life were investigated at the expense of social militancy and realistic exposition. Carl E. Schorske has shown that the political disillusionment engendered by the rise of anti-Semitism led Sigmund Freud to neutralise politics by reducing it to psychological categories.

However, despite the temporary setback caused by the stock market crash of 1873, the relative economic and social backwardness of the Austrian part of the dual monarchy was, in part, corrected by compensatory trends. In Vienna, the most striking of these was undoubtedly the increase in population, largely due, as in other big cities of Europe, to immigration. The ethnic minorities most abundantly represented were the Czechs and the Jews, followed at a distance by the Poles and Hungarians. In 1900 Vienna, like London and Paris, was a city of contrasts – on the one hand, the conspicuously wealthy; and on the other, an impoverished proletariat living under inhuman conditions. Under a Liberal, and later a Christian Social administration, the city was considerably modernised by a succession of large-scale public works projects.

In the 1850s and 1860s Vienna had lagged behind Budapest and Berlin in economic and social progress. In the two decades preceding the First World War, however, the three capitals developed at roughly the same pace, and

1

experienced similar social dislocations and changes in life-style. Thus, the notorious Viennese strategy of 'muddling through' ('Fortwursteln') was inspired largely by political problems. Observers have long been struck by the discrepancy between a neo-absolutist government encumbered by archaic survivals and a considerably modernised society. By the turn of the century the gains of 1848 had been voided of their content. The Christian Social and Social Democratic parties, which dominated political life after the decline of the Liberals, were unable to take control of the central bureaucracy or to offer a solution to the nationalities problem. The Pan-German movement, the xeno-phobia aroused by the growth of the Czech colony, and the spread of anti-Semitism made Vienna an ethnic battlefield rather than a melting pot.

For want of political outlets, many Viennese intellectuals were drawn to alternative strategies, such as the Pan-Germanist Wagnerianism of the young Hermann Bahr or of Otto Weininger; the Zionist movement in reaction to the rise of anti-Semitism; the aestheticism and introversion of the young writers and artists disillusioned by the collapse of liberalism. All these trends have one thing in common: whether drawing inspiration from historical traditions or seeking regenerative forces in art, they unconsciously fell in with the natural inclinations of the governing class. The 'Habsburg myth' (Claudio Magris) upheld by the ruling house had its counterpart in the new Germanic, biblical, or aesthetic mythologies of the intellectuals striving to fill the vacuum created by the nonexistence of an 'Austro-Hungarian' nationality. In the case of the assimilated Jews of Vienna this insecurity, linked to the quest for a national identity, was also the source of remarkable creative attitudes.

The Viennese 'moderns', products of a recent and still incomplete moderni-sation, are distinguished by the fact that they were less aggressive than those of other world capitals, and more respectful of the 'ancients'. Adolf Loos was a 'conservative revolutionary', an admirer of Biedermeier and the classicism of 1800. Karl Kraus was devoted to Nestroy, and Schoenberg was not above doing pastiches of Johann Strauss. Hofmannsthal and his group defined themselves as heirs to a grand tradition no less than as innovators. Viennese modernism was not a triumphant movement. It never threw off a strong sense of loss, a feeling that the world was falling apart and that something should be done about it. The Viennese moderns seldom thought of treating their malaise as a political problem. Although they embraced modernity as an inescapable necessity, they conceived of it in aesthetic, ethical or psychological, but always individualist terms. Without exception, they were marked by Nietzsche's contempt for such 'modern' ideas as democracy, historicism, scientism, or progress.

Yet some of the leaders of Viennese modernism took a more optimistic view. The career of the literary critic Hermann Bahr typifies a modernism combining a belief in Darwinian evolution with a naively Marxist faith in progress. The key word in his pronouncements is *überwinden*, the need to 'surmount' the past. 'Above all,' he wrote in 1887, 'no settling down, no permanency, no stasis. Anything new is better than the old, if only because it is younger.'[2] What seems specifically Viennese in this critic, always eager to champion the latest 'ism', is that for him modernism in the last analysis meant only one thing, the reign of individualism. The modern creator, he held, puts his trust in no school, no rule, no tradition; he recognises only one law, that of his nerves, his instinct, his subjectivity.

Baudelaire observed that 'the modern is the transient, the fugitive, the contingent: it is one half of art, the other being the eternal and immutable'.[3] For Bahr, the uneasiness provoked by the transient character of modernism finds its corrective in an affirmation of the individual genius of the creative artist, which, transcending all metamorphoses, guarantees the coherence and legitimacy of his undertaking. The modern concept of genius is the culmination of aesthetic individualism. Weininger devoted a detailed study to genius. Klimt, Loos, Kraus and Schoenberg believed in genius as the ultimate justification of the modernist project. The most critical minds of the time – Freud, Musil, and Wittgenstein – took a profound interest in the problem of genius.

The Viennese experience figures prominently in present-day discussions of postmodernism. The moderns of turn-of-the-century Vienna may well have prefigured certain central themes of postmodernism: the triumph and crisis of individualism (as defined by Louis Dumont and Gilles Lipovetsky); [4] the quest for mythologies capable of regenerating modern culture (from the 'total art work' of the Secession to Zionism and the various nationalisms); and the questioning of scientific and technical rationality (through the critique of language, Husserl's analysis of the inherent corruption of rational science, the critique both of functionalism and of ornament). Living in a socio-economic and political environment that long remained premodern, the Viennese intellectuals and artists were particularly alert to the crises engendered in society as well as in private life by the accelerated process of modernisation begun at the end of the nineteenth century. This specific situation no doubt explains why Viennese modernism presents in many ways the appearance of a postmodern moment in the history of European culture.

In support of his thesis that in postmodern culture 'the question of the legitimation of knowledge is formulated in different terms', Jean-François Lyotard notes (in *The Postmodern Condition*) that 'grand narrative [*le grand récit*] has lost its credibility, regardless of what mode of unification it uses, regardless of whether it is a speculative narrative or a narrative of emancipation'. It is this very pessimism which inspired the early twentieth-century generation of Viennese artists and thinkers (here Lyotard cites Musil, Kraus, Hofmannsthal, Loos, Schoenberg, and Broch, as well as Mach and Wittgenstein): 'They carried awareness of and theoretical and artistic responsibility for delegitimation as far as it could be taken.'[5]

'Vienna 1880–1939: A Joyful Apocalypse' was the title of an exhibition held in 1986 at the Centre Pompidou in Paris. This highly significant event was conceived by Jean Clair, author of *Considérations sur l'état des beaux-arts: Critique de la modernité*, an interesting contribution to the discussion of postmodernism.[6] In his preface to the catalogue, entitled 'A Sceptical Modernism', Jean Clair attacks the sterile academicism of the avant-garde movements, for ever striving to outstrip each other. The history of art, he declares, remains to be rewritten; but this will be possible only after the conformism which judges art works by

3

the criterion of 'progress towards abstraction' has been rejected. And he speaks of Viennese modernism as a privileged site for the archaeology of postmodernism. Certain observers, as was to be expected, accused Jean Clair and his associates of *Passéisme* and neoconservatism.

I myself prefer to stress another aspect of 'Viennese postmodernism': the crisis of modern individualism and its corollary, the identity crisis. In linking these two crises, I go back to the analyses of Georg Simmel, who saw individualism as an essential component of modern existence and showed that modern man, responsible only to himself for his values, lives in a state of permanent anxiety. 'For the essence of modernity is the psychologism that leads us to experience and interpret the world in accordance with the reactions of our inner life as an inner world; this means the disintegration of stable contents in the unstable element of the psyche . . . .'[7] Most critics regard individualism, that quintessentially modern achievement, as a mixed blessing; they accept it as an ethical, logical, aesthetic desideratum, but at the same time regard it as a danger to culture. Schopenhauer and Nietzsche analysed the illusions and evils of individualism, and this critique is carried over into the psychology and sociology of the late nineteenth and early twentieth centuries.

In the Vienna of 1900, the fading of political perspectives accentuated the triumph of individualist values, which brought with them an unmistakable desocialisation of the individual. The crisis of individualism, experienced in the form of a crisis of the subjective sense of identity, was at the centre of the preoccupations of literature and the sciences as represented by Hofmannsthal, Freud or Mach. Psychoanalysis reflects the human condition in an era of identity crisis. One might go so far as to say that in psychoanalysis the notion of identity vanishes, to be replaced by a relatively unstable series of identifications.

The identity crisis plays a central part in Musil's novels and in his theoretical work as well. In *The Man Without Qualities*, Musil, a contemporary of Viennese modernism, who subsequently, during the 1920s and 1930s, became a critical and detached analyst of that phenomenon, formulated observations that are fundamental to the present discussion. On the one hand, he made it clear that most of his contemporaries were trying their best to escape their identity crisis by running after the first will-o'-the-wisp, however irrational, that presented itself. On the other, he suggested that this loss of identity could prove exceedingly fruitful, since it made possible a salutary deconstruction of the sterile conventions and constraints that weigh on society. It thus provides a *tabula rasa* on which the maxims of a new ethic could be written.

In response to their feelings of solitude, ego-fragility, and instability in their inner identifications as well as their outward identities, certain creative minds at the turn of the century explored possibilities of rebuilding an identity by means of what was called a radicalised individualism. The mystic (in Hofmannsthal, for instance), the genius (as perceived by Weininger), and Narcissus (as reinterpreted by Lou Andreas-Salomé) would seem to be the three main typifications of the individual cut off from all human community, of the introverted ego directly interacting with the reality of the world. This affirmation of individual identity necessitates the reformulation of a philosophy of the identity of mind and being, the unity of subject and object.

In reality, these types (the mystic, the genius, and Narcissus) are under constant threat, dependent as they are on passing moments of beatitude or quickly dissipated illusions of omnipotence. Their inevitable collapse plunges the individual into aggravated feelings of discontinuity and identity loss. These utopias of mysticism, genius and narcissism as forms of existence have in common the striving to transcend the limitations imposed by life; they negate the male/female dichotomy and tend towards an androgynous ideal; they aim at the auto-destruction of a self that suffers because it cannot accept its contingent qualities (sex, race, etc.) and at the creation of a more perfect self.

In this perspective, it becomes possible to read the theoretical constructions of Otto Weininger's *Sex and Character* (comparable, though in a rationalised form, to the lucubrations of Daniel Paul Schreber in *Memoirs of my Nervous Illness*) and certain of the young Hofmannsthal's writings (e.g., his *Tale of the 672nd Night*) as accounts of mystical crises or of narcissistic psychoneuroses connected with disruption of sexual identity. The breakdown of male identity is the theme which suggests a connection between these three authors. It was Otto Weininger's obsession with the feminine, coupled with his anguished hostility to women, which inspired him to excoriate the decadence of the times. This also led him to formulate a programme for the regeneration of the modern world which – paradoxically enough – seems characteristic of a type of anti-modernist critique based on the battle of the sexes, running from Friedrich Nietzsche to Ludwig Klages and Walter Benjamin, and specifically in Vienna from Karl Kraus to Robert Musil. The case of Otto Gross deserves special attention in this context, because his situation was the exact opposite of Weininger's. Whereas the author of *Sex and Character*, reacting against the supposed feminisation of modern culture, carried misogyny to an extreme, the work of the maverick psychoanalyst Otto Gross culminates in an appeal for a revolution of womanhood and the abolition of father-right. The problem for contemporary feminism, wrote Rosa Mayreder in 1905, is no longer male despotism but the inability of men to administer the world order they have fashioned.

In the *Kulturkritik* of the early years of the twentieth century, another figure that features as prominently as 'the male' and 'the female' is 'the Jew'. Visions of the feminisation of culture have a parallel in visions of its 'Judaisation'; the antifeminism of certain critics of modern life follows a logic similar to that of anti-Semitism. Indeed, this analogy characterises a marked feature of the culture of the period: the relationship between, on the one hand, the crisis of male identity and the redistribution of roles between men and women, and, on the other, the confrontation between Jews and non-Jews. Historical and social analysis shows that the movement to liberate women and the movement to liberate the Jews experienced parallel successes, failures, and contradictions. Freudian theory finds a common unconscious root in anti-feminism and anti-Semitism. In the work of Arthur Schnitzler, the woman and the Jew share the difficult and sometimes tragic role of hero and victim of modern life. Adorno and Horkheimer (in their *Dialectic of Enlightenment*) also noted this parallel

5

between the lot of women and of the Jews in the modern age; both, they found, are victims *par excellence* of logico-identificatory and instrumental reason; both incarnate the individual striving to rescue the self from the mutilations of identificatory and falsely universalist thinking. If we review the thinking of Adorno and Horkheimer in the light of recent discussions of postmodernism, the woman and the Jew would seem, in the *Dialectic of Enlightenment*, to represent a new form of subjectivity which no longer corresponds to the rigid unity of the bourgeois subject but reveals a more fluid, flexible identity.

The historical situation of assimilated Jewish intellectuals in Vienna enables us to understand why they were especially prone to the modern identity crisis. The Jewish students who attended the University of Vienna during the last three decades of the nineteenth century all had to contend with anti-Semitism. The liberal assumption, inherited from 1848, that the Jews would gradually be assimilated into Viennese society and culture was brutally called into question. Their social environment denied them the identity they would spontaneously have chosen, that of German nationality. At the same time, their German education cut them off very largely from traditional Judaism. Constantly reminded of their Jewish identity, first by their enemies, then by the numerous Jewish movements that grew up in Vienna during the last quarter of the nineteenth century, they were compelled to redefine the word 'Jew' and the meaning of their Jewishness.

Ordinarily, when anti-Semitism is considered as a product of the identity crisis, it is the identity crisis of the anti-Semite that first comes to mind. Shaken by economic and demographic changes, incapable of forging a true sense of national identity, Viennese society was a privileged breeding place for the kind of identity crisis that seeks its compensations and derivatives in anti-Semitism. The case of the assimilated Jew is more complex, for here a single individual combines, on the one hand, the non-Jew with his identity pathology and, on the other, the Jew with his forgotten Judaism and the Jewishness of his actual experience, in short, the 'imaginary Jew'.[8]

The case of Sigmund Freud is particularly interesting. Determined not to deny his 'Jewishness', he nevertheless rejected in the main the religious traditions of Judaism and took a critical view of his fellow Jews. In *The Interpretation of Dreams* Freud's Jewishness seems anchored in his unconscious, but more often than not it is associated with humiliations and injustices suffered. It was a long and subtle development that led Freud to his last word on Jewish identity in *Moses and Monotheism*. This book does not represent a return to the religious sources of Judaism, but, on the contrary, a surprisingly free and sometimes provocative reinvention of a Jewish identity. Sigmund Freud's Jewishness first manifested itself in his self-analysis; it found its final formulation in a 'historical novel', whose hero, Moses, might well be regarded as an autobiographical projection and final identification of the man Sigmund Freud. Another Viennese Jew, Theodor Herzl, dreamt of becoming the modern Moses of the Jewish people. A comparison between these two lives reveals the enormous difference between them, but also explains why Freud ran into Herzl in one of the dreams recorded in *The Interpretation of Dreams*, and why he followed the progress of the Zionist movement with sympathy, though he never gave it his full support.

Paradoxically, it might be said that Karl Kraus, regarded by his admirers as the very embodiment of the critical mind free from all allegiances, often gave evidence of conformism when the question of his Jewish identity was raised. Although he did everything in his power to dissociate himself from the Viennese intellectual community, he longed all his life for complete assimilation into German culture and above all its language. Anything that seemed to cast doubt on this assimilation provoked passionate and, it must be said, none too convincing reactions in Kraus. He came out in support of the anti-Dreyfusards and, in commenting on a ritual murder trial that exposed a Jew to the worst anti-Semitic prejudices, his main concern was to dispel any suspicion of 'Jewish solidarity'. He opened the pages of *Die Fackel* to Houston Stewart Chamberlain, whom he showered with praise, and took every opportunity to express his contempt for Heinrich Heine. Would it be an exaggeration in Kraus's case to speak of 'Jewish self-hatred'?

Among the literary representatives of 'young Vienna', Richard Beer-Hofmann was alone in defending and glorifying the Jewish identity. His novel *Der Tod Georgs* begins with a critique of the Jewish mind that has forgotten Judaism and been corrupted by individualistic aestheticism. Following a schema that reminds one of Maurice Barrès's trilogy *Le culte du moi*, the 'cult of the self' leads to the rediscovery of a 'national energy'. Beer-Hofmann's originality consists in representing the affirmation of Jewish identity as a deepening of his protagonist's narcissism. To paraphrase Nietzsche's formula, he seems to suggest that Judaism can be justified only as an aesthetic phenomenon. This unorthodox reconstruction of Jewish identity takes on its full meaning when placed in the context of revivalist movements like the *jungjüdische Bewegung* and cultural Zionism, developed in the early years of the century by Martin Buber and his circle.

In analysing the crisis of culture reflected in the destabilisation of individual roles and identities, I have stressed two factors: on the one hand, the threat to male identity represented by the disruption of sexual codes of conduct and sensibility, and, on the other, the vicissitudes of the Jewish identity, undermined by assimilation, brutally reawakened by the provocations of anti-Semitism, and finally reconstructed in every individual by a difficult, often traumatic and sometimes unsuccessful process of 'working through' (Freud's *Durcharbeitung*). These two illustrations of the loss of pre-established identities, of the hazardous and always uncertain redefinition of differences, and of the lone individual undertaking to correct the disorder of the world, enable us to define Viennese modernism more precisely in the spirit of Hermann Bahr's aphorism (of 1889): 'Modernism is everything that comes after the failure of individualism: everything that is not there but is in process of becoming.'[9]

This approach makes it possible to confirm our contention that certain major themes of the *Kulturkritik* of the 1970s and 1980s were prefigured in the Viennese modernism of 1900, and to understand more clearly the Viennese vogue that has swept Europe and North America in the last ten or twelve years.

7

In retrospect we can say that interest in the German world has momentarily moved from the Weimar period, the fascination of which was felt in the 1950s and 1960s, to the years of Viennese modernism. This shift has gone hand in hand with the turn of the intellectual public away from revolutionary commitment and social critique. Interest has shifted from *homo politicus* to *homo psychologicus*. And the result has been a more complex conception of 'modernism', linked by Carl E. Schorske, the pioneer of Viennese studies, with what Heinz Kohut has called 'reshuffling of the self'.[10] Historical changes not only obliged the individual to forge a new identity but also forced entire social groups to rethink or discard extinct systems of belief. Liberal culture, Schorske points out, believed in a rational man who would master nature by means of science and master himself with the help of ethics. In the modernism of 1900, the man of reason conceived as an ideal gave way to a more unstable, changeable individual on the lookout for new forms of life and in constant danger of seeing his individualism engulfed by new collectivities.

Henri Meschonnic has recently ridiculed the 'joyful apocalypse operation' mounted by the organisers of the 'Vienna 1880–1938' exhibition at the Centre Pompidou: 'This cradle of modernism,' he writes, 'has become a coffin. I suggest that if you look closely you will recognize it as your own.' Our *fin de siècle*, says Henri Meschonnic, likes to represent the era of Viennese modernism as a period dominated by decadence and by a premonition of 'the last days of mankind', in order to convince itself that in history, as E. M. Cioran puts it, 'only the periods of decline are captivating'.[11] All this, according to Meschonnic, shows a morbid penchant for decrepitude and decay.

And yet the pessimism of Hermann Broch and Ludwig Wittgenstein, faced with the cultural void of the age and the difficulties encountered by the individual looking for ground to stand on and finding no support in any collective norm, should not make us forget that this deconstruction of identities was also a source of projects for the regeneration of mankind. Habermas recalls that Adorno sometimes spoke of Peter Altenberg's well-known 'neurasthenia' as an example of individualism carried to the extreme, a last hiding place where a private life could escape from the control of totalitarian authorities and allegiances, anticipating a freer conception of mankind.[12]

In an article entitled 'Individuality', published in *Prodromos* in 1906, Altenberg proclaims: 'In so far as individuality has any justification or even a semblance of justification, it must be nothing other than a beginning, a forerunner within some sort of organic development of mankind as such, which, however, must be consonant with the natural potentialities for development of all human beings.'[13] Egon Friedell presented his essay on Peter Altenberg as a 'natural history' of the human race in process of mutation.[14] The reduction of individual existence to a more and more simplified, more and more nonconformist and marginal life, would create the *tabula rasa* on which it would be possible to build a better form of existence, freed from all cultural conventions. Behind the nonchalance of the Bohemian poet and idler, Peter Altenberg concealed the wisdom of an ironic prophet.

Thomas Mann, who prized Altenberg's writings, pointed out that his pose

8

parodied Nietzsche's *Ecce Homo*.[15] And, indeed, Altenberg might have been called the Zarathustra of the Café Central. Obviously, the new type of man he claimed to incarnate (or at least to prefigure) had nothing in common with the strong Nietzschean superman. He was characterised, rather, by an indeterminate, fluid ego, without ties or fixed orientation, always 'available' ('disponible'), open to every combination and every temptation, a model of the new individualism in the age of emptiness.

Hermann Broch characterised the crisis of modern culture as a 'disintegration of values', that is to say, a fragmentation of collective norms into atomised value systems. Ludwig Wittgenstein held that a culture deserving of the name must assign to each individual his proper place and that the modern era on the contrary left everyone to his own devices. Similarly, Robert Musil, through his character Ulrich, observed that at the end of a century of scientific and technological progress 'we have lost in the totality all the order we have gained in detail, with the result that we have more and more orders and less and less order'.[16] In his obituary of Musil, Hermann Broch found a kinship between *The Man Without Qualities* and his own *Sleepwalkers*. Musil, he said, had called attention to 'the exhaustion and the quasi-mystical dissolution of a culture, the collapse of its complex value structure'.[17]

In his quest for a better form of life, a new ethic, Musil repeatedly insists on the necessity of remaining in a situation of subjective openness, of keeping one's character (i.e. the sum of one's 'qualities') in a state of incompleteness, so as to leave room for new combinations. What he called 'moral fertility' ('moralische Fruchtbarkeit') consists in an ability to change, to follow the mystical intuitions that enable us to see the world in a new light, and not to let ourselves be constrained by a fixed identity. The true moral law is in perpetual flux; it is not a set code, but a combinatory creativity. Freed from the roles and identifications that society tries to impose on him, the man without qualities proves to be a man of the possible, of experimentation, who is not alarmed at seeing his identity being constantly refashioned. He prefers a freedom composed of indetermination to all the certainties that enslave those around him.

Musil unflinchingly accepted the maxims of Nietzsche, who demanded for the free spirit the perilous privilege of living experimentally ('auf den Versuch hin');[18] and who also proclaimed: 'Let us scrutinise our experiences as rigorously as a scientific experiment, hour by hour, day by day. Let us, ourselves, be our experiments, our own guinea pigs.'[19] In *The Man Without Qualities* he thus presents a 'utopia of experimentalism'. 'Utopia,' he writes, 'means experiment, in which we examine the possible modifications of an element and the consequences these modifications would have for the composite phenomenon that we call life.'[20] In modernism, individuals are called upon to become 'autopoietic systems'[21] in a process of continuous creation, to proceed unremittingly to the selective reorganisation of the world's disorder and of their own lives.

In appearance, nothing is more solidly and irrevocably established than sexual identity, a fact that led Freud, paraphrasing Napoleon, to say: 'Anatomy is Destiny'.[22] In appearance, nothing is more constraining and unbending than the Jewish identity, which led Freud to say that of all the peoples of the Mediterranean basin the Jews alone have remained unchanged down through the centuries, fossils of the biblical era. How many of the ethical and aesthetic values of our cultural tradition, but also how many crimes against humanity, have resulted from these obvious, nay glaring, differences?

Yet Viennese modernism recognised that these old certainties had crumbled. The androgynism of the modern psyche and the inextricable commingling of Jew and non-Jew had given rise to the most bewildering confusion. Would the consequence be the decay and extinction of culture, or a creative, liberating redistribution? The second third of the twentieth century cruelly revived these lost identities: Fascism and Nazism reconstructed 'the female' to enslave her and 'the Jew' to destroy him. Since these regressions and this barbarity, our culture has lived under the influence of the certainties they resurrected, revived projects of liberation conceived in the days of the Enlightenment, and re-enacted some of the struggles of the nineteenth century.

Weary of reliving the eighteenth and nineteenth centuries, our own *fin de siècle* seems to be in a situation similar to that of Viennese modernism. Once again, sexual identities are merging and once again 'the Jew' is becoming imaginary. The Viennese model shows that such indeterminateness can prove extremely fruitful and provide a basis for rich combinations, provided that a new reaction does not call a halt to the postmodern reinvention of the individual.

Notes

1. Hermann Bahr, *Selbstbildnis* (Berlin, 1923), p. 127.
2. 'Nur nichts Beharrendes, nur keine Dauer, nur kein Gleichbleiben: denn jedes Neue ist besser, schon weil es jünger ist als das Alte'. Hermann Bahr, *Briefwechsel mit seinem Vater*, ed. Adalbert Schmidt (Vienna, 1971), p. 154 (letter of 11 March 1887).
3. Charles Baudelaire, 'Le peintre de la vie moderne', in *Oeuvres complètes*, ed. Claude Pichois (Paris, 1976), II, p. 696.
4. Louis Dumont, *Essais sur l'individualisme* (Paris, 1983); Gilles Lipovetsky, *L'ère du vide. Essais sur l'individualisme contemporain* (Paris, 1983).
5. Jean-François Lyotard, *The Postmodern Condition: A Report on Knowledge*, tr. Geoff Bennington and Brian Massumi (Manchester, 1984), pp. 37 and 41.
6. Jean Clair, *Considérations sur l'état des beaux-arts. Critique de la modernité* (Paris, 1983); Jean Clair (ed.), *Vienne 1880–1938: l'apocalypse joyeuse*, exhibition catalogue, Centre Georges Pompidou (Paris, 1986).
7. Georg Simmel, *Philosophische Kultur* (Berlin, 1983), p. 152.
8. Cf. Alain Finkielkraut, *Le Juif imaginaire* (Paris, 1980).
9. 'Die Moderne ist alles seit dem Zusammenbruche des Individualismus: alles, was da nicht ist, sondern wird.' Hermann Bahr, *Prophet der Moderne. Tagebücher 1888–1904*, ed. Reinhard Farkas (Vienna, 1987), p. 45.
10. Quoted in Carl E. Schorske, *Fin-de-siècle Vienna: Politics and Culture* (Cambridge, 1981), p. xviii.
11. Henri Meschonnic, *Modernité, modernité* (Lagrasse [Aude], 1988), p. 175; E. M. Cioran, 'Sissi ou la vulnérabilité', in *Vienne 1880–1938*, ed. Jean Clair, p. 19.
12. Jürgen Habermas, 'Ein philosophierender Intellektueller', in *Über Theodor W. Adorno* (Frankfurt, 1968). p. 35.
13. 'Denn insofern eine Individualität nach irgendeiner Richtung hin eine Berechtigung,

ja auch nur den Schein einer Berechtigung hat, darf sie nichts anderes sein als ein Erster, ein Vorläufer in irgendeiner organischen Entwicklung des Menschlichen überhaupt, die aber auf dem naturgemäßen Wege der möglichen Entwicklung für alle Menschen liegt!' Peter Altenberg, in *Ausgewählte Werke in zwei Bänden*, ed. Dietrich Simon (München, 1979), I, p. 129.

14. Egon Friedell, *Ecce poeta* (Berlin, 1912), p. 11 ('Eine Art Naturgeschichte des Menschen nach 1900').
15. Thomas Mann, in *Das Altenberg-Buch*, ed. Egon Friedell (Vienna-Leipzig, 1921), p. 75.
16. '[. . .] Der Erfolg ist sozusagen, daß man alles, was man an Ordnung im einzelnen gewinnt, am Ganzen wieder verliert, so daß wir immer mehr Ordnungen und immer weniger Ordnung haben.' Robert Musil, *Der Mann ohne Eigenschaften*, ed. Adolf Frisé (Reinbek/Hamburg 1978), p. 379.
17. 'Das Müdewerden und den beinahe mystischen Auflösungsprozeß einer Kultur, den Zusammenbruch ihres komplizierten Wertgebäudes [aufzeigen]'. Hermann Broch, 'Nachruf auf Robert Musil', in *Schriften zur Literatur I: Kritik*, ed. Paul Michael Lützeler (Frankfurt, 1975), p. 98.
18. '[. . .] Dem freien Geiste das gefährliche Vorrecht [. . .], *auf den Versuch hin* leben [. . .] zu dürfen.' Friedrich Nietzsche, *Menschliches, Allzumenschliches*, in *Kritische Studienausgabe*, ed. Giorgio Colli und Mazzino Montinari (Berlin-New York, 1980), II, p. 18.
19. 'Wir [. . .] wollen unseren Erlebnissen so streng in's Auge sehen, wie einem wissenschaftlichen Versuche, Stunde für Stunde, Tag um Tag! Wir selber wollen unsere Experimente und Versuchs-Tiere sein.' Nietzsche, *Die fröhliche Wissenschaft*, KSA, III, p. 551.
20. 'Utopie bedeutet das Experiment, worin die mögliche Veränderung eines Elements und die Wirkungen beobachtet werden, die sie in jener zusammengesetzten Erscheinung hervorrufen würde, die wir Leben nennen.' Musil, *Der Mann ohne Eigenschaften*, p. 246.
21. A term used by Niklas Luhmann in *Reconstructing Individualism*, ed. Thomas C. Heller, Morton Sosna and David E. Wellbery (Stanford, 1986), p. 321.
22. *Complete Psychological Works of Sigmund Freud*, ed. James Strachey (London, 1953-74), XIX, p. 178.

Karl Kraus's Oscar Wilde:
Race, Sex, and Difference
Sander L. Gilman

One powerful factor in the formation of the fictive personality is the image of representations of the self in the external world. Each of us incorporates into our fictive personality aspects of our understanding of the world's image of ourself. When the stigma associated with a stereotype in which one sees oneself placed becomes internalised, it becomes impossible to understand the representation of the self apart from understanding that internalised image.[1] However, it is only when such an image of difference has sufficient salience for an individual in the stereotyped group to become completely internalised, that the individual acts *as if* the image is a pattern for self-definition. And this is true whatever the validity or implications of the charge of difference or the image imposed. Thus the external image of the self has symbolic significance for the formation of the ego. One aspect of the fictive personality may well be the destructive (or idealised) image of a general social category to which an individual believes him/herself to belong. But, of course, it is impossible for an intact personality completely to internalise a corrosive self-image without some psychic defence measures.

Thus, one measure of Jewish identity in Western culture can be the rate of the internalisation (and projection) of anti-Semitic images of the Jew, if such images have a high enough salience to become part of an individual's definition of his/her fictive self. The complex case of the *fin-de-siècle* Viennese cultural critic and writer Karl Kraus is an excellent example of the means by which individuals, labelled as Jews, internalised and projected the qualities of differences attributed to themselves onto other subgroups. Kraus's case is of interest because it illustrates the formation of a fictive personality within the world of words, within the culture of writing during a time of an extraordinary public manifestation of anti-Semitism in Austria in the earliest stages of his career and the success of Nazism in Germany at the close of his career. This period saw the public discourse about the Jews become an accepted, if corrosive, fact within Austrian life.

The basic structure of projection is rooted in the polar sense of the world which underlies all our perceptions. But it is important to understand how this general process of distancing and projection functions within a specific historical dimension. The bipolarity which we see manifested in the creation of 'good' and 'bad' stereotypes is the reactivation of the fantasy of wholeness which existed in all of us before we distanced ourselves from our first care-giver. Our internalised sense of difference is a product of that primal moment in all our experience. We need to project the fantasised source of our anxiety onto the world. The individuals who make up the screen onto which group fantasies are projected likewise share this internalised, universal sense of difference. This sense of difference is triggered by any deep-seated sense of ontological insecurity, such as that created by the double-bind situation in which one must rationalise one's sense of self with the image of the 'Other' projected upon a group with which one is identified. This moment of insecurity, of loss of control over one's self in the world, reproduces the repressed anxiety of that primal moment when we first became aware that we were different, different from the care-giver, unable to control our world.

When we are in such a state, we desire to overcome it by reconnecting ourselves with that force, society, which has replaced the mother as the prime determinant of our sense of alienation. We thus actively seek to accept society's sense of our own difference in order to recreate our sense of oneness with the world. Thus anyone who is labelled as 'Jewish' in times of crisis, whatever the objective reality behind that label, reacts to the label by internalising the image of 'Jewishness' projected by the dominant group which he or she fears, and thus wishes to emulate. Anna Freud observed this pattern of action among the Jewish children evacuated to her London clinic during the Second World War when they played Nazis and Jews.[2] All of the children identified with the power of the aggressor as an apotropaic gesture to preserve their own sense of power. They projected those qualities of 'Jewishness' ascribed to themselves onto an appropriate subgroup of 'Jews', the victims in their games, as a means of preserving their own sense of control over their identity.

Jews who internalise the image of the Jew projected by the dominant society (as that society's means of assuring its own sense of control, its own power over a group labelled as 'different' and thus inferior) must respond to this form of self-stereotyping. They respond either by denying it (and proving to the dominant group the validity of their perception that all Jews lie, especially about their own essence) or affirming it (while projecting the negative associations about 'being Jewish' onto specific subgroups among those labelled as 'Jewish'). Thus, whenever an individual accepted the charge of being 'Jewish', he/she also accepted all the negative associations which accompanied that image. The image of the Jew possessing a damaged or damaging discourse has left those writers who were labelled as Jewish and accepted the assigned label (rather than an internally generated one) with a need to prove that their discourse was unimpaired. Thus anyone could be labelled as a Jew and could accept the implications of this category: being Jewish was not merely an attribute of the self but, more important, was the agreement of certain internalised images of the self with the projections of difference by the dominant group. The reality behind the image, whether it is the reality of the Jew, or of the homosexual, or the Black, is not at the heart of the matter. Rather it is the acceptance, for any

of Viennese Jews as an affectation which he associates with their corruption. Salten is the writer who mocks the purity of language by introducing into a discussion of the universal sense of terror attributed to the animals of the forest the image of the Jews as perpetually terrorised by the world around them. According to Kraus, this faulty analogy can be exploded if one sees the conscious use of Yiddishisms as a sign of artificial separateness, and this as the origin of fear. And yet, Kraus senses that what he perceives as artificial is seen by the anti-Semite as a permanent marker for the Jew. Kraus accuses Salten of exploiting *jüdeln* to create a false effect. With this accusation he throws the charge that the Jews possess a baser, more materialistic language back into the face of the Jew, or at least the Jew who can use better language.

When Kraus returns to the image of the 'Yiddish-accented hares' in a later essay, 'Growing Up as an Altar Boy' ('Aufgewachsen als Meßnerknabe'), he uses yet another set of quotations, this time from the Jewish weekly *Bukowinaer Volkszeitung* published in Czernowitz (Romania).[9] He apologises for using the quotations, because he feels himself hypnotised by the quality of the language of the text and drawn to it as a satirist, 'defenceless, like the hare before the glare of the boa constrictor' (p. 31). Kraus's metaphor is an ironic reversal. He, the satirist, becomes the aggressor. The 'altar boy' in this essay is Felix Salten, who recounts his youthful education in Vienna, where he attended the compulsory Catholic religious instruction and, indeed, served as an altar boy. All of this Kraus recounts using the text that he cites from the newspaper written by Eastern Jews for Eastern Jews, a paper that glorified Salten as one who had maintained his Jewish identity in spite of the pressures applied to him while he was growing up. Kraus's attack on Salten is of secondary importance: his barbs are aimed at the language of the report of Salten's visit to what had been one of the frontier towns of the Habsburg Empire. Kraus himself had been born in a similar frontier town, Jičin (now in Czechoslovakia). For Kraus's point is not that Salten, like Max Reinhardt, has proven the baseness of both the Jews and the Catholic Church, but that it is in the language of these Jews that their perversity can be read, and read like an open book.

Kraus, Wilde, and the discourse of difference

The complexity of Kraus's understanding of the perversity embedded in the Jews' discourse can be traced back to his reading of another perverse text, Oscar Wilde's *Salome*, in 1903.[10] Wilde, tried in 1895–6 on the charge of sodomy, and released from prison only to die in ignominy in Paris during 1900, became for the German and Austrian liberal of the turn of the century the icon of the persecuted genius. Quite the antithesis of the successful author of *Bambi*, Felix Salten! Kraus's analysis of Wilde's drama *Salome*, first performed in German in Breslau during 1901, provides the reader with a detailed presentation of Kraus's understanding of a seemingly positive discourse of difference. Kraus's analysis of the discussions of Wilde's play (and its dialogue) reveals it to be a bench-mark for the discourse of the Jews' difference.

In December 1903, Kraus opened his discussion of Wilde and his works with

16

a comment on a German book on sexual life in Britain: 'The uncomplicated German can only gaze upward jealously at the British nation which is so far above the continent in the culture of sexual perversity and the development of sexual hypocrisy, which can bring forth as well as murder the genius of Oscar Wilde, and which has flagellation-bordellos and laws which can threaten the nuances of sexual activity with a ten-year jail sentence.'[11] The importance of this gloss is not merely that Kraus points out the parallels to British sexual attitudes in contemporary Viennese society, even in terms of the popularity of public executions and the sadistic pleasure they aroused (a parallel to the Wilde trials); it is rather that Kraus introduces that term which is central to any understanding of the complex linkage between language, difference, and the avant-garde — the term 'perversity'. Kraus's manner of indirect citation shows here that he is using a term from the generalised discourse of difference of his time.

It is the category of the 'perverse', not merely the unnatural but the anti-natural, which provides the link which can help us to understand the power of reading Wilde through the prism of Kraus's sense of the nature of the Jews' discourse. At the close of that same issue of *Die Fackel*, he reports two items of gossip back to back: the anti-Semitic attacks abetted by the official city government to limit the promotion of Jewish civil servants; and the permission granted to perform Wilde's *Salome* in Vienna but only '"if the head of John the Baptist, which Salome brings in, is covered with a cloth". Too dumb!'[12] Kraus retorts. This seemingly random juxtaposition makes one aware how closely Kraus links various categories of difference such as anti-Semitism and homophobia; the Jews and Oscar Wilde.

In his Christmas number of 1903 Kraus devotes the first fourteen pages to a detailed review (and review of the reviews) of this production of *Salome*.[13] It was performed in the Deutsches Volkstheater, the Viennese counterpart to Max Reinhardt's Kleines Theater, a theatre which was able to produce the European avant-garde plays, otherwise banned in Austria by the censor, through the means of inviting German guest productions. On 12 December 1903 Adele Hartwig brought her version of *Salome* from the Neues Theater in Berlin to Vienna, where it was a *succès de scandale*. Kraus begins his review (as was his usual practice) with an attack on an existing review, on that by Friedrich Schütz in the *Neue Freie Presse*, the paper edited by Kraus's *bête noire*, Moriz Benedikt. It is important to read Kraus's opening of this review in the light of the rhetoric to which he is responding and in which he clothes his understanding of the play:

> 'When critics disagree the artist is in accord with himself', wrote Wilde in the introduction to his wonderful 'Picture of Dorian Gray'. In the sphere of his noble culture of the spirit, the argument of proletarian idea-mongers can only be heard like the Yiddish-accented German *(Gemauschel)* of the Pharisees, modulated by the excellent direction of *Salome*. I am denied the privilege of enjoying works of art as an observer. A fatal sharpness of hearing forces me to listen to the voices which come from the depths and I cannot pray before I curse those who have committed sacrilege. Like the *Gemauschel* of the Pharisees in *Salome*: 'Nay, but he ain't the prophet Elias!' cries one who has forced himself gesticulating into the foremost row and his name is Friedrich Schütz (p. 1).

17

Kraus uses this review to defend Wilde and his drama (with the parodied cry echoing the closing of the play: 'Kill that critic!' ('Man erschlage diesen Kritiker. . .' p. 2); but it is his attempt to decouple the linkage of homo-sexuality and the Jews which makes up the majority of his long and detailed examination of Schütz's review. ('Homosexuality' is a 'scientific' label for a new 'disease', coined by Karoly Benkert in 1869 at the very moment in history when the new 'scientific' term for Jew-hating, 'anti-Semitism', was created by Wilhelm Marr.) He observes that 'Mr Friedrich Schütz is not a pederast' (p. 2). The unspoken theme of Schütz's review, according to Kraus's reading, is: if in a review of a work by a known homosexual such as Oscar Wilde, I, as a reviewer, do not attack homosexuality, then am I not 'one of them'? Kraus's defence of Wilde is linked to his opposition to the prosecution of homosexuality and his libertarian view that sexuality has no business being within the control of the state. But the central thrust of the first paragraph has little to do with this question and Kraus himself drops this theme after the first few pages. His main concern, the centre of his review, is also the central theme of the opening paragraph of his review. It is his focus on the role of the Jews, represented for Kraus (but not for Schütz) by their discourse, the language of the 'Pharisees' in the debates before Herod about the divinity of Christ and the mission of John the Baptist. Kraus takes issue, in this opening paraphrase from the review, with Schütz's critique of allegedly anti-Semitic elements in Wilde's play. For Schütz, Wilde is merely an anti-Semite, a 'Briten-Goi' (p. 8) who attacks Jews in the basest manner. Kraus quotes Schütz's assertion that the Jews are reduced to '"a quintet of tottering Jews represented with ugly gestures, which are infused with the deepest sense of subjugation". The direction of the Volkstheater does even more and "lets these Hebrews *mauscheln*". And that has to happen to Mr Schütz, who wishes to extract from every work of art the same message: "Jews can do no wrong"' (p. 9). But even Kraus admits that the use of *Gemauschel* on the Viennese stage was a bit of strong business: 'Indeed the jargon [*Jargon*] of the group of Pharisees should have been moderated — at least with an eye toward the audience at the premiere, which succumbed to a family mood that damaged the overall effect' (p. 9). For the use of *Gemauschel* points, as I have indicated in much more detail elsewhere, to the double-bind of Jewish writers in German such as Kraus.[14] Kraus, Theodor Herzl's most outspoken early opponent in Vienna, rejects the Zionist call for an Orientalisation of the European Jews. He sees acculturation, if not assimilation, as the only possible means of overcoming the hostility to the Jews of the world in which he lives. He shares the general assimilationist point of view, that the recent political opposition to the Jews, at least in Vienna, is the result of having large numbers of unacculturated Eastern Jews from the provinces of the Austro-Hungarian Empire in Vienna. With his focus on the *Gemauschel* of Wilde's Jews, Kraus points to the inadequacies of a specific group of Jews, the Eastern, Yiddish-speaking Jews from the provinces of the Austro-Hungarian Empire, the Jewish parvenus in Vienna, the object onto which Viennese Jews projected their anxieties. These anxieties arose because of the charge, heard in the political speeches and read in the pamphlets and scholarly monographs of anti-Semites of all persuasions, that all Jews (not merely the newly arrived) did not, could not, command the discourse of high culture, the discourse of Germans. It is, of course, in a central work of the canon of cultural anti-Semitism, Richard Wagner's 'Jews in Music', that this view had its most often quoted formulation.[15] Kraus points to his separation from those designated by this charge with his own 'translation' into 'Pharisees' of Wilde's designation of those argumentative figures as 'Jews'. For Kraus, Wilde's stage Jews are but 'Pharisees', with all of the negative connotations in Christian-German rhetoric of that term. They are not merely 'Juden', as the German translation of the text states, for that designation, read as a racial category by a German reader, would also include Karl Kraus.

In Kraus's review of *Salome*, he condemns the German (Berlin) version as unnecessarily altering Wilde's intent in the drama; but his main target is the thin-skinnedness of the critic of the *Neue Freie Presse*, that daily paper which both anti-Semites and Jews such as Kraus understood as 'Jewish', and which saw in every representation of the Jews an oblique attack. Kraus mockingly asks Schütz to allow some 'perverse' tastes, so that the theatre can serve up peacock's tongues as well as peasant dumplings [*Bauernknödel*] (p. 12). The use of the word 'perverse' in this context ironically links the defender of the Jews (Schütz/Benedikt) with the 'perversity' of homosexuality which Kraus himself defends. 'Perversity' becomes a positive label, the label of libertarian aesthetics, of the cultural avant-garde with which Kraus, on one level, identifies himself. He thus closes his review of the reviews with the acerbic observation that the clerical newspaper *Vaterland* as well as Benedikt's *Neue Freie Presse* have both condemned the play. Both Catholics and Jews conspire to damn true art, while Kraus, whose discourse (in his own estimation) is pure and neither Jewish nor conservative, represents the defender of the 'perverse'.

Let us for a moment examine not Kraus's response, that is the response of a Viennese 'Jew' who is internalising his own ambiguity about the hidden language attributed to the Jews by the anti-Semites, but rather Friedrich Schütz's original *feuilleton*.[16] Kraus's reading of Schütz presents a clear case of his projection onto the 'Jewish' writer (Schütz as the agent of the 'Jewish' newspaper, Moriz Benedikt's *Neue Freie Presse*) of his own fears about the nature of Jewish (i.e. 'perverse') discourse. Schütz does, indeed, spend over half of his review recounting the biography of Wilde in a condemnatory manner, contrasting him with Byron and Heine. Kraus reads quite correctly Schütz's condemnation of the poet as homosexual. But his reading of Schütz's discussion of *Salome* as a text and of the visiting Berlin production has a different slant. Schütz stresses the historical marginality of the court of Herod, does not glorify the history of the Jews under the Romans, and only in his penultimate paragraph condemns the Volkstheater for having 'the Hebrews *mauschel*': 'if such a concept were correct then one would need to play [such dramas as Hebbel's] *Judith*... which are set on the soil of Judea in Yiddish (*Jargon*)'. Kraus places this condemnation of the representation at the very opening of his review, since it was the quality of the production (and the language of the review) which spoke most directly to his own sense of identity. He reads Schütz's review as an attack on the homosexual poet Wilde from the standpoint of the Jewish press, an attack which reveals the discrepancy between the corrupt discourse of the self-conscious Jew, Schütz, and the forces of pure art, represented by Wilde. Kraus reads the review as an attack on the avant-garde from the side of the forces of reaction, but a Jewish reaction, which he labels ironically as no different from the forces of Catholic reaction. But, of course, the perversity of the Jews' discourse, no matter what the ideological identity of the actual individual, was inexorably linked with the polluted language of the homosexual. Thus Kraus needed to separate his discourse about the avant-garde (which was not 'Jewish' but in this case about Jews) from that of the narrow-minded Jews, such as Friedrich Schütz, and their discourse about the Jews.

Kraus's view was not an unambiguous affirmation of the label of the 'perverse' for the cultural avant-garde, any more than Nietzsche had glorified the 'degenerate' as the sole image of the true artist. On 4 January 1904 Kraus followed his review of *Salome* with a further attack on Friedrich Schütz under the title 'The Picture of Dorian Gray (Toward a Picture of Friedrich Schütz)', which again begins with a paraphrase of the homophobic rhetoric of the period:

> In that rag, the advertising pages of which are open to the offering of every perversity and whose owners notoriously benefit financially from the procuring of pederastic contacts, a certain F. Sch. has, as is well known, become consumed with moral indignation about Oscar Wilde.[17]

While Kraus proceeds to quote from Wilde on the corruption of critics in general, as he had at the beginning of the earlier review, he has begun by condemning the homophobic Schütz as writing for a mere homosexual rag. The Jew who condemns the homosexual is not above pandering to (and for) him. The importance of this statement is the ambiguity of Kraus's use of the term 'perversity', applying not merely to the homosexual but also to the Jewish press. Jews such as Moriz Benedikt are by implication no better than their own image of the homosexual.

The function which the Eastern Jew has as the negative projection for Kraus's sense of self and the antithetical role ascribed to the figure of the gay playwright provide the boundaries for the definition of the self, of the fictive image of Karl Kraus, within his world of words, his periodical *Die Fackel*. The complexity of Kraus's sexual identity is also implicated, the sexual identity of one whose desire was publicly to establish himself as a heterosexual member of the culture of Vienna. When he proposed to Sidonie Nadherny, no less a figure than Rainer Maria Rilke undertook to write to her to point out the potentially miscegenational nature of the relationship.[18] The model is set by the nineteenth-century French writer Abel Hermant:

> Differences of race are irreducible and between two beings who love each other they cannot fail to produce exceptional and instructive reactions. In the first superficial ebullition of love, indeed, nothing notable may be manifested, but in a fairly short time the two lovers, innately hostile, in striving to approach each other strike against an invisible partition which separates them. Their sensibilities are divergent; everything in each shocks the other; even their anatomical conformation, even the language of their gestures; all is foreign.[19]

The very language of the Jew, his internalised *Gemauschel*, the sound which Kraus tries so hard not to hear when he delivers his much-vaunted public readings of the classics, is a sound of his sexual difference. For being Jewish is associated, as least by Jewish men whose sexual identity was closely linked to their internalisation of their label as a 'Jew', with being gay. And the link is always made through the world of words, the creation of the fictive categories of 'Jew' and 'gay'. This was present in the charge that Jews were inherently feminised. David Friedrich Strauss, the great critic of Christianity during the late nineteenth century and Friedrich Nietzsche's *bête noire*, was able quite off-handedly to dismiss the 'humbug' of the Resurrection as the result of the 'fantastic', 'oriental', 'especially female' nature of the Jews.[20] The evils of Christianity lie in the mentality of its Jewish origin – a view to which Nietzsche, like many of the 'Christian' critics of Christianity during the late nineteenth century, also subscribed. It is the very biological (or ontological) difference of the Jew which is the source of his feminised nature. For gay Jews (that is, for men who understood these labels as describing aspects of their identity) the stigma associated with this double category led them to see these categories as socially, rather than biologically, determined. Marcel Proust, whose confusion of the stigma of 'race' and of sexuality was certainly no less complicated than was Kraus's, records this confusion in *Cities of the Plain* (within *Remembrance of Things Past*), when he observed that the gays are 'portrayed in a mirror which, ceasing to flatter them, accentuates every blemish that they have refused to observe in themselves, and makes them understand that what they have been calling their love (and to which, playing upon the word, they have by association annexed all that poetry, painting, music, chivalry, asceticism have contrived to add to love) springs not from an ideal of beauty which they have chosen but from an incurable disease; like the Jews again . . . [they are] invested, by a persecution similar to that of Israel, with the physical and moral characteristics of a race, sometimes beautiful, often hideous. . .'.[21] Gays come to look different, to speak differently, to act like a race apart, that is, to be like Jews, because of their treatment in society. What Proust, Kraus, and other Jews reject is any intimation that their own sexual difference is the result of inherent rather than acquired characteristics. Thus, circumcision is understood by assimilated Jews to be written 'on the skin'; for anti-Semites it is a sign of the inner nature of the Jew.

Hoist with his own petard

In 1913, shortly after the publication of his aphorisms, *Pro domo et mundo* (1912), there appeared in a Viennese satiric journal a caricature of Kraus hawking his books and accompanied by a series of aphorisms, written in a mock Viennese Yiddish accent (Fig. 1).[22] This caricature was very much in the same vein as the postcards widely sold at every kiosk in Vienna recounting the 'adventures' of little 'Herr Kohn', whose tiny, deformed body and macrocephalitic head surmounted by a giant nose became the given image of the Jew. (So much so that Max Nordau could simply call his widely performed drama of 1899

Figure 1. Caricature of Karl Kraus by Fritz Schönpflug

attacking anti-Semitism *Doktor Kohn*, without elaborating its context, and call forth an immediate and clear reaction to the anti-Semite's image of the Jew.) The image of the out-of-proportion nose was, by popular association, understood as a reference to the circumcised penis which set the Jew apart and was thus a symbolic reference to the sexuality of the Jew. 'Herr Kohn' is the exemplary Jew, he is a merchant, selling cheap goods dearly. All of these aspects rattled Kraus's sense of the protection given him by the wall of words he constructed in *Die Fackel*.

The satire, entitled 'Pro domo et loco', called forth a complex reaction. Kraus reprinted the entire page, with the caricature, and then proceeded to parallel the crude image of the peddler Jew with long citations from a text that praised Kraus as one of the few writers to free German from the double curse of Jewish and journalistic language. The contrast between the mock Yiddish attributed to Kraus, which revealed the basest anti-Semitic stereotypes, and the quotations from Jörg Lanz von Liebenfels, one of Adolf Hitler's main sources of inspiration, highlights Kraus's need to distance himself from the accusation of speaking in a Jewish mode, even if this was merely the accusation of his enemies.[23]

In the same year, Kraus published his answer to a correspondent who was subtle enough to pick up the implication of Kraus's use of Lanz von Liebenfels's essay and cited the racist dictum 'One cannot leave one's race' in order to elicit Kraus's response. In this essay, entitled 'He's Still a Jew' ('Er ist doch ä Jud'), Kraus presents the theoretical presuppositions of his understanding of the essence of a Jewish language. Kraus relates the essence of language to its function in the society or group in which it is found. He does not argue with the fact that he is a 'Jew', at least in the terms of the definitions offered by racist critics, but he sees a distinction between materialistic Jews and those Jews who reject materialism. Thus the language of the Jews is the language of materialism. 'The others [non-Jews] are also capable of acquiring this intonation, for it is this intonation that accompanies the rolling of money. It is the language of the world, it is its desire, and we may – we must – address it as a Jewish tendency, for it was the mission of the Jews, thanks to their gift of persuasion, fortitude, and greater gift at making it in the world, to attach to the world these qualities.'[24] Kraus sees a specific language of worldliness, of commerce, as typical of the Jews. He also perceives certain Jews' ability to transcend this baseness. He has his category of Jews who speak good German, including Peter Altenberg and Else Lasker-Schüler (and, of course, Karl Kraus). What makes their German good German, and not the language of the Jews, is that they use a language that is non-materialistic. Here is the clue to Kraus's sense of the validity of language. For the language attributed to his enemies is the language of lies, of the market-place, of the Jew as dissembler. Thus Kraus, in tabulating the quality of a truthful perception of the world, observes: 'I do not know whether it is a Jewish quality to find an old whisky drinker in a caftan more cultured than a member of the German-Austrian Association of Authors in his tuxedo.'[25] The Eastern Jew, with his whisky and in his distinctive dress, is more truthful than is the hidden Jew disguised as a German-Austrian author. So, too, is his language.

The cathexis of Kraus's sense of the importance of language lies in the hidden agenda attributed to the producers of Jewish language with whom he wishes not to be identified. He selects as his models for the ideal Jewish language writers such as Peter Altenberg and Else Lasker-Schüler, writers who avoid any association with the 'official' (and, thus, in Kraus's mind's eye 'Jewish') cultural institutions and therefore can produce 'good' German. Kraus himself undertook to create such an institution in his periodical *Die Fackel*, which was independent of all the existing, corrupting, cultural and linguistic structures of his time. Kraus's desire to withdraw from the cultural market-place moved him to create yet another object for cultural consumption. This double-bind situation was heightened by the constant attacks on Kraus as the Jewish writer *par excellence*. Kraus seemed to relish these attacks. He reprinted any number of them with his own commentaries.[26]

But the overall effect of these attacks and Kraus's responses was to generate an image of the author as a consciously non-Jewish Jew, a paradox that even Kraus senses. Here the centrality of Heine's image as a writer for late nineteenth-century writers, both Jewish (such as Kraus) and non-Jewish (such as Nietzsche), cannot be overestimated.[27] In his polemic against Heine, published in 1910, Kraus selects as his antithesis the one Jewish writer who both had been compared to him and had become the anti-Semites' image of the essential Jewish writer. Kraus is careful not to attack Heine directly as a Jew; rather, he uses the markers that for his audience pointed to the image of the Jews' language. Heine is the father of modern journalism. He is the great 'Frenchifier' of the German language. Heine sexualised the language of poetry: 'Heine has so loosened the corsets of the German language that today every little merchant can fondle her breasts.'[28] This attack on Heine using the rhetoric of the anti-Semitic views of the nature of the Jews' language is seen by Kraus as a defence of 'good' language, language that does not blur the line between ornament and philosophy, and an attack on the 'bad' language attributed by Kraus to the journalists and Jews. But it is important to contrast these comments with Kraus's defence of Wilde and the language of the Jews in *Salome*.[29] For Heine is seen as a raving heterosexual, following the German xenophobic image of the Frenchman; Wilde as a persecuted homosexual, following the xenophobic image of the British. The sexualisation of the poet's discourse is a mark of his difference. But if he is a Jew, such as Heine, his discourse is perverse; if he is the non-Jewish creator of an image of the Jews' discourse, his is a truthful discourse. The hidden language of the Jews is made manifest by Wilde; in Heine's works, it remains hidden until it is revealed by the insightful Jew, Karl Kraus, a clandestine convert to Catholicism. Perversity is a quality only of the Jews' discourse, as the anti-Semites of the period claim. As a measure of Kraus's success in identifying with the anti-Semites' characterisation of Heine's discourse as corrupt and corrupting, one should note that while Fritz Mauthner used Heine as a negative example in his writings on the philosophy of language, published before Kraus's attack on Heine, he wrote a defence of Heine, which he published in 1914, after Kraus's polemic appeared.[30] It is, of course, true that Kraus's identification with Wilde, the artist persecuted for his sexual orientation, drew no credence from the Viennese anti-Semites. From their standpoint, Kraus is labelled over and over again as the 'arch-Jew'.

With the rise of the Nazis in Germany (and Austria), Karl Kraus began to see the attack on the language of the Jews for what it was, an attack on the idea of the Jews as separate and inferior. The publication of Theodor Herzl's diaries in the 1920s provided Kraus with what he perceived to be some insight into Herzl's character, and he revised his opinion of the man, his work, and, one presumes, his language. In Kraus's last work, *The Third Walpurgis Night (Die Dritte Walpurgisnacht)* (1933), he ironically admits to using the language of the Jews. In the book he includes the text of a letter to the West German Radio in Cologne, which had asked for a review copy of his version of Shakespeare's sonnets. In the letter, written in the complex style of official German correspondence and mocking this essentially Teutonic bureaucratic style, Kraus observes that they really do not want to review the book, for the translations

24

of Shakespeare's sonnets published by Kraus are 'really translations from the Hebrew'.[31] Shakespeare's sonnets in German are Kraus's 'Hebrew Melodies', the title of Heine's last great work of poetry. This labelling signifies Kraus's ironic awareness that the charges levelled at the Jews for writing in their 'Jewish manner' constitute an attack on the Jews' ability to function in Western culture. Kraus's response followed the demand from official Nazi circles that all works written by Jews in German be labelled as translations. Kraus's desire to purge himself of the 'bad' language of the Jew is replaced by his need to see this distinction as spurious.

For Kraus, the presence of the Nazis in Vienna, where the problem of linguistic and literary criticism played out in the city's journals was converted into street brawls, marked the necessary turning point in his self-awareness. The complex literary boundaries which he had established to encapsulate his identity began to crumble once his ability to hide within his own world of words, with his journal and his criticism, began to be threatened. Suddenly all the devices to distance his identity as a Jew, his identification with libertarian causes, his condemnation of 'bad' Jews, all was for naught. For his ability to function in the public sphere as a critic, not as Jew, not as male, but as critic, was compromised. Kraus, like so many acculturated and assimilated Jews, suddenly discovered that it was not the 'other' Jews about whom the anti-Semites were speaking, it was themselves. And the careful creation of a fictive personality of Kraus the pure 'critical ear', cultivated for more than three decades in the pages of *Die Fackel*, finally collapsed.

Notes

1. See my *Jewish Self-Hatred: Anti-Semitism and the Hidden Language of the Jews* (Baltimore, 1986). This is a counter-reading of the construction of the subaltern personality as given by Gilles Deleuze and Félix Guattari in *A Thousand Plateaus: Capitalism and Schizophrenia*, tr. Brian Massumi (Minneapolis, 1987), pp. 291–3.
2. Anna Freud, *The Ego and the Mechanisms of Defense* (New York, 1966), pp. 109–21.
3. On Kraus and his Jewish identity see Wilma Abeles Iggers, *Karl Kraus: A Viennese Critic of the Twentieth Century* (The Hague, 1967), pp. 33–6, 171–91; and Harry Zohn, 'Karl Kraus: 'Jüdischer Selbsthasser' oder 'Erzjude'?', *Modern Austrian Literature*, 8 (1975), 1–18. Kraus's association of the newspapers of Vienna with *mauscheln* may be based partly on the columns of Daniel Spitzer, who created the speculator Itzig Kneipeles as a stock comic character for the *Neue Freie Presse* during the late nineteenth century. Martin Buber, in a letter to Werner Kraft dated 20 March 1917, labels Kraus as a 'Jew unhappy with himself' (Martin Buber, *Briefwechsel aus sieben Jahrzehnten*, ed. Grete Schaeder, 3 vols [Heidelberg, 1972], 1, p. 487). On Kraus's ideas on language see Josef Quack, *Bemerkungen zum Sprachverständnis von Karl Kraus* (Bonn, 1976), p. 189; and J. P. Stern, 'Karl Kraus's vision of language', *Modern Language Review*, 61 (1966), 71–84.
4. On Kraus and his opposition to the new (Jewish) language of psychoanalysis, see Thomas Szasz, *Karl Kraus and the Soul-Doctors* (Baton Rouge, 1976).
5. *Die Fackel*, 378–9 (1913), 58.
6. bid., 17 (1899), 21.
7. An illuminating aside from the end of the twentieth century might be appropriate here. The career of Jackie Mason, the last of the 'borscht belt' comics, had an

extraordinary rebirth during 1987. An act designed for the Catskills which had brought Mason to fame during the 1960s led to bankruptcy in 1983. Suddenly this same act became the vehicle which brought him stardom (again) in the late 1980s. Mason understood what had happened: 'The Jewish people took me for granted, the young people saw me as an anachronism, then I went to Broadway where I never ever thought I'd succeed.' And the reason for his invisibility was his *mauscheln*: 'People said I was too Jewish – and I even suffered from anti-Jewish prejudice from Jews themselves. There was a profound rejection problem: the reverse discrimination of Jews against other Jews who talk like me in show business. I think they were ashamed and embarrassed about my accent, that I was somehow symbolic of the whole fear that Jews would be discriminated against again' (Glenn Collins, 'Jackie Mason, Top Banana at Last', *New York Times*, 24 July 1988, Section 2: 1, 14). The move to Broadway provided a neutral space in which *mauscheln* was no longer associated with a 'Jewish' environment, that is, the audience (Jewish or not) no longer identified with the comic as a representative of the self. This was the process which Kraus desired for himself as he created a persona as the editor of *Die Fackel*. *Die Fackel* was his neutral space, a space which was quickly labelled as 'Jewish'. Thus Kraus found it necessary to label the 'good' and the 'bad' Jews in his world of words, so as to create a boundary between them and make his position as a 'good' Jew secure.

8. *Die Fackel*, 820–6 (1929), 45–6.
9. Ibid., 847 (1931), 31–4.
10. The only essay on this topic is the narrowly focused piece by Hugh Salvesen, 'Zu den Wilde-Übersetzungen in der 'Fackel'', *Kraus Hefte*, 24 (1982), 5–11.
11. *Die Fackel*, 148 (1903), 19–20.
12. Ibid., 31.
13. Ibid., 150 (1903), 1–14.
14. See my *Jewish Self-Hatred*, especially pp. 209–60.
15. See Jacob Katz, *Richard Wagner: Vorbote des Antisemitismus* (Königstein/Ts, 1985) as well as my *Jewish Self-Hatred*, pp. 209–11.
16. F[riedrich] Sch[ütz], 'Oskar Wilde: Zur Aufführung seiner 'Salome' im Deutschen Volkstheater', *Neue Freie Presse*, 15 December 1903, 1–3.
17. 'Das Bildnis Dorian Gray's (Zum Bildnis des Friedrich Schütz)', *Die Fackel*, 151 (1904), 18–23.
18. Rainer Maria Rilke, *Briefe an Sidonie Nadherny von Borutin*, ed. Bernard Blume (Frankfurt, 1973), pp. 214–16; cf. Ilse Blumenthal-Weis, 'Rilke and the Jews,' *Jewish Frontier*, 26 (1959), 18.
19. Abel Hermant, *Confession d'un enfant d'hier*, cited by Havelock Ellis, *Studies in the Psychology of Sex*, 4: *Sexual Selection in Man* (Philadelphia, 1920), p. 176, note 1.
20. David Friedrich Strauss, *Der alte und der neue Glaube: Ein Bekenntnis* (Leipzig, 1872), p. 71.
21. Marcel Proust, *Remembrance of Things Past*, tr. C. K. Scott Moncrieff and Terence Kilmartin (Harmondsworth, 1986), 2, pp. 638–9. On the structural problems of the relationship between concepts of difference mirrored in texts see Seymour Kleinberg, '*The Merchant of Venice*: the homosexual as anti-Semite in nascent capitalism', *Journal of Homosexuality*, 8 (1983), 113–24.
22. Reprinted with a commentary by Kraus in *Die Fackel*, 381-3 (1913), 42–8. The following is a rough equivalent of the *Gemauschel* attributed by the caricaturist to Kraus: 'Der are tree kinds of pipple: dem, who when dey bodder me, I h'ignore; udders, who I look at wid distain; de tird, I slap aroun'.'
23. See Gerald Stieg, *Der Brenner and Die Fackel: Ein Beitrag zur Wirkungsgeschichte von Karl Kraus* (Salzburg, 1976), pp. 255–60.
24. *Die Fackel*, 386 (1913), 1–8.
25. Ibid., 6.

26. Ibid., 531–43 (1920), 163–77.
27 Anon., 'Heinrich Heine im Urteil Nietzsches und Karl Kraus", *Psychologische Monatshefte*, 9 (1960), 49–50.
28. Reprinted in Karl Kraus, *Untergang der Welt durch schwarze Magie* (Munich, 1960), pp. 188–219 (p. 193).
29. One of the most interesting de-couplings in Kraus's work is the fact that the *Salome* theme was widely read in Heine's long poem 'Atta Troll', Heinrich Heine, *Sämtliche Schriften*, ed. Klaus Briegleb, 12 vols (Berlin, 1981), 7, pp. 540–4 . This contains some verbal parallels to Wilde's drama, including the famous dance of Salome.
30. Fritz Mauthner, *Beiträge zu einer Kritik der Sprache*, vol. 2, *Zur Sprachwissenschaft* (Stuttgart, 1901), p. 645, and vol. 3, *Zur Grammatik and Logik* (Stuttgart, 1902), p. 525; see also the section on 'Heinrich Heine', in Mauthner, *Gespräche im Himmel* (Munich, 1914), pp. 59–91, which is directed against Bartels but with clear reference to Kraus.
31. Karl Kraus, *Die Dritte Walpurgisnacht* (Munich, 1952), p. 139.

Aus einem Skizzenbuch

Five Unpublished Sketches

by

Peter Altenberg

Edited (with an introduction and notes) by Andrew Barker

After an absence of almost twenty years, Henrik Ibsen returned to Vienna in the spring of 1891 to attend a festival organised in his honour by the emerging generation of young writers soon to be known collectively as *Jung Wien*.[1] That Ibsen was thus fêted by writers who are seen today as heralding the movement away from literary Naturalism is not always accorded its due weight by modern commentators, even though as early as 1887 Hermann Bahr had detected in Ibsen's divergence from Naturalism a factor of the greatest importance in the development of a new kind of literature.[2] In this Ibsen essay, written two years before Hauptmann's *Vor Sonnenaufgang*, Bahr had expressed for the first time his unhappiness with literary Naturalism, a dissatisfaction which achieved its most famous expression in the essay 'Die Überwindung des Naturalismus', published in 1891, the same year as Ibsen's triumphant visit to the Austrian capital.[3] If, today, we nevertheless feel that the undoubted enthusiasm for Ibsen amongst the *Jung Wiener* has left hardly a trace in their writings, the evidence of 'Wahrheit' ('Truth'), the last and most extended of the five sketches presented here, would suggest that Altenberg takes for granted his readers' acquaintance with the intricacies of *The Wild Duck*. That Altenberg's own interest in Ibsen goes back to the very beginnings of his literary career emerges from a reference in the correspondence between Schnitzler and Hofmannsthal dated 9 January 1893 to a now lost essay of Altenberg's on Solness, the main character in *The Master Builder*, a play whose first performance in the theatre did not take place until 19 January, when it was put on simultaneously in Trondheim and Berlin.[4]

Altenberg's struggle for truthfulness, his desire for the genuine and the unspoilt were attributes of his personality and writing which made him such an attractive figure for Karl Kraus. They may be seen also as reflecting Altenberg's response to Ibsen's problematic notion of the 'saving lie' which makes life possible, a quandary which lies at the heart of *The Wild Duck*, the play which Altenberg quotes from in his preface to 'Wahrheit'.[5] The impossibly idealistic Gregers Wehrle, who in Altenberg's version becomes Gregor Werle, expresses his disgust at what he sees as the hypocrisy upon which life in the Ekdal family (Altenberg writes Egdal) is based. In his mania for truth at all costs, Wehrle is determined that his friend Hjalmar Ekdal shall know that his wife Gina is the former mistress of Wehrle's father and that their daughter Hedwig might well not be Hjalmar's child. Dr Relling discounts the absolute nature of truth as propounded by Wehrle and argues instead for the necessity of the 'saving lie' to make life livable. The drama ends in tragedy, for Hedwig kills herself in response to Wehrle's 'truth'.

The intricate and disconcerting relationship between literature and life for Peter Altenberg (né Richard Engländer) is revealed in the fate of his sketch 'Familienleben' ('Family Life'), found only in the first edition of *Wie ich es sehe* (*'As I See It'*, 1896), and thereafter withdrawn, presumably upon the insistence of the Engländer family, who felt that literature had come too close to home for comfort. In this very Ibsenesque sketch, much of it written in the form of dramatic dialogue, the already pseudonymous Peter Altenberg is replaced by the still more extreme persona of the 'revolutionary' Albert Königsberg, a name which itself is a partial anagram of Peter Altenberg. Looking at his assembled family, Engländer/Altenberg/Königsberg remarks, in a manner reminiscent of Wehrle:

> Dieses Leben nach außen, dieser Selbstbetrug, dieser Mangel an Einkehr, diese ewig rastlose Selbstbetäubung! Seid ihr Kinder oder seid ihr Wahnsinnige ?! Was seid ihr ?! Ich sehe die Krankheit der Welt und ihr seid Babies.[6]

> [This superficial living, this self-deception, this lack of introspection, this eternal unremitting self-inflicted anaesthesia ! Are you children or are you madmen ?! What are you ?! I see the sickness of the world and you are babies.]

The particular butt of the Revolutionary's passion for 'truth' is Albert's brother-in-law, but towards the end of the sketch a dispassionate third-person narrator remarks, in words directly echoing Ibsen's notion of the 'saving lie':

> Die Schwester saß da mit ihren feuchten Augen und ihrem traurigen Gesichterl. Sie hatte sich so gefreut auf dieses Abschiedssouper mit ihren Brüdern.
> War das die Freiheit und die Wahrheit. . . ?!
> Da liebte sie mehr die 'schöne Lüge' des Lebens und seine süße Knechtschaft.[7]

> [His sister sat there with her moist eyes and sad little face. She had so looked forward to this farewell supper with her brothers.
> Was this freedom and truth. . . ?!
> She preferred the 'saving lie' of life and its sweet servitude.]

That Peter Altenberg was prepared to withdraw 'Familienleben' from all future editions of *Wie ich es sehe* is an indication that unlike his *alter ego* Albert, whose revolutionary philosophy is given considerable airing, he is ultimately prepared to adopt a relativistic stance towards the nature of truth. Reference to the struggle which clearly was taking place between 'Peter Altenberg' and 'Albert Königsberg' as Richard Engländer sloughed his bourgeois identity might thus shed light on his failure to publish 'Wahrheit', a text which is nevertheless alluded to in the first edition of *Wie ich es sehe*, where there is a cryptic reference in the text 'Idylle' to an 'essay on "Truth"' written by Albert Königsberg.[8] That reference apart, nothing bearing the title 'Wahrheit' appears in this edition, whereas the text 'Wahrheit' which is found in the second, 1898, edition of *Wie ich es sehe* is not an essay, but rather an embittered anecdote on the nature of romantic love. The discovery in the Leo Baeck Institute in New York of the text 'Wahrheit' thus not only elucidates the reference in 'Idylle', it further enlarges our understanding of what was taking place in the mid-1890s, when Peter Altenberg, the reformatory artist with revolutionary tendencies, rather than Albert Königsberg, the 'Revolutionär' *per se*, conclusively displaced the burgher Richard Engländer.

In 'Wahrheit' the narrative voice which we might dub 'Peter Altenberg' clearly disapproves of the actions of Gregor Werle, a 'revolutionary' figure from the same mould as Albert Königsberg, who brings calamity upon the Egdal family. That Richard Engländer (born in 1859) may well have felt a certain kinship with this character is nevertheless a strong possibility, given that both are highly impractical, already in their mid-thirties, searching for a role in life, and obsessed with an ideological version of the nature of truth.[9] In the literary text, however, Altenberg contends that as truth is a two-edged sword which can do both good and evil ('Deine Wahrheit kann Gutes, kann Böses bewirken'), it is incumbent upon us to proceed with the greatest of care and to act in a spirit of Christian brotherhood. When truth-telling is merely the function of an overweening ego it contradicts 'der menschlichste Gott, der göttlichste Mensch' ('the most human God, the most divine human being'), who is not only the way and the life but also 'die Wahrheit' ('the truth'). It may be recalled that Altenberg converted to Christianity in 1900, and the sentiments expressed here, as well as the manner of their expression, suggest that the conversion may have had more substance than that of many other Jewish apostates. Just as insistent as the tone of Christian mildness, however, are the echoes of Haeckel's monism, with its stress on 'Bewegung' ('movement') in the evolutionary progress of mankind. In *Wie ich es sehe* the 'Revolutionary' states quite simply 'Mensch heißt sich bewegen' ('to move is to be human').[10] And it is clear that the unself-conscious admixture of the spiritual, the psychological, and the evolutionary-biological so characteristic of Altenberg's first book are equally typical of *Aus einem Skizzenbuch* as a whole. For Peter Altenberg (as opposed to the more extreme persona of the 'Revolutionary') truth is thus relative. Gregor Werle's 'truth' is destructive rather than life-enhancing, and, hence, it becomes a negative rather than a positive factor.

'Wahrheit' is not, however, the only text in *Aus einem Skizzenbuch* in which Altenberg examines the relative nature of truth. In 'Subjectivität und Objectivität' Altenberg presents in uncommented fashion an exchange of letters between Albert (the 'Revolutionary') and Katharina, in which stock bourgeois prejudices are immediately upturned by the attribution of cool objectivity to the female, and dreamy, love-lorn subjectivity to the male. (This typecasting is encapsulated by the husband in the third sketch 'Ehebruch' ['Adultery'], when he quotes the view 'Der Mann hat Geist, das Weib hat Gemüth' ['A man has a mind, a woman has a heart']). In each of the letters, however, the truth is expressed as it is perceived by the subject, and each of the truths is seen to have validity. 'Ehebruch' examines truth in the context of a societal institution whose survival depends upon its participants' attitude towards the truth of their relationships. Like Schnitzler in *Reigen (La Ronde)*, Altenberg characterises his dramatis personae in this dialogue, soon to become a favourite form for his analysis of relationships between the sexes, not by name but by function, e.g. husband, wife, third party. The third party, the incipient threat to the marriage, voices an evolutionary, Haeckel-inspired philosophy which again echoes the 'Revolutionary' in *Wie ich es sehe*, but he forcibly reminds us, too, of the proximity of this sketch to the world of Henrik Ibsen when he characterises the young husband's attitude to marriage as an example of the 'Lebenslüge', the 'saving lie': '"Das ist eben die Lüge *Eures* Lebens. . .".'

These five sketches *Aus einem Skizzenbuch* well illustrate both the evolutionary philosophy and the sensitivity towards young women which will be already familiar to readers of Altenberg's early work. Yet whereas hitherto it has been customary to see that work more in the context of the French tradition which he openly acknowledged (and especially the work of Huysmans and Maeterlinck), the evidence of *Aus einem Skizzenbuch* would suggest that in Altenberg's case at least, the well-attested Viennese enthusiasm for Ibsen of the early 1890s led to an artistic response at both a thematic and formal level.

A note on editorial principles:

The many inconsistencies and apparent errors in the texts as reproduced below result from the decision to publish *Aus einem Skizzenbuch* in the most faithful manner possible. Spelling has, therefore, not been normalised, inaccuracies in the introduction and closing of quotation marks have been retained, as have also the eccentric use of capital letters and the unusual spellings of characters from Ibsen's *The Wild Duck*. The use of italics corresponds to those parts of the manuscript where Altenberg's handwriting switches from German to Roman.

Aus einem Skizzenbuch
von
Peter Altenberg

Nacht-Café

Warum lächelt die Cäcilia, wenn Sie mich grüßt?!

Warum lächelt die Josepha, wenn Sie mich grüßt?!

Aber warum liegt Dein süßes Antlitz in dunkler Ruhe, wenn Du mich grüßt, Camilla?!

Auch die Sterne am Himmel grüßen und lächeln herab – – –;
hat er mich denn lieb, der Stern am Himmel, hat er mich denn lieb
– – – Und dennoch leuchtet er mir – – mir – – in die Seele hinein

Gesunken, gesunken – – – !

Rasch ist ein Gott in Mensch-Werdung gestorben – –,
Langsam ersteht in Gott-Werdung der Mensch – – – !

Langsam – – –, langsam!

Wohin blickst Du, Camilla, Du Aschblonde, Du Zarte?!
Senkst Du den Blick, den müden Blick, in die weißen Tage Deiner
Kindheit?! – – – Damals, damals, als Du im Garten unter den
Obstbäumen Blumensamen eingrubst – – und Deine Blumen
Dein Glück, Deine Liebe waren – – – ?!

Da standest Du, Du mit Deinen zarten Gliedern, mit Deinen
feinen Händchen und Füßchen, mit Deinem Antlitz, das Gott
geweiht zu haben schien zur Reinheit, da standest Du zwischen
Deinen Blumen – – – in Deinem stummen, kindlichen Glück – – –.
Und wie Du so dastandst, zwischen Deinen Rosen, Deinen Nelken,
in Deinem stummen kindlichen Glück – – –,
da fieng ein Engel droben im Himmel bitterlich zu weinen an – –,
Und Gott, der ewig milde Vater, sagte: Engel, warum weinst Du?!
Und der Engel zeigte hinab – – –

Da sah Gott einen großen Garten, voll von Obstbäumen; unter
jedem Baum wuchs eine Blume – –; und ein kleines Mädchen,
mit einer zarten Gestalt, mit feinen weißen Händchen und Füßchen,
mit einem Antlitz, das geweiht schien zur Reinheit, gieng von
einer Blume zur anderen, und berührte leise die Blüthen, die
Blätter – – in ihrem stummen kindlichen Glück – – –.
Sie stand da, in dem großen Garten, und war schön und einsam – – –,
und ihr kleines Herz war voll von Rosen und Nelken – – – –
– – – in der Ferne aber lag das Leben, das schwere
dunkle Leben – !
Da wusste Gott, warum der Engel so bitterlich weinte – –.

Andrew Barker

Subjectivität und Objectivität

Erster Brief: (*Subjectivität*)

Liebes, theures, wunderschönes Fräulein Käthchen!

– – – – – und das Alltägliche breitet wieder seine schweren dumpfen Schleier über meine Seele aus – – –; ah, wie empfinde ich das, seitdem Sie, liebe, süße Lichtgestalt, mir entschwunden sind; in die öde träge Stimmung meiner Seele ist durch Sie, blonde Katharina, ein Schimmer von Sonnenglanz gedrungen, und hat mich tief bewegt – – – !

Warum stürmen so viele Menschen in Leidenschaft und Unruhe dahin?!

Wie tief, wie ruhig und still kann das Menschenherz sich einem holden Zauber hingeben und ungestört dem Tönen seiner Seele nachlauschen – – – !

Damals, als wir neben einander den stillen dunklen Weg am Flusse wandelten, sagte ich, erfüllt von dem süßen Zauber Ihrer Nähe: „Sie werden mir sehr abgehen, Käthchen – –;"

Und so ist es geworden – – – !

Ihre Nähe that mir so wohl, so wohl – –;

Wie wenn der Leib, in Sonnen-Wärme, in Licht und Luft gebadet, rosig und frisch wird – – – so ist es mit der Seele; auch sie wird rosig und fröhlich, und still und zufrieden – – und Du hörst sie gleichsam tiefer athmen – –;

so strömte unbewusst von Ihrer süßen Gestalt Wärme und Licht und machte meine Seele rosig und fröhlich – – –.

Am Morgen Ihrer Abreise gieng ich an Ihren Fenstern vorüber – – –;

dann setzte ich mich im See-Park auf eine Bank und sah hinaus in den Sonnen-Nebel;

das heiße Holz der Bank verbreitete Harzduft, die warme Luft roch nach verwelkten Blättern, die Berge waren matt wie blau-graue Kreide, und hie und da glänzte und schimmerte ein Streifen vom See – –;

Herbst, Abreise, letzte Grüße, eine letzte Berührung einer lieben, lieben, Hand; ach, wie gern hätte ich an ihrem Gartenthore allein von Ihnen Abschied genommen – – – dann hätte ich einfach und ruhig gefragt: darf ich ihre liebe, liebe Hand küssen?! – – –

Adieu, adieu, diese schönen, hellen, liebenswürdigen Tage sind vorüber; Alles ist matt und farblos geworden, und das Alltägliche senkt wieder seine schweren dumpfen Schleier über meine Seele herab – – –.

Albert.

Antwort. (*Objectivität*)

Lieber Herr Albert!

Ich fühle es, es ist am besten, frei und natürlich, und einfach und wahr zu sein – – –; das will ich, das möchte ich so gerne, nachdem ich, lange unschlüssig, ein wenig verwirrt, und von vielen Erwägungen belastet, mich damit beschäftigt habe, ob ich Ihren Brief beantworten solle oder nicht!?

Ich sage Ihnen also frei und einfach mein liebenswürdiges Wort: Ihre poëtische und schwärmerische Huldigung hat mich freudig überrascht und – – ein wenig gerührt – – –;

aber bitte, bitte, haben Sie dabei nicht die verschleierte Empfindung, als ob dieses, was ich da sage, mich Ihnen irgendwie ein bischen näher rückte – – –.

Die schwärmerische begeisterte Stimmung, die den sonst etwas schwerfälligen Mann zu einem bewegteren, zarteren Geschöpfe macht, scheint seine geheimnisvolle Quelle in uns Frauen zu haben.

Sind wir es also nicht, die Ihn dem Ideal-Menschen, wenn auch für Augenblicke, näher rücken?!

Und sollte uns das nicht ein edles, ruhiges Vergnügen bereiten?! Sollte es uns nicht ein wenig rühren können, wenn wir den Mann, den schweren Kämpfer im dunklen Leben, sanft und zart, und mild und rücksichtsvoll werden sehen, und ein Schimmer von melankolischer Selbstvergessenheit sich über sein rauheres Wesen breitet?!

Wie wenn der Sommer-Abend sich freuen würde, daß gute Menschen, ausruhend vom Tage, andächtig und still und zufrieden werden, – – – so ist unsere Freude!

Aber wie?!

Ist denn da eine persönliche Beziehung zwischen der Natur und dem Menschen, den sie in diese Stimmung versetzt?!

Ich habe die Empfindung, als ob es keinen Mann gäbe, der diese unsere natürliche Freude an seiner Huldigung, seiner *sympatie*, so und gerade so, und nicht ein bischen anders, erfassen und begreifen würde, als es wirklich und einfach empfunden ist!!

Eitelkeit, Eitelkeit, Eitelkeit – – – !

Und müssen wir denn nicht jene Ansprüche an unsere Seele fürchten, die sie auf ein gutes Wort, eine freundliche Geberde gründen?! Sollen wir unsere Natürlichkeit, unsere Aufrichtigkeit, unsere Wahrhaftigkeit, unsere Menschlichkeit, mit dem Vorwurf, *coquett* gewesen zu sein, büßen?!

Müssen wir nicht jeden Hauch von *Sympatie*, von Freundschaft, ängstlich verbergen, damit Er in seiner Eitelkeit und Maßlosigkeit, in seinem unsanften, stürmischen Wesen nicht wähne, diesen Hauch leicht und mühelos zu schweren dunklen Stürmen in unseren Tiefen anfachen zu können??!

Eitelkeit, Eitelkeit, Eitelkeit – – –!

Statt mit unseren neunzehn Jahren, mit unserer Unfähigkeit, das Leben und den Mann zu durchdringen, zu ergründen, zu begreifen, statt in Ihm einen lieben guten Bruder, einen natürlichen Freund, einen milden Lehrer, einen freien ritterlichen Menschen zu finden, fühlen wir mit jedem Tage mehr, daß wir uns gegen etwas Unedles, Unschönes, Unheiliges und Feindliches im Manne wehren müssen, und daß wir von sehr viel Lüge umgeben sind! Du schönes, großes, kindliches Vertrauen, wohin schwindest Du?! Weinend verlässt Du unsere dumme, kindliche Seele, – – – und uns umringt das Geheimnis!?

Und Sie, Albert?!

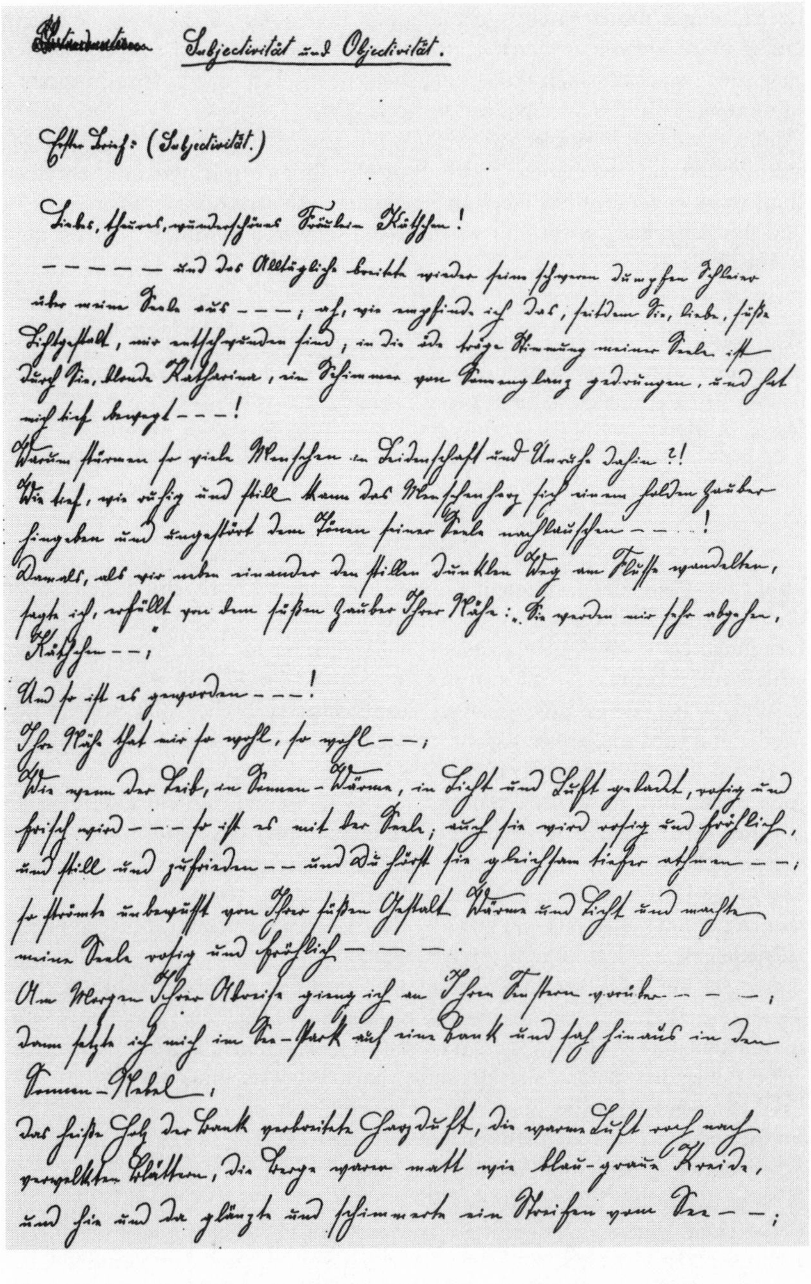

Figure 2. Page from Peter Altenberg's manuscript 'Subjektivität und Objektivität'

Ein unruhiges, dunkles Leben scheint hinter Ihnen, scheint vor Ihnen zu liegen; und in einer Art von großer Resignation auf Sonne und Glanz, geben Sie sich ganz den weichen, melankolischen, den poëtischen und schwärmerischen Stimmungen Ihrer *Ideale* bildenden Seele hin!

Dankbar und voll Freundschaft schauen Sie dem Menschen in's Auge, den Sie als die Quelle dieser schönen Empfindungen in Ihnen betrachten, und schreiben Ihm, wenn er ferne weilt, die wunderschönen, schwermüthigen Worte: „– – – und das Alltägliche senkt nun wieder seine schweren dumpfen Schleier über meine Seele herab – – –."

Und ich?!

Wie wenn der Sommer-Abend sich freuen würde, daß gute Menschen, ausruhend vom Tage, andächtig und still und zufrieden werden – – – so ist unsere Freude, unsere Rührung – – – – –.

Adieu, Albert!

Katharina.

Ehebruch

Drei Menschen sitzen in einem Zimmer: ein junger Gatte, eine junge Gattin und – – – ein Dritter.

Der junge Gatte ist – – ein anständiger Mensch; er hat eine gute Verdauung, schläft gut, arbeitet – – – alles ist in Ordnung an Ihm: Er gibt alle seine Kräfte in organischer Weise aus, geistige, körperliche, seelische; alles ersetzt sich wieder und wird wieder verausgabt – – – sein Leben ist ein kleinlicher, reinlicher Kreislauf unbedeutender Kräfte;

jedes *organ* thut, in weiser *Ökonomie,* so viel als es darf, um ein anderes nicht in seiner Thätigkeit zu stören – – –; besonders nimmt Geist und Seele auf den Körper Rücksicht – – –; denn da ist der *vegetative* Stoffwechsel!

Die junge Gattin ist fein, gebildet, zufrieden;

fein ist sie von Natur aus – –; gebildet durch Lehrer, Bücher, Menschen – – –, zufrieden ist – – – sie durch ihren Willen;

dieser „schöne Wille" ist die Wirkung der feinen Natur und der Bildung; denn durch die Bildung erkennt man „das Nothwendige", die „schönen Nothwendigkeiten des Lebens"; die Erkenntnis dieser „schönen Nothwendigkeiten" gebiert aber den Willen, sich denselben in Frieden zu unterwerfen;

das Nothwendige wollen aber heißt „frei sein"!

Freiheit aber ist die edle Mutter der *Zufriedenheit!*

So ist der Weg des guten Weibes zur Zufriedenheit.

Was ist der Dritte für ein Mensch?!

Er ist einer, der in der dumpfen *Harmonie* des täglichen Lebens einen Ton erklingen lässt, der nicht hinein gehört, einen Ton, der den dämmernden Geist wach ruft, die dämmernde Seele erbeben macht; vielleicht einen höheren, helleren – – gleichviel!!

Diese drei Menschen sitzen beisammen;

man spricht über Alles – – irgend Einer soll heiraten – – man spricht über das

36

Heiraten – – –;

der Gatte: „– – – Ihr, mit Euren Ideen! – – – Ihr glaubt, man müsse sich in der Welt, in den Büchern für die Ehe vorbereiten, im Leben – – –;

ich denke das Leben nicht, ich lebe es – – – und so ist es einfach und leicht; aber Ihr, Ihr wollt das Leben erst denken, und dann dieses gedachte leben – – – so wird es *complicirt* und schwerfällig; und dann – habt Ihr denn so viel Zeit?!

der Dritte: „Das ist eben die Lüge *Eures* Lebens – – – : das Eure ist zuerst einfach – – – aber plötzlich, eine Störung, eine Hemmung, und es wird *complicirt*! – – –, Ihr Einfachen sind verloren!

Aber unseres ist erst *complicirt* – – – dann, spät, wird es einfach, tief, ideal – – – es ist aber eine *Idee*, die sich verwirklicht!

Die Gattin, sanft vermittelnd: „Aber habt Ihr denn so viel Zeit?!“

Der Gatte: „Was gehört denn, zum Beispiel, dazu, um mit einem Weib zu leben?! Das, was man gerade ist, – – oft sogar ein bischen weniger !?“ – – –

Pause – – – !

der Dritte, der einen langen Blick voll Milde auf die etwas abgemagerte Gestalt des jungen Weibes gerichtet hatte, – – – ruhig, sanft, wie selbstverständliches, aus dem innersten *organismus* Hervorkommendes sprechend:

„Was Du bist, gibst Du Deinem Weib – – –! Bist Du viel, gibst Du Ihr viel; sei ein Schwärmer, und Du gibst Deinem Weib das Schwärmerische; sei ein Geist, Geist; eine Seele, Seele – – – –

– – – brauchen aber tut sie nichts! Denn sieh! Sei nichts, kein Mensch, keine Seele, kein Geist – – – und sie gibt Dir doch ruhig ihren Leib und ein Stückchen von ihrer Seele – – –; nur ihr Geist bleibt in Ihr, tief verborgen, und der ist Dein Feind – – – !

Der Gatte: „Was ist denn der Geist des Weibes, worin liegt er? Man sagt immer: Der Mann hat Geist, das Weib hat Gemüth“.

Der Dritte: Ihr Geistiges in Ihr ist nicht etwas Bewusstes, wie beim Mann, keine Gedanken, Ideen, und ihr Zusammenhang mit dem und jenem, mit allem! – – –

Die junge Gattin: „Natürlich, ich verstehe Dich jetzt, das Geistige im Weibe ist eben etwas Weibliches, etwas Halb-Bewusstes über sich selbst!?“

Der Dritte: „Ihr Geist, der Geist des Weibes, das Geistige im Weib, ist ganz einfach die Ahnung dessen, was Ihr fehlt, und was sie sein könnte, sollte – – –; es ist die Sehnsucht nach dem eigenen *Ideale*, die Sehnsucht nach der Entwicklung ihres möglichen *Ideal*-Zustandes, der, tief verborgen, als *latente* Spannkraft, in Ihr ruht, und nach Erlösung, nach Befreiung, nach der Geburt in's Leben, zum Lebendigsein, ringt und drängt! Der Auslöser der *latenten* Spannkraft in lebendige Kraft ist die Liebe!

So wie die unorganische *Materie* nach *Organisirung* strebt und drängt, wie die erste *organisirte Substanz*, die Zelle, sich nach Weiter-*Organisirung*, Vervollkommnung sehnt in der ersten Pflanze, dem Faden-Pilz, der Flechte, dem Moose, wie die Pflanze sich sehnt nach dem Thier mit seiner erhöhten *organisation*, das Thier nach dem Menschen, der Mensch nach Gott-Werdung, nach *Jesus Christus*, so sehnt das Weib sich nach dem in ihrem Innern tief versteckten Leben, nach Höher-*Organisirung* ihres seelisch-leiblichen Lebens!

Dieses in seiner Fülle, seiner Tiefe, seiner edlen Größe zur Entwicklung zu bringen, zum Leben, zur That – – – erwartet Sie, erhofft Sie, und ersehnt Sie *vom Mann*! Er allein kann es Ihr geben – – –;
Das ist ihre Sehnsucht, ihre namenlose, tiefe Sehnsucht – – – das ist ihr Geistiges in Ihr, ihre *Idee*!! – – –

Du aber, Mann mit dem einfachen Leben, sagst:„Was gehört denn dazu, um mit einem Weibe zu leben?! Das, was man gerade ist – oft sogar ein bischen weniger – – –;
Aber siehe! auch Deine Stunde wird kommen !!! – – – – –

Da sitzest Du eines Abends, still, ausruhend, neben Deinem Weib – – –;
plötzlich sieht sie wie gelangweilt aus, müde, etwas starr, verworren – –;
Du betrachtest sie theilnahmsvoll – besorgt –; sie erscheint Dir fremd – fern – –!

Du Ruhiger, Guter, Einfacher, erbleiche!
Dein Feind ist bei Ihr!

Sie denkt – – –;

Sie denkt an ihre Idee! – – –.

Die Gattin: „Du *quälst* – – –;"
Der Gatte: „Du *zerstörst* – – –;"
Der Dritte: „ich *erwecke* – – –"!!

Pastell-Bild

Fräulein G.L. hat röthlich-blonde matte Haare, feine lange weiße Hände, und eine silberne Stimme

Sie ist ein bischen *anämisch* – – – wenn Sie angeregt ist, wenn Sie Furcht oder Freude empfindet, erhält Ihr Gesicht einen Schimmer von Ruhe – – –. Solche Mädchen haben die Stimmung eines zarten jungfräulichen Ernstes; sie haben etwas Ruhiges, Harmonisches; sie kommen selten aus dem Gleichgewicht – – –; nie sind die überspannt oder ironisch; aber oft berührt sie ein Hauch von melancholischem *Phlegma* – – –; bewegt, erzittern sie leise; gerüttelt, sinken sie zusammen, und verwelken;
manchmal raffen sie sich auf, und mit einer etwas zaghaften, kreischenden Stimme sagen sie: „ich will, ich werde, ich muß – – –";
aber was kommt denn dabei heraus?!
Wenn sich die Aufregung gelegt hat, werden sie nachdenklich, trübe, und erschlaffen;
ihre Nerven haben eine geringe Spannkraft und sind auf einen einzigen *Accord* gestimmt: „Sanfte *Passivität*" – – – !
Solche Mädchen glauben immer, ihre milden verschwommenen Empfindungen könnten plötzlich groß und erdrückend werden – –
– – – und doch bleibt das alles lange, lange unverändert;

es gährt nichts, es treibt nichts;
als Kinder sind sie schon ruhige ausgeglichene Weibchen; den zufriedenen
Eltern bieten sie für sprunghafte Entwicklung ein liebliches Ebenmaß. Wenn
sie einen Mann lieb gewinnen, so werden sie weder stiller noch lebhafter;
wenn der Liebling ihrer Seele nicht da ist, so liegt eine sanfte, gemüthliche
Monotonie über sie ausgebreitet – – –, manchesmal sogar etwas gleichgiltiges,
fades, unaufmerksames – – –; dann raffen sie sich plötzlich auf und lächeln –
– – –;
und wenn der Liebling hereintritt – – – vielleicht erwartet Ihr von ihnen etwas
außergewöhnliches, etwas leidenschaftliches?!
Keineswegs!
Sie reichen Ihm ruhig die Hand und küssen Ihn mit ihrem sanften Augenaufschlag;
wie Er auch gestimmt ist, angeregt oder kühl, – – – sie werden bewegter und
heiter gestimmt durch seine Nähe; es ist wie ein Ruck, der durch ihre Natur
geht – – – sie empfinden eine lang anhaltende stille Freude – – –.
Was machen sich dann solche Mädchen für *Ideen* vom Leben, vom Manne oder
vom Glück?! – – –
Sie machen sich gar keine *Ideen* vom Leben, vom Manne oder vom Glück!
Die unfertigen kindischen Mädchen überkleben ihre *Ideale* mit Muth,
Entschlossenheit und Ehrgeiz – – –;
was sind denn das für grobe dicke Striche: „*Energie*", „*Courage*", „*genialität*" – –
– ?! Man denkt ja gar nichts dabei;
aber so sind diese gezierten, *conventionellen* Mädchen;
Puppen, Puppen, Puppen – – –!
Jene aber treten aus der sittsamen duftigen Kinderstube frei und anspruchslos
heraus;
einfach und natürlich entrollt sich das Treiben des Lebens vor ihren klaren
sanften Augen, und treuherzig reichen sie den treuherzigen Gestalten ihre
weiche Hand – – –.
Bisweilen nur gleitet ein leiser Schatten von Unmuth über ihr friedliches
Antlitz, wenn auch sie gemahnt werden, daß das Gute, Zarte, minder gilt;
verwundert und wehmüthig betrachten sie den Jüngling, wie er bequemer und
geselliger mit dem lebhafteren Mädchen tändelt – – –; da fühlen sie sich
schwerfällig, matt und farblos; sie sind eben schüchtern und beengt bei den
keckeren *Melodieen* des Lebens – – –;
Ihr kalten, frechen Melodieen, wo fliegt ihr hin, wer lauscht Euch nach?! – –
–
Aber Ihr, schwerfälligere, einfachere Klänge, Ihr, uralte, unvergängliche,
keusche *Chorale*, wie bebt unser Herz bei Eurem Lied – – –!
Rauscht, rauscht an uns hinan, und Ihr, sanfte, ewig weibliche Gestalten, bleibt
uns nah – – –; bei Euren reinen, ruhigen Melodieen wollen auch wir reiner,
ruhiger werden!

Wahrheit

„Wildente von Ibsen, Akt, Scene

Relling zu Gregor: nun, finden Sie es nicht ganz schön, einmal zur Abwechslung an einem gut besetzten Tisch, in einem glücklichen Familienkreise, zu sitzen?!
Gregor: Ich für meinen Theil, gedeihe nicht in Sumpfluft!
Hjalmar: ach, komme doch nicht wieder auf diesen Unsinn;
Gina: Hier ist keine Sumpfluft, Herr Werle; ich lüfte jeden Tag aus;
Gregor (steht vom Tisch auf): den Gestank, den ich meine, lüften Sie gewiss nicht aus!
Hjalmar: Gestank?!
Gina: ja, was sagst Du dazu, Hjalmar?!
Relling: Um Verzeihung, sind Sie es nicht selber, der den Gestank mitbringt?!
Gregor: Es wäre Ihnen ähnlich, das Gestank zu nennen, was ich ins Haus bringe!
Relling (geht zu Ihm): Hören Sie, Herr Werle, ich habe sie stark in Verdacht, daß Sie noch immer die *„ideale* Forderung" unverkürzt mit sich in der Hintertasche herumtragen;
Gregor: In der Brust trage ich sie mit mir herum –;
Relling: Ja, zum Teufel, wo sie dieselbe auch haben mögen, möchte ich Ihnen nicht rathen, hier den Einkassierer zu spielen, so lange ich da bin; –"

Die Wahrheit, die Du den Menschen, Deinen Nebenmenschen, gibst, muß groß, gesund und stark sein!
So allein bewirkt sie Großes, Gesundes, Gutes und Kraftvolles;
So allein bewirkt sie Bewegung des Innern, Veränderung, Reinigung, Licht und Leben;
Sie ist der *Motor*, der die *„latenten* Spannkräfte" erhöhten, gesteigerten Menschentums in *„vitale* Kräfte", in lebendige Bewegung, umzusetzen hat;
Dazu gehört Kraft, Kraft, Kraft!
Die Wahrheit, die Segenspenderin, kann nicht aus den Bedürfnissen eines verstörten, in Selbst-Quälerei erkrankten, eines geschwächten, unbefriedigten, unklaren, versumpften, sich selbst hemmenden geistigen oder seelischen *organismus* hervorgehen.
Sie ist Krankheit, wenn sie auf einen *organismus* als Hemmung zurückwirkt; Sie ist Gesundheit, wenn sie vorwärts bewegend, befreiend, Werde-Prozesse des Seelisch-Geistigen im Menschen beschleunigend wirkt.
Sie kann nur dort, sie darf nur dort eindringen, wo der Mensch leise und sanft auf sie, die Schöne, Starke, vorbereitet ist, wo die physische und geistige *organisation* vorhanden ist für ihre *Assimilirung*, wo der *organismus assimilirungs*fähig ist;
Die Wahrheit, die Du Deinen Brüdern gibst, muß eine solche sein, daß sie erlösend, daß sie *christlich* wirken kann, wie die Wahrheit in der Lehre *Jesu* von der Nächstenliebe und dem Reich der Armen erlösend und befreiend wirkt, weil sie aber die wirkliche Wahrheit mit ihren *immanenten motorischen* Kräften ist, welche lebendige, befruchtende Bewegung im Menschen-Geiste, in der Menschen-Seele zeugt.

Zum Beispiel:

Du bist verstimmt, unruhig in Dir, unbefriedigt, körperlich, seelisch oder
geistig; Du sitzt in Deinem Zimmer; alles ist unordentlich; eine trübe Reue
hockt in dir;
ein Mensch kommt herein, jung, lebendig;
Du sagst ihm: Du bist heute hässlich, oder gelb, oder eingefallen – – –; es ist
vielleicht, gewiss eine Wahrheit – – – aber siehe! Alles hast Du an Ihm gestört;
sein Stoffwechsel ist verlangsamt, du hast Ihm die Tugend, die Lebendigkeit,
die Lebensfülle dieser Stunde genommen!
Und was hast Du Ihm dafür gegeben?
Eine Wahrheit!!
Sage diese Wahrheit einem Schwachen, einem Mädchen, zum Beispiel, und es
setzt sich zu Dir hin, wird gelber, hässlicher, schwächer – – – es wird krank;
– – – sage sie einem Starken: Er nimmt einen Mantel und geht hinaus in die
frische sonnige oder auch feuchte kalte Luft, oder er trinkt ein Glas *Malaga*,
oder zwei, oder drei, oder er nimmt kleine eiserne Hanteln und schwingt sie,
stößt sie, hebt sie, macht die tiefe Kniebeuge, die Rumpfbeuge, dreißigmal,
mehr, – – – er dampft – – – Deine Wahrheit hat Ihn gerettet!! Er ist nicht mehr
gelb, hässlich, nein, gesunder, schöner!
Deine Wahrheit kann gutes, kann Böses bewirken – – –.
Aber sitze Du, ruhig in Dir, zufrieden, gut, rein gestimmt, körperlich, seelisch
oder geistig in Deinem Zimmer;
es kommt Einer herein; Er ist gelb, hässlich – – –;
Du betrachtest Ihn liebevoll, suchst Ihn zu durchdringen, findest den Schmerz
der Seele, des Leibes; Du knüpfst ein schönes, ruhiges Gespräch an, Du ziehst
mit Deinem Geist, Deinem Gemüth, leise an seiner Wunde vorbei, berührst sie
sanft, heilst sie oder machst sie vergessen – – er wird schöner, reiner gestimmt,
Alles *functionirt* besser – – –; oder Du nimmst Ihn und führst Ihn sanft in die
liebe warme Sonne, oder in den Schatten eines Gartens, einer *Allée*, oder Du
sagst es Ihm blos: gehe ein wenig spazieren, bitte – – –, und er wird schöner
werden, reiner gestimmt, menschlicher – – –.
Das ist eine Wahrheit, die aus einem freien, durch nichts Krankes gehemmten
Menschengemüthe hervorgeht, eine *christliche* Wahrheit, wie sie aus dem
reinen, befreiten Gemüthe des sanften, milden, einzig gerechten Heiland's
hervorging, eine Wahrheit, die nichts Anderes ist, als die zum Ausdruck in's
Wort, zum tönenden Leben beseelten Klanges gebrachte Menschenliebe,
Menschenfreundschaft und Selbstvergessenheit;
es ist eine Wahrheit, welche der *organismus*, auf den sie wirken soll, liebevoll
bedenkt, wie die erste, wirkliche, gute Kirche, und *Jesus* selbst, welche die
schwere drückende Wahrheit von dem Elend des irdischen Lebens der nach
Erlösung ringenden Menschheit, in schöne weiche Hüllen einschlugen, damit
sie dem kindlichen *Organismus* der Menschheit nicht wehe thun und so in diesen
Hüllen zu männlicher Menschheit erwachse, erstehe!
Die Wahrheit des Gregor Werle ist eine unwahre Wahrheit, im kranken
Gemüthe krank und unfruchtbar geboren und wieder Krankes, Unfruchtbares
zeugend; es ist eine Wahrheit des bedrängten Ich-Lebens, nicht eine Wahrheit

der freien Nächsten-Liebe; es ist eine *unchristliche* Wahrheit, die in dem kleinen, rührend beschränkten Kreis der Familie Egdal nicht fruchtbares Leben, sondern Zerstörung auslöst, indem sie den armen Menschen den poëtischen Frieden raubt, den Sie sich so tapfer, so herzig einfach, im beschwerlichen Dasein erkämpft haben – – –; es ist eine Wahrheit, die nicht von dem freien, jungen, ungestümen Drange eines schönen Menschengemüthes zum Leben in's Wort, in Wort-That gedrängt wird, sondern aus einem kranken, unfreien, trübe Dinge von sich gebenden Gemüth, zur eigenen Erleichterung, schwerfällig und mühselig abgesondert wird – – –.

Ego, Ego, Ego – – –!!

Die *„Idealen* Forderungen" aber liegen in der Durchsetzung, dem zum Sieg Verhelfen, zum Leben, der wirklichen Wahrheiten, welche für alle Menschen, für die Menschheit befreiend und erlösend wirken müssen, insofern sie eins sind mit den tief verborgenen und unbesiegbaren Gesetzen der menschlichen *Organisation* und ihrer *Organisirung* zum *idealen* Ende; sie allein können und werden den Menschen zu seinem körperlichen, seelischen und geistigen Frieden führen.

Die Wissenschaft sucht diese wirklichen Wahrheiten, diese unbesiegbaren, unentrinnbaren Gesetze der menschlichen *Organisirung* zu ergründen, die *Religion* erschaut sie in ahnungsvollen *Visionen* – – –.

Und darum sagte der menschlichste Gott, der göttlichste Mensch:

„Folget mir, denn Ich bin der Weg, die Wahrheit, und das Leben"!!!

Author's note

A list of locations of manuscripts by Peter Altenberg is being compiled by the author of this article. Enquiries and offers of information should be sent to him at the following address: Dr Andrew Barker, Department of German, David Hume Tower, University of Edinburgh, George Square, Edinburgh EH8 9JX, Scotland.

Although Peter Altenberg published eleven books in a literary career of just over twenty-two years, these volumes, along with three posthumous collections, by no means account for all he wrote. His voluminous correspondence remains virtually unknown, and a considerable amount of imaginative writing lies unpublished. Indeed, its very whereabouts remain largely uncharted. Much is located in European libraries and archives, but the USA is also a rich source for hunters of Altenbergiana. Indeed, perhaps the richest collection, gathered by the art dealer and connoisseur Otto Kallir (1894–1978), is now in private hands in New York City. Besides a great deal of unpublished material, it also contains large portions of the manuscripts for the later collections *Vita Ipsa* (1918) and *Mein Lebensabend* (1919). Examination of these manuscripts, most of them hitherto unknown to scholars working on Altenberg, reveals that longheld opinions about the writer will have to be considerably revised.

The *Skizzenbuch* manuscripts, located in the Leo Baeck Institute in New York, came into the Institute's collection in 1959 via the art dealers Karl & Faber of Munich.[11] They do not appear in the recent *Gesammelte Werke in fünf Bänden*, whose first two volumes comprise the 'Gesammelte Skizzen' from 1895–1918. The title page of *Aus einem Skizzenbuch* bears in the top right-hand corner a pencil entry of modern but unknown provenance 'ca 1893/94', a putative dating which goes counter to statements made both by Altenberg himself and by subsequent critics concerning the dating of his first works. Altenberg himself claims that he wrote his first sketch 'Neun und Elf' in September 1894;[12] but the dubious nature of this assertion emerges from a letter he wrote to Arthur Schnitzler dated July 1894 which makes clear that by this date Altenberg was already well embarked on a literary career. Altenberg's letter is itself obviously a reply to an enquiry from Schnitzler about Altenberg's methods of composition, and in it he states his gratitude that he is able to display his talent 'in einem Kreise von feinen gebildeten jungen Leuten', a clear reference to his work already being known to other members of the *Jung Wien* clique by the summer of 1894.[13]

To judge from the calligraphy, the texts of *Aus einem Skizzenbuch* are very early examples of Altenberg's writing. Peter de Mendelssohn quotes Frau Hedwig Fischer's appreciation of Altenberg's neat, almost feminine hand when she received the manuscripts for *Wie ich es sehe* in the summer of 1895.[14] At that time she was acting as a reader for S. Fischer Verlag, and when her husband found her in tears over the manuscripts that was recommendation enough for him to publish them.[15] The neatness of the texts in *Aus einem Skizzenbuch* underlines not only the reactions of Frau Fischer, it underpins also the claims made in *Bilderbögen des kleinen Lebens* where Altenberg lauds his 'wunderbar deutliche Schrift', acquired through eight days of hard labour at the Stuttgart booksellers Hühnersdorf & Keil in the early 1880s.[16] The contrast between the orthography of these early texts and the large, untidy scrawl of later ones is very marked. The purely visual evidence of the manuscripts thus supports an early dating, and as the reference to the Solness essay in the Schnitzler–Hofmannsthal correspondence early in January 1893 reveals, it is clear that Altenberg had indeed begun writing as early as 1892.

The very term 'Skizzenbuch' allies these texts with others printed in the earliest two versions of *Wie ich es sehe*, whose first edition appeared in the spring of 1896. In this, as also in the second edition of 1898 and the third edition of 1901, we find four series of texts grouped together under the rubric '*Skizzenreihe*', whereas in the fourth edition of 1904 this term is replaced by '*Studienreihe*'. At the latest, then, these texts might conceivably have been written in 1904. All internal evidence, however, shows this later dating to be untenable, for the material of *Aus einem Skizzenbuch* quite clearly relates to the first and second editions of *Wie ich es sehe*.

In the 1896 edition of *Wie ich es sehe* the 'Skizzenreihe' entitled 'Der Revolutionär dichtet' contains five, the edition of 1898 seven, examples of 'Albert Königsberg's' writing. The titles of the pieces in the 1896 edition are 'Wachstum', 'Le coeur', 'Genie und homme médiocre', 'Fidélité', 'Nacht-Café', and added to them in 1898 come 'Wahrheit' and 'De amore'. *Aus einem Skizzenbuch* also consists of five pieces, these bearing the titles: 'Nacht-Café',

'Subjectivität und Objectivität' (an exchange of letters between 'Albert' and 'Katharina'), 'Ehebruch', 'Pastell-Bild', and 'Wahrheit'. As they are unpaginated, I have reproduced the manuscripts according to the order in which I found them in the Leo Baeck Institute. It will be clear from these listings that two of the titles in the unpublished collection, namely 'Nacht-Café' and 'Wahrheit', correspond to titles found in the 1896 and 1898 editions of *Wie ich es sehe*.

Examination of the present version of 'Nacht-Café' with the version Altenberg came to publish in the 1896 edition of *Wie ich es sehe* will show, I believe, the manner in which the writer was prepared to revise work before publication. This, of course, goes against the evidence of Altenberg's letter to Schnitzler where he says how much he hates 'Retouche', and how his works are born in their finished form:

> Meine Sachen haben das Malheur, daß Sie immer für kleine Proben betrachtet werden, während sie leider bereits das sind, was ich überhaupt zu leisten im Stand bin.

In the present manuscripts the presentation is notably fluent and clear, with virtually no sign of correction or afterthought. Yet, as Peter Wagner has shown in his analysis of the changes which 'Roman am Lande' underwent from first to second edition of *Wie ich es sehe*,[17] Altenberg was, on occasion, prepared to modify his work after publication. It might, therefore, be argued that *Aus einem Skizzenbuch* was completed *after* the publication of the 1896 edition but before the second edition of 1898. The example of 'Wahrheit', which did not appear until the 1898 edition, might seem initially to confirm this dating of the texts, but, as I argue above, it is most likely the text which Albert/Altenberg refers to in 'Idylle' in the 1896 edition of *Wie ich es sehe*. Given the unitary nature of *Aus einem Skizzenbuch* to which 'Wahrheit' belongs, I therefore suggest a date of composition sometime before publication of the first edition of *Wie ich es sehe* in April 1896, with 'Nacht-Café' representing the original version of a piece revised for publication, rather than the reworking of an already published work.[18]

Why these pieces, with the exception of the revised 'Nacht-Café', remained unpublished must remain in the realm of speculation. One reason may lie in the lack of any formal relationship between the various items, especially when compared with the various 'Skizzenreihen' in *Wie ich es sehe* which are genuinely cyclical, linked together by a variety of formal and thematic devices. The pieces in the 'Skizzenbuch' are much more obviously random and thus at odds with the through-composed nature of much of *Wie ich es sehe* in its original guise. At the level of content, 'Subjectivität und Objectivität' may well have been too personal in nature to permit publication, just as 'Familienleben', with its clear allusions to the author's own family, was dropped after the first edition of *Wie ich es sehe*. Finally, in 'Wahrheit', Altenberg criticises unequivocally the excesses of a 'revolutionary' figure, whereas in *Wie ich es sehe* the similar figure of Albert Königsberg functions as an example of incorruptibility in a flawed world. To have published 'Wahrheit' would thus have contradicted one of the central thrusts of *Wie ich es sehe* as a whole.

Notes

1. The plays performed were *The Pretenders, An Enemy of the People,* and *The Wild Duck.* See Michael Meyer, *Henrik Ibsen: The Top of a Cold Mountain 1883–1906* (London, 1976), p. 176. On 16 April Ibsen attended the first Viennese performance of *The Wild Duck* at the Deutsches Volkstheater with Friedrich Mitterwurzer, a great favourite of Peter Altenberg, playing the role of Hjalmar. Rudolf Lothar writes of Mitterwurzer: 'Sein Hjalmar Ekdal war ebenso ein Meisterstück des natürlichen Modernen wie sein König Philipp im Klassischen', quoted from Heinz Kindermann, *Theatergeschichte Europas,* vol. 8 (Salzburg, 1968), p. 148.
2. Hermann Bahr, 'Henrik Ibsen', reprinted in *Österreichische Literatur- und Kunstkritik 1887–1902,* ed. Gotthart Wunberg, vol. 1 (Tübingen, 1976), pp. 1–17.
3. Hermann Bahr, 'Die Überwindung des Naturalismus', reprinted in *Österreichische Literatur- und Kunstkritik 1887–1902,* vol. 1, pp. 155–9.
4. See *Peter Altenberg. Leben und Werk in Texten und Bildern,* ed. H. C. Kosler (Munich, 1981), p. 243. Reviewing Ernst Rosmer's *Peter Kron,* a drama which survived three performances at the Burgtheater in April 1899, Altenberg noted in the Vienna *Extrapost:* 'Unser Publikum goutiert vielleicht *noch nicht* "Baumeister Solneß", sicher aber *nicht mehr* "Peter Kron".' See Robert Werba, 'Ein Außenseiter der Theaterkritik. Peter Altenberg und das Wiener Theaterjahr 1898/99', *Maske und Kothurn,* 20 (1974), p. 184.
5. Altenberg's quotation is most likely adapted from E. Brausewetter's translation for the Reclam edition (p. 63). Although undated, it appeared in all probability in Leipzig in 1887. Minor divergences from this translation in both nomenclature and punctuation can be put down to Altenberg himself. Professor M. Dietrich (personal communication) has suggested that Altenberg may have been working from a 'Regieexemplar'.
6. Peter Altenberg, 'Familienleben', quoted from *Gesammelte Werke in 5 Bänden,* ed. W. J. Schweiger (Vienna and Frankfurt, 1987), vol. 1, p. 94. The reflection of enthusiasm for Ibsen in narrative rather than dramatic form is also a feature of the early Rilke, as George C. Schoolfield has shown in his essay 'A Bad Story by Young Rilke', *From Vormärz to Fin de Siècle. Essays in 19th Century Austrian Literature,* ed. Mark G. Ward (Blairgowrie, 1986), pp. 107–32.
7. Ibid., p. 99.
8. Ibid., p. 49.
9. Emil Reich remarks that Gregers Werle (*sic*) is 'ein geistig wenig bedeutender, praktisch unfähiger Mensch [. . .], der bis zu seinem 37. Jahr (so alt ungefähr wäre er zu denken) eine Lebensaufgabe sucht und sie endlich in dem Unternehmen zu finden glaubt, das Heim eines Jugendfreundes [. . .] von der Lüge zu reinigen'. Emil Reich, *Henrik Ibsens Dramen,* 7–8th edn (Berlin, 1910), p. 285.
10. Ibid., p. 87.
11. Since finding *Aus einem Skizzenbuch* in June 1988, I discover that its existence is recorded in the *Verzeichnis der schriftlichen Nachlässe in deutschen Archiven und Bibliotheken,* ed. W. A. Mommsen, vol. 1, pt II (Boppard am Rhein, 1983), p. 558, cited in Irene Köwer, *Peter Altenberg als Autor der literarischen Kleinform* (Frankfurt, 1987), p. 281.
12. Peter Altenberg, 'Wie ich "Schriftsteller" wurde', *Mein Lebensabend* (Berlin, 1919), p. 9; W. J. Schweiger (op. cit., p. 343) nevertheless claims that Altenberg did not begin writing until 1895.
13. *Das Altenbergbuch,* ed. Egon Friedell (Leipzig, Vienna and Zürich, 1921), p. 79.
14. Peter de Mendelssohn, *S. Fischer und sein Verlag* (Frankfurt, 1970), p. 214ff.
15. Ibid., p. 214ff.
16. Peter Altenberg, *Bilderbögen des kleinen Lebens* (Berlin, 1909), p. 84.

17. Peter Wagner, 'Peter Altenbergs Prosadichtung. Untersuchungen zur Thematik und Struktur des Frühwerks', Ph.D. thesis (Münster, 1965), p. 149.
18. There exists a further, unrelated piece called 'Nachtcafé' in *Neues Altes* (Berlin, 1911), pp. 135–6.

Acknowledgements

My thanks go to Dr Diane Spielmann of the Leo Baeck Institute in New York for her friendly and efficient service, and to the Institute itself for granting permission to publish these texts. I am also indebted to Professor Margret Dietrich for her kindness in locating the source of Altenberg's quotation from *Die Wildente*. For their help and advice I am also most grateful to Leo Lensing, who shared in the excitement of discovering these texts, and to Edward Timms.

Peter Altenberg's Fabricated Photographs
Literature and Photography in Fin-de-Siècle Vienna
Leo A. Lensing

Although Peter Altenberg has begun to emerge as a key figure in Viennese modernism, the visual orientation of his literary production has not yet received the critical attention it deserves. Altenberg's ongoing concern with the act of seeing and the ethics of vision, announced in the title of his first book *Wie ich es sehe* (*As I See It*), made him an avid collector of photographs and picture postcards. These objects, which Altenberg usually signed and inscribed with aphoristic or lyrical commentaries, constitute a second *oeuvre*, one that is arguably just as significant as the sketches and prose poems upon which his literary reputation currently rests. Understanding Altenberg's photographs constitutes an important step towards defining his literary individuality and evaluating the innovative character of his work.

The intensity of Altenberg's interest in photography may be measured by the circumstance that he once described the genesis of his literary career as the written response to a photographic image. His first published sketch, 'Lokale Chronik', took its inspiration from an illustrated notice about the disappearance of a young girl. In 'So wurde ich' ('How I Became What I Am'), a brief memoir about the composition of the sketch, Altenberg remembered the illustration as a photograph. But the photograph turns out actually to have been a drawing, and Altenberg changed and added other details to the brief account he found in a 1894 issue of the *Illustriertes Extrablatt*.[1] Why Altenberg, consciously or unconsciously, transformed the sketched portrait into a photograph is suggested by the situation in which he dramatises his literary beginnings. He depicts himself becoming a writer as he is 'discovered' by the 'Young Vienna' circle. Arthur Schnitzler, Hugo von Hofmannsthal, Felix Salten, Richard Beer-Hofmann, and Hermann Bahr enter the Café Central and catch him in the act of writing. While they recognise his literary talent, they also question his naturalistic procedures. Even to Schnitzler, the writer in the group most committed to critical observation, the act of composing a commentary on a visual image seems 'suspicious'.[2] Altenberg's stylised recollection in 'So wurde ich' fictionalises the difference he sensed between himself and the aesthetes of Young Vienna, between his own perceptional immediacy and the form-conscious literature cultivated especially by Hofmannsthal and Beer-Hofmann.

For Peter Altenberg, who once wrote that he hated all modern writers who denounced Zola as a mere photographer, there was no contradiction between photography and literary art.[3] Young Vienna, however, equated photography with Naturalism, which, under Hermann Bahr's leadership, had been rejected as too mechanistic and too inattentive to the unconscious life. Hofmannsthal, for example, noted in his diary in 1892: 'Photographie/Naturalismus verzichten auf die Mitwirkung der Suggestion (der Farbe), welche sie durch Genauigkeit ersetzen wollen.' ('Photography/naturalism dispense with the attendant effects of suggestion (of colour), which they claim to replace with exactitude').[4] Not only did this view underestimate the complexity of Naturalism; it also ignored the contemporary movement among Austria's most talented photographers towards a highly self-conscious pictorial photography.

As early as 1891, Hugo Henneberg, Hans Watzek and Heinrich Kühn, the self-designated TRIFOLIUM of Austrian art photography, began to introduce pictorial nuance and painterly composition into their images. As a programmatic statement published by Watzek in 1895 indicates, their aesthetic project expressly sought to overcome the apparent objectivity of the medium:

> In the photographed image (. . .) all spatial qualities of the depicted object are not accorded the same value. Instead, in keeping with the subjective disposition of the artist, certain characteristics of the phenomenon are emphasized, whereas others are suppressed or eliminated. In this way the image presents a harmonious whole that produces the effect on the viewer intended by the artist.[5]

The practical results of this ambitious theorising might have pleased even Hofmannsthal. Photographic portraits subtly adapted the look of Old Masters, and photographed landscapes acquired the symbolic texture of Böcklin's canvases.[6] Watzek and his colleagues achieved their artistic effects by modifying the photographic apparatus and by complicating the printing process. First of all, they used special lenses that softened the focus and exploited the tone values of diffused light. Secondly, they printed their images painstakingly, often superimposing multiple impressions produced by the 'Gummidruck' or gum-bichromate method. In addition to the experimental fusion of positive prints, they also combined negatives and scratched or retouched their surface.[7] This decisive manipulation of the image won the admiration of the photographic and the artistic avant-garde alike. Alfred Stieglitz published photographs by Henneberg, Kühn, and Watzek in *Camera Work;*[8] and *Ver sacrum* reproduced their exquisite images alongside drawings by Klimt and Khnopff, the Belgian Symbolist.[9]

It is unlikely that Altenberg sympathised with the ideal of these costly, sometimes canvas-sized photographs that were displayed at Secession exhibitions in both Munich and Vienna. More than once, he argued that the diminutive reproductions in his picture-postcard albums rendered pilgrimages to '"famous" art collections' (*PAB*, p. 61) superfluous. Nevertheless, art photography influenced his work decisively through its effect on stylish practitioners of photographic portraiture. Many of the reproduced images he collected and inscribed came from the commercial studios of Hermann Clemens Kosel, Dora

Kallmus (better known as Madame D'Ora), and other talented adaptors of the Trifolium's aesthetic principles. Kosel, whose 'Künstlerische Porträtphotographien' ('Artistic Portrait Photographs') were even advertised in *Die Fackel* in 1906,[10] deserves special mention. He is the only prominent photographer identified so far as having taken photographs under Altenberg's direction. The poet commissioned him to take '*half-nude* and *nude*' portraits of one of the many young women whose photographic images he transformed into verbal–visual collages.[11] Kosel also acted as the guiding spirit behind a photography supplement that first appeared in 1904 in the sixth issue of *Kunst*, Altenberg's short-lived art magazine. *Der Gummidruck. Blätter zur Förderung der modernen Kunstphotographie* ('The Gum Print. Papers for the Promotion of Modern Art Photography') took its name from the printing method that Kosel had popularised in 1896 with the publication of a widely acclaimed instruction manual.[12] Friedrich Krauss, the editor of *Der Gummidruck*, stressed his indebtedness not only to Kosel's technical explanations but also to Altenberg's aesthetic conception of photography. He begins his essay on the importance of the gum print with a motto borrowed from the poet's programmatic introduction to the first issue of *Kunst*: 'Die größte Künstlerin vor allem ist die Natur und mit einem Kodak in einer wirklich menschlich-zärtlichen Hand erwirbt man mühelos ihre Schätze' ('The greatest artist of all is nature, and with a Kodak in a truly tender human hand one can acquire her treasures effortlessly').[13] Krauss is clearly speculating on the publicity value of this statement and may well have expected his readers to overlook its contradiction of the principles of technical manipulation inherent in the gum-bichromate process.

Altenberg was apparently not as willing as the pictorial photographers to play down the medium's documentary power. Describing his writing method in a 1894 letter to Schnitzler, he exclaimed: 'Ich hasse die Retouche' ('I hate retouching').[14] Altenberg chooses to celebrate the sensitive hand that wields the camera rather than the skilled manipulator who operates in the darkroom. This preference is in keeping with his frequent use of photography as a technological metaphor for his own poetic vision. When Altenberg was asked, in 1901, to explain how he imagined texts before committing them to paper, he replied that the events of the day seemed to be recorded in his mind unconsciously and automatically as photographs.[15] He went on to say that he then tried to associate titles with these mental images without resorting to the logic of traditional formal connnections. This statement shows how importantly photography figured in Altenberg's attempt to find an innovative literary form which would both shape his experience adequately and suit his eccentric creative temperament. In view of this goal, it is not surprising that his earliest visually oriented texts take their inspiration from picture postcards rather than from art photographs or modern paintings.

The postcard presented Altenberg with a congenial modern form that had originated in Austria–Hungary. The 'Correspondenzkarte', issued in 1869, became the world's first postcard. Picture postcards were produced for the first time soon after, and by 1898 they had begun to evolve into a distinct art form, used in Vienna by the Secession and later by the Wiener Werkstätte both to represent and to publicise their aesthetic programme. What prompted Altenberg to explore the aesthetic potential of this postal novelty emerges quite clearly from the reflections of James Douglas, an English journalist writing in 1907:

> Like many great inventions the postcard has brought a silent revolution in our habits. [. . .] The postcard is really a very short and unceremonious missive. It contains neither affectionate preambles nor reassuring conclusions. It begins without a prelude and finishes without a conclusion. The picture postcard takes coarseness to the extreme. There is no space for courtesy. Often one writes on a blue sky or a white road, but usually there is space only for a short breathless sigh.[16]

By subverting the stilted conventions of the traditional letter, the postcard offered a model for a new form which could convey a narrative without resorting to traditional story-telling. The illustrated card could, potentially, go even further by substituting the ambiguous interplay between word and image for the narrative comforts of well-defined beginnings and ends.

For Peter Altenberg, picture postcards were, for all practical purposes, photographic postcards. In one of several references to the fascination they held for him, he stated that he had collected 1,500 cards since 1897 and specified that they were 'ausschließlich photographische Aufnahmen von Landschaften, Frauen, Kindern, Tieren' ('exclusively photographic pictures of landscapes, women, children, animals') (*PAB*, p. 60). Even if archival sources indicate that this is not strictly true, the overwhelming majority of his inscribed images prove that for him the picture postcard was — literally rather than metaphorically as it was for James Douglas — 'a candid camera recording our amusements and pastimes, our habits and customs, our moral attitudes and behaviour'.[17]

In 'Ansichtskarten' ('Picture Postcards'), first published in 1899 and the first of several texts with the same or a similar title, he investigates these cultural snapshots for the first time. The text consists of fourteen postcard messages sent by an unnamed him to an unnamed her. The cards themselves are evoked by titles, which also provide a point of reference for the brief texts. 'Inneres einer Kirche' ('Inside a Church'), for example, undermines the putative visual image rather than simply invoking it. Instead of what we might imagine as an meditative interior, the writer sees a despondent space:

> Hier ist der Raum, in welchem besiegte Menschenseelen ihre Sedan-Capitulationen unterzeichnen!
>
> [Here is the space where conquered human souls sign their Sedan capitulations!][18]

This deft inscription apparently overrides the visual codes of the image, which was probably meant to convey religious consolation. The use of a political metaphor — the surrender of Napoleon III's army to the Prussians at Sedan in 1870 — intensifies the unsettling effect of the interpretive juxtaposition of word and image.

Altenberg's commentaries not only appropriate the image; they also occasionally subsume it, as in the wryly humorous text for the card entitled 'Donau bei Y.' ('Danube near Y.'):

Stundenlang sah er dem breiten, flimmernden Strome zu, an Weidenzweigen vorüber säuseln! Und er gedachte ihrer. Denn immer gedachte
er ihrer; auch wenn er nicht stundenlang dem breiten, flimmernden
Strome zusah, an Weidenzweigen vorübersäuseln!

[For hours he gazed at the wide, shimmering stream, as it gurgled past
the willow branches! And he thought of her. Because he was always
thinking of her, even when he was not gazing for hours at the wide,
shimmering stream, as it gurgled past the willow branches!] (WT, p. 310)
This card dispenses with its visual antecedent for the purpose of gently mocking
the lover, who is so absorbed by his passion that he merely looks at rather than
sees the world around him. The critical effect achieved here by rhetorical
repetition derives in some of the other texts from a more direct engagement with
the absent visual image. 'Perchtoldsdorf, Platz', for example, questions the
picturesque quality of a still lovely square in one of Vienna's outlying wine
districts:

Hier ist ein kleines Café. Morgens leer. Vormittags leer. Mittags leer.
Nachmittags kommen einige Gäste. Das 'Interessante Blatt' ist ganz
zerfetzt. Man liest eben gern von Mord und Kälbern mit zwei Köpfen [...]
in dem kleinen Café am Platze.

[Here is a small café. Empty early in the morning. Empty later in the
morning. Empty at noon. In the afternoon several guests arrive. The
'Interesting News' is completely tattered. It's just that people like to read
about murder and calves with two heads [. . .] in the small café on the
square.] (*WT*, p. 311)

This sparely drawn vignette implies a critique of the false images generated by
the dominant visual culture. *Das interessante Blatt* became one of Vienna's first
photographically illustrated magazines. It specialised in reproductions of
extremely high quality, geared chiefly to monitoring the doings of high society
and illustrating the more sensational aspects of everyday life. In *The Last Days
of Mankind* Karl Kraus uses the same magazine to demonstrate how the visual
mass media exploit the suffering caused by the war. Act I, Scene 20 shows an
Austrian lieutenant excitedly describing his photograph of a dying Russian
soldier that he hopes will be right 'fürs *Intressante*'.[19] Altenberg's critique focuses
on the consumption rather than the production of such images. The deserted
café, emphasised by the threefold repetition of 'leer', also reflects metaphorically on the lives of the patrons who will soon sit at its tables. The detail of a
tattered, repeatedly devoured copy of the illustrated magazine suggests that
these guests are compulsive readers who still their hunger for experience with
images that have little to do with their own existence.

As these examples demonstrate, Altenberg's method in 'Ansichtskarten' is
to subvert the reader's expectation of formulaic greetings. He offers instead
rhetorical repetition, invented details, and even unseen miniature narratives. It
would be incorrect, however, to assume that these postcard texts were not
originally keyed to visual images. In at least one instance, the actual postcard

with its inscribed text, published first as a pictureless 'Ansichtskarte', has survived.[20] It is more likely that editorial policy, based on the high costs of good reproductions, rather than Altenberg's choice dictated the omission of the postcards themselves.

More than any other writer of turn-of-the-century Vienna, with the possible exception of Karl Kraus,[21] Peter Altenberg not only brought a photographic sensibility to bear on his literary production but he also incorporated actual photographs into his written *oeuvre*. His complex response to the medium has no parallel among his own contemporaries, and invites comparison instead with the work of the most inventive artist–photographers of the last two decades. His images may, in fact, be understood as fabricated photographs, or 'fabrications' — Anne Hoy's collective term for the most innovative work in photography since 1970.[22] Altenberg's imaginative transformation of photographic images anticipated the staged, altered, and appropriated photographs that mark the experiments of Arnulf Rainer, Duane Michals, Cindy Sherman, and others.

Rainer's aggressively 'overpainted' and 'overdrawn' photographic self-portraits, for example, exaggerate the histrionic self-observation already present in Altenberg's numerous inscribed photographs of himself. While Rainer (born in 1929), one of contemporary Austria's most important artists, mainly scratches and brushes intricate but indecipherable marks onto the image, the American Duane Michals (born in 1932) inscribes his photographs with provocative comments. These carefully calculated texts enliven a deliberately unremarkable image or create a verbal narrative that conflicts with the denotation of the photograph. Similarly, in Altenberg's inscribed images the calligraphically applied text frequently surrounds and occasionally threatens to write over and violate the image. Such comparisons, abbreviated as they must remain on this occasion, provide a valuable diachronic perspective on Altenberg's fabricated photographs, the innovative aesthetic of which has generally been overlooked in favour of more conventional biographical explications.

The recent major 'Vienna 1900' exhibitions held in Venice, in Vienna itself, and in Paris contained Altenberg displays which tended to equate the poet's photographs with the framed pictures that covered the walls of his garret room in the Graben Hotel. This conception was derived from what remains of the poet's pictorial *Nachlaß* in the Historical Museum of the City of Vienna, some 350 objects including photographs and postcards, and can be traced back ultimately to the 'Peter-Altenberg-Zimmer' in Otto Kallir's Neue Galerie. After buying the *Nachlaß* from Altenberg's sister, Kallir set up the Altenberg Room as a memorial to the poet, which remained open to the public from 1929 to 1938.[23] Hans Bisanz's recent book, which provides the first systematic sampling of the photographs in the *Nachlaß*, interprets Altenberg's inscribed images almost exclusively as the furnishings of an 'aesthetic temple'.[24] The assumptions behind this metaphor lead all too easily to the misconception that these images amount to a permanent exhibition of private obsessions. Yet Altenberg did not simply buy and collect these images for himself. He commissioned, staged, and mounted photographs, and had them reproduced as picture postcards. He inscribed them and often gave (rather than mailed) them to friends and admirers. In several instances, he even published his commentaries together with the images that inspired them. He not only transformed single photographs into composite images but he also mounted these images in albums and created pictorial narratives complicated further by marginal commentaries. Towards the end of his life, he wrote of having collected '10,000 postcards with and without texts' (*PAB*, p. 61). Given this daunting number, it seems prudent to avoid any pretence of interpretive generalisation. Although several images will be introduced in the following discussion, the interpretation will focus on a few particularly interesting examples that function as acts of aesthetic communication.

The images to be examined closely belong to the two most important, and probably the two most extensive, categories in Altenberg's collection: photographs of himself and photographs of girls and women. There is, in fact, good reason to see these two motifs as variations on the same theme. From the very beginning of his literary career Altenberg's literary 'otherness' was explained as femininity. In a formulation that perhaps owes more to consternation than conviction, Hofmannsthal identified the autobiographical substratum in *Wie ich es sehe* emerging from the fragmentary sketches as a portrait of the poet:

> So ist das Gesicht des Dichters schattenhaft in die hundert Geschichten eingesenkt und schwebt empor. Ein sehr stilisiertes Gesicht, mit einer großen raffinierten Einfachheit. Mit weiblichen Augen sozusagen; was man an Männern weiblich nennt.

> [Thus the face of the poet, which was submerged in a hundred stories, floats to the surface. A very stylised face, with a great complicated simplicity. With feminine eyes so to speak, or what is called feminine in men.][25]

Almost as an afterthought, Hofmannsthal adds to the image of the stylised face the detail of feminine eyes. This hesitant acknowledgement of a female perspective in Altenberg's work, which seems to suppress the pejorative adjective 'effeminate' only with difficulty, undergoes a positive revision in a more sophisticated commentary by Hans Heinz Ewers.

In 1914 Madame D'Ora, easily the most important portraitist of the Viennese cultural elite, published a brochure advertising her photography studio. Besides sixteen photographs the brochure contained an essay by Ewers entitled 'Bild und Photo'. Ewers articulates an aesthetic distinction between the standard painterly likeness, which he illustrates with an insightful critique of the ubiquitous portraits of Franz Joseph, and the artistic portrait photograph. Then, giving an original twist to the standard period dichotomy between male intellect and female sensuality, he defines painting as male inwardness and photography as female outwardness. True to his promotional purpose, he then maintains that the mastery of surfaces is an inherently female talent which explains why the most artistic photographs are being produced by women. Unexpectedly, he introduces Peter Altenberg as a possible synthesis of the male painter and the female photographer:

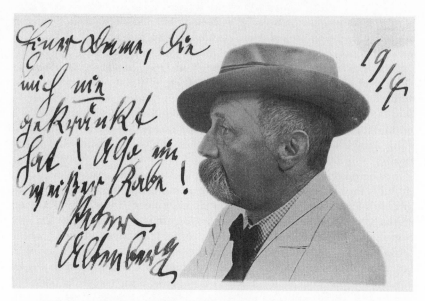

Figure 3. Altenberg in profile (inscribed postcard)

Peter Altenberg does not know what a Danae he is himself nor that every artist must be one: masculine and feminine alike, impregnating and giving birth. The purely male man will never have a profound relationship to art, nor will the entirely female woman: Hermes and Aphrodite created the soul of the artist *together*.[26]

What is remarkable about this characterisation is not the *fin-de-siècle* sexual mythology, but rather the link between Altenberg's artistic individuality and the creative talent of the woman photographer. As might be expected, the sexual ambiguity that marked Altenberg's life and art did not allow for the harmonious hermaphroditism evoked by Ewers.

Two photographic portraits from 1914 (Figures 3 and 4), the year of Ewers's essay, provide a good starting point for examining the complexities of Altenberg's fabricated photographs. The first of these shows the poet in a standard bust portrait rendered even more conventional by the profile view; the frontal pose often signalled a more confrontational posture. But Altenberg takes advantage of this position by arranging the caption in such a way that it seems to trace and extend the visual image. The text, 'Einer Dame, die mich *nie* gekränkt hat! Also ein weißer Rabe! Peter Altenberg' ['To a lady who has never injured me! Therefore, to a white raven!'), represents at best a backhanded compliment to the lady in question.[27] In German, the distinction of being a rare bird of the type 'weißer Rabe' is dubious enough, but there is also the pejorative expression 'to steal like a raven'. What distinguishes this dedication from Altenberg's usual complaints about his maltreatment at the hands of women is its interaction with the image. Altenberg's attire, especially his white jacket and light-coloured hat, associates him with 'white', thus suggesting that he is an odd bird himself. The

54

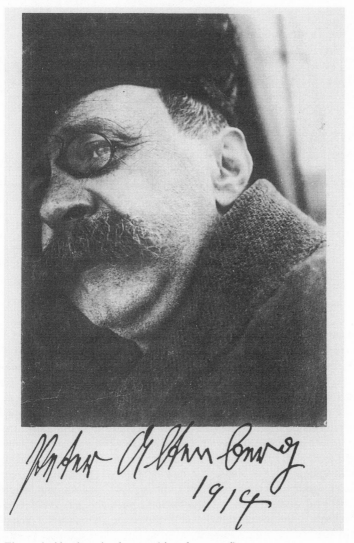

Figure 4. Altenberg in close-up (signed postcard)

connotations of eccentricity implicit in the word 'Vogel' would have immediately occurred to the contemporary viewer. Not only were Altenberg's outlandish dress and eccentric behaviour part of his public persona; his intermittent confinement in Vienna's mental hospitals had become part of the public record.

A second photo postcard from 1914 (Figure 4) presents a radically different face: instead of the artful co-ordination of a restrained pose with an allusive text, a disturbing close-up which is merely signed and dated. In this case, however, we are reminded that 1914 is the year of the outbreak of the First World War. Whether the photo actually reflects Altenberg's anxiety about the war is

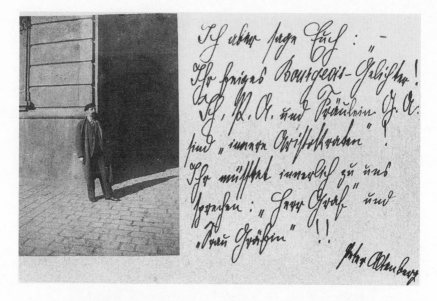

Figure 5. Altenberg (photograph mounted on a postcard)

impossible to know. The erratic quality of his writing during this period, which includes a number of blatantly propagandistic texts, indicates that his declining health also clouded his judgment. The composition of the image does allow for a further reading, however. An extreme close-up of this type was certainly unusual and is, to the best of my knowledge, unique among Altenberg's portrait photographs. The angle of the head is also noteworthy; it seems as though the poet were looking over his shoulder at the camera or trying to escape its gaze. At the same time, the organisation of the frame draws the viewer to Altenberg's eye and to the left half of his pince-nez, which looks like a monocle. Does the visual emphasis on the single eye looking through a glass lens suggest a fabricated image of the poet as photographer? This, too, is impossible to say, but Altenberg's connections with professional photographers make it possible that he knew of the so-called 'Monokel-Aufnahme', a procedure developed by Hans Watzek for creating a soft-focus photograph which was publicised in *Ver sacrum* in 1898.[28]

The extent to which Altenberg planned and even rehearsed his photographic portraits becomes evident in a simple collage which consists of a small photograph mounted onto a regular postcard and paired with a handwritten caption (Figure 5). The text represents a variant of the first postcard message in the previously mentioned sketch 'Ansichtskarten'. There, under the title 'Schloss in P.', the text reads:

> Hier müssten 'innere Aristokraten' wohnen! Solche, zu welchen jeder Fremde innerlich spräche: 'Herr Graf', 'Frau Gräfin'!
>
> ['Inner aristocrats' should live here! The kind of people whom every

56

Figure 6. Altenberg in front of the Hofburg (inscribed postcard)

stranger would address inwardly as 'Your Lordship', 'Your Ladyship'!]
[*WT*, p. 310]

On the card, the third-person subjunctive becomes an aggressive vocative:

> Ich aber sage Euch: Ihr feiges Bourgeois-Gelichter! Ich, P. A. und
> Fräulein G. A. sind 'innere Aristokraten'! Ihr müsstet innerlich zu uns
> sprechen: 'Herr Graf' und 'Frau Gräfin'!!

> [I, however, say unto you: You cowardly bourgeois riff-raff! I, P. A. and
> Fräulein G. A. are 'inner aristocrats'! You should address us inwardly as
> 'Your Lordship' and 'Your Ladyship'!!]

Paraphrasing Jesus's formulaic admonition in the Gospels ('Ich sage euch'), this defiant address also revises the published text through its visible interaction with the photograph.[29] The imaginary location is no longer a castle in which unnamed noble spirits might realise a domestic fantasy. Instead we see an urban street, where the poet provokingly identifies himself and Gertrude Auspitz, a member of the Auspitz-Lieben family with whom Altenberg had several connections, as 'inner aristocrats'.[30] The repetition of 'A', their common initial, links the letter to the spirit of 'inner aristocracy' and thereby reinforces the gesture of self-definition. The fusion of the male and female names, accomplished by the use of initials, may also belong to Altenberg's need to articulate the feminine aspect of his persona.

The simple artfulness of the text corresponds to the careful composition of the photograph. Altenberg chose the location for this portrait quite deliberately. A similar photo in his *Nachlaß* (Figure 6) identifies the setting as the private entrance to the Hofburg in Vienna.[31] Posing in front of the imperial residence associates the poet's 'inner aristocracy' with the ultimate actual nobility, that of the Habsburgs. Comparison of the two photographs indicates that Altenberg experimented with the camera distance and settled on a shot which removed him further from the viewer. This decision calls attention to the ideological implications of this visual trope. Altenberg positions himself on the periphery rather than within the perimeter of the Hofburg. While his shadow crosses the threshold of the portal, his body remains dwarfed by the dark entrance. The shadow's angular shape indicates the direction of Altenberg's desire, but it also visualises his insubstantiality. The photograph exploits codes of proximity and chiaroscuro to create an image of ambiguity. While the image does not negate the text, the visual message does question its biblical assertiveness. Altenberg's hatred of the bourgeoisie and its domination of Viennese culture sometimes took the form of a cult not only of the nobility in general but also of the Habsburgs in particular. In this portrait the act of identification remains tentative and understated. The photograph concretises the poet's outsider status rather than celebrating imperial power. Although some of Altenberg's photographs of himself are more expressive than others, the best examples create searching self-portraits by staging his poses and endowing his images with textual voices. As this example documents, they also revise his published texts and attempt a more assertive self-definition than conventional literary forms allowed.

The second major group of Altenberg's inscribed images are those depicting women and young girls. At first glance, many of these images, sometimes appropriated by little more than the poet's initials, could easily pass as objects labelled for possession by a tasteful, slightly prurient collector. Besides more or less appealing nudes photographed anonymously, there are artistically executed portraits by Madame D'Ora, Franz Xaver Setzer, Anton Trčka, and other prominent Viennese photographers. Although in many cases Altenberg was acquainted with the women whose images he signed and framed, he also apparently searched for and purchased images of beautiful women whom he did not know. Included in his *Nachlaß*, for example, are several portraits of the German dancer Clotilde Derp from the studio of Rudolf Dührkoop, an important *Jugendstil* photographer. Images such as the one reproduced here (Figure 7) have an undeniable aesthetic appeal; but Altenberg's inscriptions, which often ascribe an 'ideal' quality to the sitters, seem to do little more than acknowledge the photographer's stylisation of the dominant fashion of female beauty.

Photographs or picture postcards of Clotilde Derp and other artistic personalities belonged, of course, to the sphere of public images. They functioned as an early form of publicity photo and were readily available in specialty stores. It is characteristic of Altenberg's attitude towards the visualisation of his poetic activity that even his habit of purchasing these images should itself be documented. His *Nachlaß* contains a postcard made from a photograph showing him standing in front of a photographer's shop (Figure 8). Although Altenberg appropriates the image with a caption that expresses the ageing poet's affinity with young women, the arrangement of the photographic frame implies that this

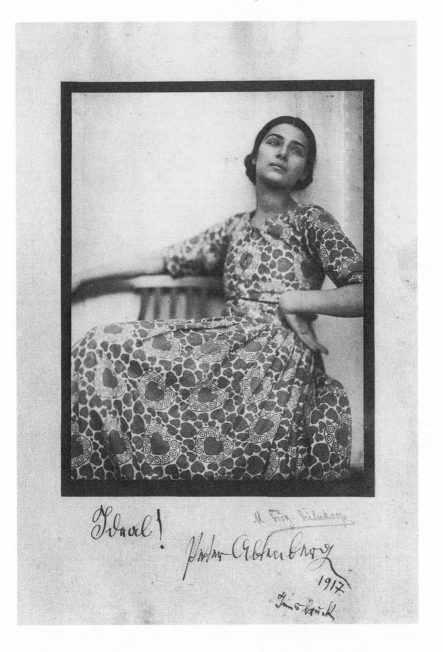

Figure 7. Clotilde Derp (photograph by M. Diez-Dührkoop, inscribed by Altenberg).

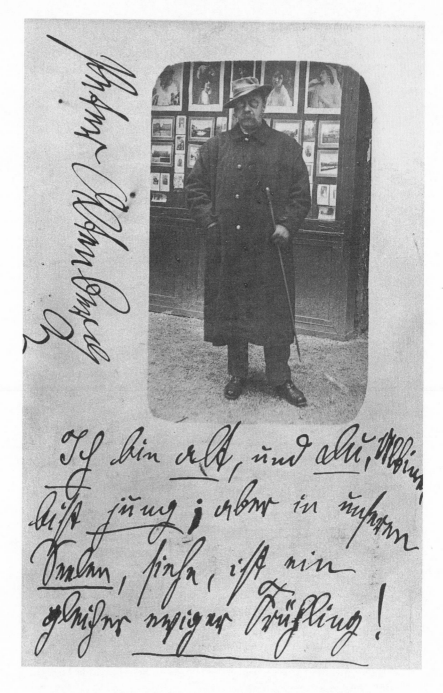

Figure 8. Altenberg in front of a photographer's shop (inscribed postcard)

Figure 9. Ideal Legs (photograph inscribed by Altenberg)

affinity is visual and symbolic rather than physical and actual. The photograph constitutes a self-reflexive depiction of the poet as gazing subject and of photographed women as objectified images of the gaze. This gesture of experimental self-consciousness notwithstanding, two further photos (Figures 9 and 10) in the *Nachlaß* look like classic examples of what feminist film theory has

Figure 10. Paula Schweitzer (photograph inscribed by Altenberg)

defined as the fetishisation of the female body through the aggressive 'male gaze'.[32] When these images, both of which focus on the legs of female bodies, are inscribed with Altenberg's favourite adjective 'ideal', the result seems much less ideologically innocuous than does the stylised feminine figure of Clotilde Derp.

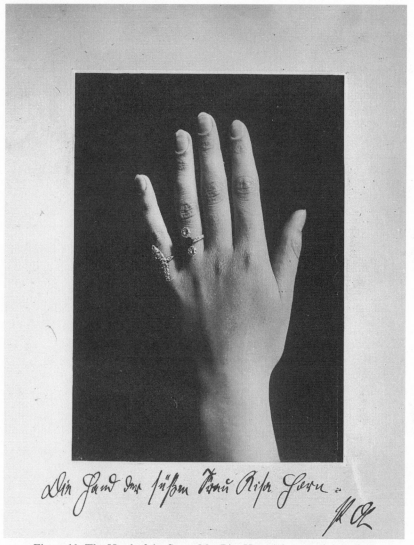

Figure 11. The Hand of the Sweet Mrs Risa Horn (photograph inscribed by Altenberg)

A photograph inscribed as 'The Hand of the Sweet Mrs Risa Horn' (Figure 11) also belonged to the furnishings of Altenberg's last domicile. This image partialises the female body even more radically than the two photographs of 'ideal legs'. The exaggerated close-up combines with extreme sharp focus to produce the striking effect of an image that seems to duplicate the object it represents. The slight bluish tint of the original photograph reinforces the tactile quality of the image achieved by making even the pores of the skin visible. Altenberg accorded this image a special place among his fabricated photographs

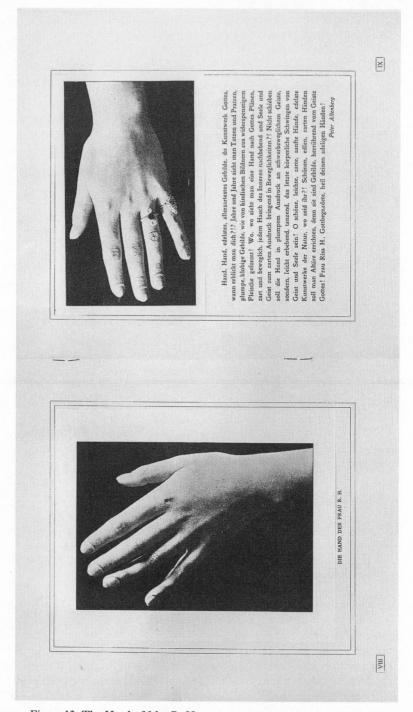

Figure 12. The Hand of Mrs R. H.

by publishing it in 1903 in the first issue of his art magazine *Kunst* (Figure 12). This issue also featured two rather more conventional photographs of women, both variations on the standard three-quarter portrait. In the programmatic introduction to *Kunst*, it is the hand, however, rather than these ostensibly more complete images that Altenberg celebrates as the exemplary art work:

> Wir wollen die Kunst, dieses Exzeptionelle, dem Alltage vermählen. Die Hand der Dame R. H. ist ein Kunstwerk Gottes. Wir bringen sie photographiert.

> [We want to wed art, the exceptional, with the everyday. The hand of the lady R. H. is God's work of art. We present it as a photograph.][33]

In the text of the magazine, both the original photograph (Figure 11) and another image of the same hand, this time without the rings, are reproduced (Figure 12). The impact of the nearly life-sized images is enhanced by the close cropping of the reproductions; in the case of the bejewelled hand, the area of the background has been substantially reduced over against the original photograph. By using two images of the same hand, one positioned vertically and the other horizontally, Altenberg simulates visually the delicate, expressive motion evoked in the accompanying text.

Risa Horn (1878–1939) would have been twenty-five when her hand was photographed. She is mentioned occasionally in Schnitzler's diaries around 1910, and a few surviving letters from the early 1930s indicate that she was on good terms with Karl Kraus and attended his readings regularly.[34] Whatever Altenberg's own relationship with Risa Horn may have been, the photograph used to represent her cannot be the result of a snapshot, nor would it have been a likely motif for a commercial postcard. As might be expected, Altenberg himself arranged to have the photograph taken.

In a letter written to Karl Kraus in late September 1903, soon after the first issue of *Kunst* appeared, Altenberg recounts the pertinent circumstances of the photograph's production and also complains about a journalistic reaction to its reproduction in the magazine:

> Was sagst Du zu der frechen Anrempelei des 'Wiener Journal'?!? Es ist wirklich zu schäbig, daß wenn in Wien eine neue vornehme Kunstzeitschrift, anders wie die bisherigen, erscheint, Herr Tann-Bergler die Gelegenheit ergreift, mit billigstem Humor die ganze Sache in den Dreck zu zerren!

> Nicht daß er mich oder die Zeitschrift angreift, berührt mich, sondern seine schamlose Bemerkung über diese süße wirklich ein lebendiges Kunstwerk darstellende Risa Horn, die so liebenswürdig war, meiner dringenden Bitte zufolge, mir ihre edlen Hände zur photogr. Reproduktion zu überlassen! Ich stellte es ihr direkt als eine künstlerische Verpflichtung dar [. . .]

> [What do you say to the insolent attack in the 'Wiener Journal'? It's really too shabby that when a new, elegant art magazine different from the others is published, Herr Tann-Bergler takes the opportunity to drag the entire

enterprise through the mud with cheap humour. I'm not bothered by the fact that he attacked me or the magazine. What bothers me is his shameless remark about this really sweet Risa Horn, who is a living work of art and was kind enough to grant my urgent request and to turn over her noble hands to me for a photographic reproduction. I told her that she had an artistic responsibility to do so [. . . .][35]

The evidence contained in this letter should not be underestimated. First of all, it shows that, on occasion, Altenberg actively participated in making the images that he fabricated by means of inscriptions or commentaries. Even his choice of words — 'to turn over her noble hands to me for a photographic reproduction' — reflects the poet's belief in the aesthetic power inherent in the medium's technical capabilities. At the same time, however, this phrase unwittingly articulates the inevitable effect of the photographic frame; it reduces and partialises the object captured by the lens. The hands are, in effect, separated from the body. What for Altenberg was undoubtedly an aesthetic strategy provided an occasion for journalistic ridicule.

In the *Neues Wiener Journal* Ottokar Tann-Bergler greeted the first issue of *Kunst* with a facetiously laudatory review, which takes special notice of Risa Horn's hand. At first, he dismisses it as the 'Hand mit den schönen Ringen und schlechtgepflegten Nägeln' ('the hand with the beautiful rings and the poorly manicured nails'), but then he reveals the taboo that Altenberg's photographs had apparently violated:

> Um es aufrichtig zu sagen, sind wir insbesondere neugierig, zu erfahren, welche Körperteile der zur ratenweise Veröffentlichung bestimmten, gottbegnadeten Frau Risa H. demnächst zur Anbetung ausgesetzt werden sollen.

> [To be honest, we are especially curious to learn which parts of the body of the divinely endowed Mrs Risa H., who is scheduled for publication in instalments, are destined to be exposed for adoration next.][36]

This reading of the photographed hands, sarcastically expressed as genuine curiosity about more intimate body parts, amounts to an act of journalistic dismemberment. Above all, the critic's reaction suggests that Altenberg's presentation of the photographs conveys an unusual corporeality that revises conventional images of the female body.

Altenberg may very well have meant the hand to function as *pars pro toto*. In a sketch which appeared in *Kunst* just two issues later, he reports the following exchange between a young countess and a poet:

> Die junge Gräfin sagte: 'Was sagen Herr Dichter zu dem süßen Fräulein, das sich auf einer Schilf-Insel splitternackt von Herrn so und so photographieren ließ?!?'

> 'Ich sage, daß wenn die Frau Fabriksdirektor von C. dazu seinerzeit den Mut gefunden hätte, sie jetzt nicht jahrelang ihre Mitmenschen mit den Berichten vergangener Schönheit belästigen würde müssen [...] Eine schöne Hand dürfte nicht lange im Handschuh bleiben wollen [...]'

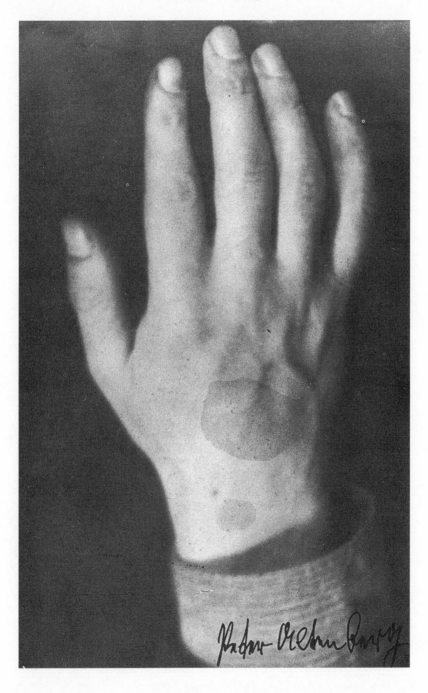

Figure 13. A man's hand (photograph signed by Altenberg)

Figure 14. Emperor Karl with his son Otto (photograph inscribed by Altenberg)

[The young countess said: 'What does the esteemed poet have to say about the sweet young Fräulein who allowed herself to be photographed completely in the nude by Herr so-and-so?!?'

'I say that if the wife of the factory owner von C. had found the courage at the time, she wouldn't have to bother her fellow human beings with reports of faded beauty [...] A beautiful hand would hardly want to remain in a glove for long [...]³⁷

The parallel motifs of a photographed nude and of the hand that should shed its glove leave little doubt that the photographed hand serves as a metonym of nudity. In this context, the emblematic hand is certainly meant to convey a message of social-aesthetic liberation rather than engage in a fetishisation of the female body.

The iconological argument of Altenberg's fabricated photograph may be compared with Klimt's provocative gesture of aesthetic defiance in 'Nuda veritas', a drawing published in *Ver sacrum* in which a nude woman holds a mirror up to the viewer, and in the allegorical painting with the same title and a similar motif.³⁸ Altenberg's admiration for Klimt is documented in several texts, including one published in *Kunst*.³⁹ In a later text, a review of the famous Kunstschau 1908, Altenberg discusses Klimt's portraits of women and describes the hands of the models in terms very similar to those he used for the hand of Risa Horn.⁴⁰ Finally though, it is possible to read the constellation of the hands as something more than an aesthetic revision of female beauty.

Even before the hand of Risa Horn is reproduced within the text of the magazine, it is announced in the introduction as 'God's work of art' and associated with the 'tender human hand' that wields the kodak and collaborates with nature, the greatest 'Künstlerin' of all.⁴¹ The use of the feminine form of 'artist' encourages the interpretation that the hand represents not only the photographed object, but also the photographing subject. This means that in the text which accompanies the photographs, Altenberg's dialogue with the hand is also a dialogue with himself and with the feminine aspect of his persona. Given this perspective, the two photographs of the same hand — one bare and vertical, the other ornamented and horizontal — symbolises a conjunction of the male and the female artist. A photograph of his own hand (Figure 13), a mirror image of the vertical version of Risa Horn's, suggests that he identified with the role of female photographer.

Both formally and ideologically, Altenberg's fabricated photographs constitute a complex *oeuvre* which can only be introduced here. Seen as a whole, these appropriated and inscribed images encompass differing, sometimes contradictory positions. On the one hand, Altenberg's calligraphic commentaries often undermine the visual codes of traditional motifs and conventional poses; and his predilection for images of corporeal details insinuates a potentially subversive discourse of the body into repressive images of female sexuality. On the other hand, such images can also embody exploitation; and some of Altenberg's inscribed photographs betray his susceptibility to political mystification. His inscribed portraits of the imperial family, which reinforce the 'Habsburg Myth', provide a case in point. An almost Biedermeier-like portrait of the last emperor, Karl, and his young son, Otto (Figure 14), for example, bears the inscription: '*Father* and *Son*! Incidentally: Emperor and Crown Prince!' This sentiment confused paternal affection with patriarchal power, and thereby supported the dynasty's political propaganda. There is no evidence that

Altenberg published this patriotic exercise and others like it, but he did reproduce in private the journalistic strategy followed by loyal illustrated magazines such as *Das interessante Blatt*.

In conclusion, it is important to stress that Altenberg's fabricated photographs have been examined here as individual aesthetic assemblages. Taken together, however, these images coalesce into visual–verbal narratives, a point which the poet himself made. In his last photo album, which has survived in a private collection, Altenberg insisted that the album represented '*absolut* keine *Ansichtskarten-Sammlungen, sondern* [...] also eine ganze und *eigentliche vollständige Biografie* meines sonst nur *in Worten*, ziemlich unverständlichen und komplizierten *Denkens* und *Fühlens!*' ('definitely not a postcard collection, but rather an entire and actual complete biography of my rather obtuse and complicated thoughts and feelings, which are otherwise expressed only in words').[42] This declaration makes it clear that any comprehensive evaluation of Altenberg's work will not only have to consider this pictorial biography but will also have to face the complex issues raised by his innovative experiments with words and photographs.[43]

Figures

Figure 3. Peter Altenberg. Portrait postcard, 1914. Vienna City Library, I.N. 115.807.

Figure 4. Peter Altenberg. Portrait postcard, 1914. Vienna City Library, I.N. 115.806.

Figure 5. Peter Altenberg. Portrait photograph mounted on postcard. Private Collection.

Figure 6. Peter Altenberg. Portrait postcard. Historical Museum of the City of Vienna, I.N. 94.779.

Figure 7. M. Diez-Dührkoop. Portrait Photograph of Clotilde Derp. Inscribed by Peter Altenberg, 1917. Historical Museum of the City of Vienna, I.N. 94.994.

Figure 8. Peter Altenberg. Portrait postcard. Historical Museum of the City of Vienna, I.N. 94.798.

Figure 9. Peter Altenberg. 'Die absolut *idealen* Beine! Die 13jährige Evelyne H. . . . '. Inscribed photograph, 1916. Historical Museum of the City of Vienna, I.N. 94.910.

Figure 10. Peter Altenberg. 'Paula, *noch* Frln. *Schweitzer! Idealste* Beine!'. Inscribed photograph, 1917. Historical Museum of the City of Vienna, I.N. 94.956.

Figure 11. Peter Altenberg. 'Die Hand der süßen Frau Risa Horn'. Inscribed photograph. Historical Museum of the City of Vienna, I.N. 94.909.

Figure 12. Peter Altenberg. 'Die Hand der Frau R. H.' in *Kunst*, No. 1 (1903). By permission of the Houghton Library, Harvard University.

Figure 13. Peter Altenberg. Signed photograph of a man's hand. Historical Museum of the City of Vienna, I. N. 94.783.

Figure 14. Helene von Zimmerauer. Photo portrait of Emperor Karl with his son Otto. Inscribed and signed by Peter Altenberg, 1917. Historical Museum of the City of Vienna, I.N. 94.892.

Notes

1. Werner J. Schweiger, 'Wiener Literatencafés. VI. Ein Dichter wird entdeckt', *Die Pestsäule*, 10 (March 1974), 947.

2. *Das große Peter Altenberg Buch*, ed. Werner J. Schweiger (Vienna and Hamburg, 1977), p. 65, cited hereafter in the text as *PAB*.

3. Peter Altenberg, *Vita ipsa* (Berlin, 1918), p. 267.
4. Hugo von Hofmannsthal, *Reden und Aufsätze III/ Buch der Freunde/ Aufzeichnungen 1889–1929*, ed. Bernd Schoeller and Ingeborg Beyer-Ahlert with Rudolf Hirsch (Frankfurt, 1980), p. 349.
5. Quoted by Monika Faber, 'Photographie als künstlerisches Medium', in *Das Zeitalter Kaiser Franz Josephs, II. Teil, Beiträge*, Exhibition Catalogue (Vienna, 1987), p. 326.
6. For an example of the latter, see Henneberg's photograph 'Italian Villa in Autumn', *Ver sacrum*, I, 4 (1898), 32.
7. See August von Loehr, 'Die Malerei mit der Platte', *Ver sacrum*, I, 7 (1898), 30–2.
8. See the complete bibliography of their contributions in *Alfred Stieglitz, Camera Work: A Pictorial Guide*, ed. Marianne Fulton Margolis (New York, 1978), pp. 143–4, 146.
9. *Ver sacrum*, I, 4 (1898), 25–7; I, 7 (1898), 30–1; I, 10 (1898), 31.
10. See Karl Kraus, *Die Fackel* No. 210 and the following issues. Beginning with No. 213 the advertisement was moved from the back cover to the inside of the front cover.
11. Peter Altenberg, *Leben und Werk in Texten und Bildern*, ed. Hans Christian Kosler (Munich, 1981), p. 101.
12. See Otto Hochreiter and Timm Starl, 'Lexikon der österreichischen Fotografie', in *Geschichte der Fotografie in Österreich*, ed. Hochreiter and Starl, 2 vols (Bad Ischl, 1983), II, pp. 139–40.
13. Peter Altenberg, 'KUNST. Ein Vorwort von Peter Altenberg', *Kunst*, No. 1 (1903), 1.
14. The letter is published in *Das Altenbergbuch*, ed. Egon Friedell (Vienna, 1921), p. 81.
15. F. Bernhard, 'Unveröffentlichte Briefe über die dichterische Inspiration', *Die literarische Welt* (1932), No. 23, p. 3.
16. Quoted by Giovanni Fanelli and Ezio Godoli, *Art Nouveau Postcards*, tr. Linda Fairbairn (New York, 1987), p. 14f.
17. Ibid., p. 7.
18. Peter Altenberg, *Was der Tag mir zuträgt*, 4th edn (Berlin, 1924), p. 312, cited hereafter as *WT* in the text.
19. Karl Kraus, *Die letzten Tage der Menschheit* (Frankfurt, 1986), pp. 148–9.
20. Cf. the text 'Traunfall bei Gmunden' in *WT*, p. 314f, and the card 'Traunfall', No. 1116 in Deutsch's Postkartenverlag, which shows a view of the waterfall with the same text written in Altenberg's hand across the bottom of the image. The card belongs to the Altenberg-*Nachlaß* in the Vienna City Library.
21. See Leo A. Lensing, '"Photographischer Alpdruck" oder politische Fotomontage? Karl Kraus, Kurt Tucholsky und die satirischen Möglichkeiten der Fotografie', *Zeitschrift für Deutsche Philologie*, 107 (1988), 556–71.
22. Anne H. Hoy, *Fabrications: Staged, Altered, and Appropriated Photographs* (New York, 1987).
23. *Otto Kallir-Nirenstein: Ein Wegbereiter österreichischer Kunst*, exhibition catalogue, ed. Jane Kallir and Hans Bisanz (Vienna, 1986), p. 8.
24. Hans Bisanz, *Peter Altenberg: Mein äußerstes Ideal. Altenbergs Photosammlung von geliebten Frauen, Freunden und Orten* (Vienna and Munich, 1987), p. 7. Although Bisanz has little to say about the making of individual images, he does provide useful guidelines for understanding Altenberg's photographs aesthetically (in relation to his artistic contemporaries Klimt, Schiele, and Kokoschka) and thematically (from a diachronic literary perspective that includes Lewis Carroll and Nabokov).
25. Quoted from *Das Altenbergbuch*, ed. Egon Friedell (Vienna, 1921), p. 154–5. Hofmannsthal's comment was made in a review of *Wie ich es sehe* first published in 1896.
26. Quoted from Monika Faber, *Madame D'Ora Wien-Paris: Portraits aus Kunst und*

Gesellschaft 1907–1957 (Vienna and Munich, 1983), p. 172.

27. The cards in both Figures 1 and 2 are addressed to Lotte Franzos on the reverse side.
28. See August von Loehr, 'Die Malerie mit der Platte', *Ver sacrum*, I, 7 (1898), 31.
29. There is also a third variant of the text from 1899, which is almost identical to the version published as part of 'Ansichtskarten'. The text is written on a picture postcard with the title 'Gruß aus Grafenegg' and dedicated to Emma Rudolf. The card belongs to the Altenberg collection of the Galerie St Etienne in New York.
30. I am indebted to Werner J. Schweiger for this information.
31. The caption next to the image reads 'An dem Kaiserlichen Privat-Eingangs-Thore in der Wiener Hofburg. PA'. On the back of the card there is a similar text: 'Aufgenommen im Thore der Hofburg in Wien. Peter Altenberg. / Für Anna Konrad'.
32. See Laura Mulvey, 'Visual Pleasure and Narrative Cinema', in Philip Rosen (ed.), *Narrative, Apparatus, Ideology: A Film Theory Reader* (New York, 1986), pp. 198, 200–2.
33. *Kunst*, No. 1 (1903), p. II.
34. See Arthur Schnitzler, *Tagebuch 1909–1912*, ed. Werner Welzig (Vienna, 1981), pp. 69, 252; and four unpublished letters from Risa Horn to Karl Kraus, written between December 1931 and May 1932, in the Vienna City Library.
35. Unpublished letter from Peter Altenberg to Karl Kraus, after 19 September 1903. Vienna City Library.
36. '"Kunst." Eine Wiener Offenbarung', *Neues Wiener Journal*, 19 September 1903, p. 9.
37. Peter Altenberg, 'Konditorei im Seestädtchen', *Kunst*, December 1903, p. II.
38. Gustav Klimt, 'Nuda veritas', *Ver sacrum*, 1 (1899), 12. The drawing contains the text 'WAHRHEIT IST FEUER und WAHRHEIT REDEN HEISST LEUCHTEN und BRENNEN'.
39. Peter Altenberg, 'Gustav Klimt', *Kunst*, December 1903, p. VII.
40. Peter Altenberg, 'Kunstschau 1908 in Wien', *Bilderbögen des kleinen Lebens* (Berlin, 1909), pp. 115–16.
41. *Kunst*, No. 1 (1903), p. I.
42. The album belongs to the Galerie St Etienne, New York. I am very grateful to Jane Kallir and Hildegard Bachert for allowing me to examine it and to quote this passage.
43. The photographs and cards included in the text have been reproduced with the kind permission of the Vienna City Library (figs. 3–4), the Historical Museum of the City of Vienna (figs. 6–11 and 13–14), and Harvard University (fig. 12). I wish to acknowledge the kind assistance of Hans Bisanz, who aided me in examining the objects in Altenberg's *Nachlaß*. My very special thanks go to my colleague Andrew Barker, who not only generously shared his research with me but also provided an excellent critical reading of an early verson of this essay.

Feminism as a Vocation

Motives for joining the Austrian women's movement

Harriet Anderson

The middle-class Austrian women's movement has received relatively little attention either in the context of turn-of-the-century Vienna or of early feminism as a whole. Most has been restricted to the various women's organisations and their campaigns for concrete goals such as women's suffrage and the improvement of their education, working conditions, and employment possibilities. Indeed, even the important ideological women's groupings on either side of the non-aligned middle-class movement – the Social Democrats on the one and the Christian-Social Catholics on the other – have been the object of only limited interest.[1] The intellectual traditions within which early feminists worked, the complex arguments they used in support of their demands, and the attitudes which underlay those arguments have also been largely ignored.[2] By trying to shed light on the motives which led a number of Austrian women to support the non-confessional middle-class women's movement at the turn of the century, I hope that the various meanings attached to feminism by the feminists themselves will be revealed, and that our appreciation of their pioneering work will be enriched by a new perspective.[3] Of course, my approach in no way implies a devaluation of their commitment and the conviction which sustained it. I do not wish to suggest that personal motives for political engagement are of a lower order than 'objective' criteria, but rather to deepen our understanding of early feminism. I shall focus on three prominent figures of the first generation of the radical Austrian movement – Auguste Fickert, Rosa Mayreder, and Marie Lang – all of whom were members of its organisation, the *Allgemeiner Österreichischer Frauenverein* (General Austrian Women's Association, AÖFV). I then turn to Marianne Hainisch, the leading moderate, and finally to the question of how the different meanings each saw in her engagement influenced her contribution to the feminist cause. In each case my argument will draw on previously unpublished sources, which make it possible to sketch an alternative history of feminism 'from the inside'.

Auguste Fickert (1855–1910) was notably reticent about her motives for her feminist engagement. The only source to have come to light so far is her diary, begun on New Year's Eve 1871 at the age of sixteen and continued until 7 March 1910, three months before her death. Her inner life dominates the frequent and effusive entries of the early years of the diary at the expense of any coverage of everyday life. After about 1876, however, the entries become sporadic and often take the form of poems. Nowhere in the diary does Fickert refer directly to her activities in the women's movement. Yet reticent though she is as regards her external life, her diary voice betrays much as regards the *emotional* origins of her feminism.

Like many young people in Vienna in the final third of the nineteenth century, Fickert (as the diary reveals) was an *aficionado* of the Burgtheater, and passionate admirer of certain actors and dramatists. The early entries are full of her comments on the plays she saw which made a deep impression on her: Hebbel's *Judith* and *Agnes Bernauer*; Gutzkow's *Uriel Acosta*; but above all Schiller's plays on the theme of liberation. Indeed, over many years she cherished the wish to become an actress and even sought advice from the leading Burgtheater actor Josef Lewinsky. This is perhaps surprising for a girl of a respectable, if humble, family considering the highly dubious reputation of the profession at that time, but becomes more comprehensible when the significance she attached to the theatre becomes clear. It was for the young Fickert by no means a place of entertainment, but, on the contrary, one of revelation, moral uplift and missionary activity: 'Oh, the playwright's art is the most noble gift God has given man,' she records in her diary on 29 April 1872 after seeing a performance of *Wilhelm Tell*, 'it is through it alone that I have become aware of what man ['der Mensch'] *is*, what he *can* be, and what he *must* do. He *is* the being created free by the highest master's hand, put into this world to govern it with his free spirit; he *can* achieve what is highest with his soaring thoughts and deeds; he *must* break the bonds which bind him to what is base, must liberate his spirit from its chains, [. . .] must strive to achieve a goal higher than that of this world's miserable transiences.[. . .] The wish to become an actress grows ever stronger in me, the wish to repeat the great, beautiful thoughts of noble, immortal men ['Männer'], ever again to call them back to the heart and mind of those who have come after.' Although her use of the word 'Männer' here reflects the male monopoly in serious theatre, she saw it as her mission as an actress to spread the word of human emancipation. And from there it is but a small step to a similar passionate belief in the only other form of public performance with an emancipatory goal open to middle-class women: engagement in the women's movement.

A further, perhaps surprising, aspect revealed in Fickert's diary is her adolescent attitude to romantic love, marriage, and men. Like many middle-class young women, Fickert yearned to be needed, to have a role in life; her early diary abounds in pathetically self-conscious laments about her lack of purpose and the resulting feelings of alienation from her family and herself. And, also like many middle-class young women, she imagined the solution to lie in a love relationship which was to conform to the propagated romantic ideal of female submission: 'Oh how elevating it is to gaze up to that being which we adore like a god,' she exclaimed in her diary on 15 June 1874:

> How I would be humble and quiet, and in shy humility happily care for the loved one, live only for him, in him, be happy when his eye shines and weep with him when a frown of sadness furrows the high, clear brow. Then at last I could be myself, as I really am, known by the one and only, could laugh and cry at my heart's desire, would no longer withdraw coldly when my whole soul is aglow, for I will be understood.

Fickert had a clear image of this dream man. He would be modelled on Schiller and would, like him, shape and ennoble her, being 'the strong man, on whom I can lean, at whose heart the burning longing in my breast can be quenched'.[4] She was to yearn for this ideal for several years, but was never to find it – inevitably so, as she herself eventually recognised. In December 1887 she rejected a marriage proposal with the justification to herself that she would not find the love she sought in marriage; indeed she commented with resignation: 'I now no longer believe that this love can come true at all in our poor lives – it is the magic blue flower'.[5] Six months later she recorded in her diary the change which had taken place in her view of love over the last decade: 'Everything in our thinking and feeling which relates to what is particular, individual is changeable – steady and constant is only the love of the good. In the individual is manifested always only a part of the ideal we strive after.'[6]

Her love, then, was now to be directed towards an ideal, the good. This ideal also included a vision of love between the sexes which finds expression in the unpublished novella 'Ahnungen' ('Presentiments').[7] 'Love is the most certain protection against the atavistic desires of the bestial in human beings,' Fickert has Frieda, an emancipated woman, say there, 'and the more it extends its bright empire, the more it takes possession of the hearts of people and sets them free from narrowness, limitation and pettiness, the freer, stronger and therefore nobler those human hearts will beat, the happier they will be.' This path of love is that of the new woman's pilgrimage; thus the queenly woman will emerge, Fickert has Frieda say, and humanity be redeemed for a second time, not for the Beyond but for this world. Fickert's vision of love has, therefore, changed significantly; no longer is it the bringer of individual happiness but of collective salvation. It has thereby acquired a religious, indeed messianic function: love will redeem. But not the base love of conventional marriage; only a higher order of love, an emancipatory love, will achieve this, and it is this love which is the new woman's destiny. Fickert thus willingly submits to the conventions of her day in her adherence to an ideology which sees love as particularly a woman's destiny but gives it a new content by uniting with it unmistakable elements of Christian religiosity, a vision of human emancipation through love and the emergence of the new woman as missionary and second saviour.

Fickert was thus fired by a missionary zeal to spread the word of human emancipation she had heard in the theatre and then later combined with an ideology of love. Why, however, did she choose the women's movement as her platform of public missionary activity? Here her social background becomes significant. Fickert's family belonged to the lower middle class, and it was clear

75

that she would have to become self-supporting. Obviously the stage was not an acceptable source of income in the eyes of such parents, and Fickert was destined to take up the profession of a very large number of girls from middle-class families of moderate means: that of primary-school teacher. This destiny became a reality when Fickert's father died in the autumn of 1881, after which she was forced to earn in order to support not only herself but also her family. This she viewed as her duty and her debt to her parents but it did not make her happy, as she noted guiltily a few months later:

> Of course I *do* know Kant's categorical imperative, I tell myself daily that it is my life's task, particularly since the death of my dear father, to live for my mother, brothers and sisters. And yet I cannot suppress the egoistic instinct to wish for happiness which often rises up in my heart with its old, undiminished strength.[8]

Fickert was, therefore, typical of a large number of women who were seen to constitute the 'woman problem' at the end of the nineteenth century: unmarried, thrown back on their own resources, and forced into the only profession open to those with educational pretensions. And she is, therefore, also typical of the first wave of feminists, for it was above all from this group, teachers, that the early women's movement recruited its supporters. There were good reasons for this: these women were amongst the most highly educated; they probably had through their profession more self-confidence and practice in speaking before an audience than most, they had more time than married women with family (in Lower Austria in the final third of the nineteenth century marriage for female teachers was tantamount to voluntary resignation); and, above all, it was these women who came into very direct contact with the harsh realities of discrimination on grounds of sex.[9] In 1870 the *Verein der Lehrerinnen und Erzieherinnen* (Association of Women Teachers and Governesses) was founded in order to represent women teachers' interests – among their members was Auguste Fickert. And in 1889, as a response to the withdrawal of tax-paying women's vote for the *Landtag* (Provincial Assembly) in Lower Austria in the previous year, it was the teachers who in protest organised the first women's political meeting. Fickert was one of the prime movers.

Fickert thus turned to the women's movement because it promised to fulfil a combination of emotional needs. It satisfied her thwarted desire for the theatre by offering her another kind of public platform for her histrionic talents and her missionary desire to spread the word of freedom, and thereby also a platform for her vision of the emancipatory and redeeming love of the new woman. It needed only the right combination of circumstances found in Fickert's professional and political context to give the final impulse to a practical feminist engagement which was to dominate the rest of her life.

Rosa Mayreder (1858–1938) came to the movement and feminism along a very different route. Although her social background was also that of the lower middle class, it was combined with *nouveau riche* wealth and she was never confronted with the hard reality of financial need. On the contrary, she enjoyed (or endured) all the trappings of a young lady's upbringing – music, drawing, dancing and French lessons – intended for the salon rather than the schoolroom.

This perhaps makes her feminist engagement all the more surprising, as Mayreder herself was ready to acknowledge, for, unlike Fickert, she was anxious to address the question of how she came to feminism. Indeed, she was perhaps too ready, for where Fickert tells us too little, Mayreder protests too much. Until she was almost fifteen, she, like Fickert, held highly traditional views on the role of women and their relations to men, as she relates in her memoirs.[10] The change in her attitude occurred in the autumn of 1873 and was, claims Mayreder, a result of her increasing sense of her own individuality and the accompanying necessity of rebellion against the norms governing femininity which restricted her inner growth. It was her innate disposition which led her to feminism: emancipatory ideas developed spontaneously, she stresses. There was no external framework to encourage her in the shape of the need to earn or a strong female figure to identify with (*MP*, pp. 17, 77). She also explains her emphasis: 'I place such special value on the fact that these ideas arose spontaneously in me,' she writes, 'because I therein see the symptom of a certain state of culture, indeed even the symptom of a certain stage of human development' (*MP*, p. 77). Aware of her outsider position and the accusation of degeneration from her uncomprehending family, and despite the self-doubts she tortured herself with as an adolescent, she thus remained adamant and defiantly insisted on her right to individual development and rebellion against conventional femininity.

Mayreder's diary and her autobiography reveal the nature of this rebellion. It was to be emancipation to female intellectuality and creativity, which, for the adolescent Mayreder, meant above all writing. The intellectual woman was no longer to be regarded as a freak but as the representative of an evolutionary higher form of femininity, one who had developed the natural talents a constraining culture sought to suppress. And as an adolescent Mayreder associated intellectuality with masculinity, understandably so, given the obvious privilege of men on that score. 'At that time I had no greater wish than to be a man,' she in consequence confesses of her adolescence. 'My emancipation was anything but hostile to men; in fact it was connected rather with an overestimation of men as the leaders of intellectual life' (*MP*, p. 81). Her own intellectuality, however, soon led her to come to the conclusion that intellectual development is independent of sex and that the leading position held by men is not justified (*MP*, p. 73).

Mayreder's feminism was, therefore, largely a result of her striving for personal development in the face of conventions which stultified women's intellectual growth in particular. Yet there is another aspect to this ideology of the intellect, although one not emphasised by Mayreder herself, and that is the element of religiosity. She stresses that she feels a calling to write, that she is thereby following a path predestined by nature (*MP*, pp. 18, 180), allowing her inner voice which is the voice of nature to speak (*MP*, p. 184). That this is also the voice of God becomes clear in her fable 'Die Stimme Gottes' ('The Voice of God'),[11] which Mayreder herself called her 'mystical, poetical' (*MP*, p. 48) answer to the question of why she wrote. There it is made clear that the soul enters the public sphere at the call of God to reveal by its own example the divine potential in humanity. Mayreder felt, then, that she had a mission: to be the herald by virtue of her intellectuality of the new femininity, the product of a natural evolution to a higher, more divine level of human existence (*MP*, p. 77). At about the time of her adolescent rebellion, she also turned away from conventional Christian religious belief, considering this to be a constraint on the development of the free personality. However, although she had 'fallen from God', she explains, 'God had not fallen from me. He continued to rule as the almighty will of the intellect' (*MP*, p. 29). The intellect is divine for Mayreder; it is the voice of God in man and the path to personal development and, therefore, freedom. 'In an age deserted by God,' Mayreder remarks at the end of her memoirs, 'the religious need searches for expression along many different paths' (*MP*, p. 187); Mayreder's path was belief in the intellect expressed in her feminism and writing. Mayreder's intellectual feminism fulfils the role of a substitute religion.

This is an interpretation of Mayreder's route to feminism which largely conforms to the self-image she herself wishes to project in her memoirs: that of the unconventional outsider at odds with her environment, fired by a spontaneous drive to individual development. It is an image which, however, could be modified. Mayreder's girlhood was by no means exclusively the conventional one of a young lady of good family, as she would have it. Unusual and probably significant for her development was her father's toleration of his obviously gifted daughter's intellectual curiosity. She was, after a struggle, allowed to learn Greek and Latin, and enjoyed freedom in choice of reading matter, even being given the complete works of Richard Wagner for Christmas in 1874. Her reading was dominated first by Schiller, and then by Goethe, Wagner, and Nietzsche (*MP*, pp. 147–87). This selection of writers was widely shared by critical young people in Vienna in the last third of the nineteenth century, and, indeed, Mayreder herself, far from being isolated, was a member of a group interested in these authors. Yet, instead of acknowledging how, in fact, she was participating in an intellectual trend of the time, she is concerned in her memoirs to individualise the phenomenon and again to stress her independence of external factors when she comes to describe her intellectual development.

Wagner, for example, 'confirmed with his divine authority the goal of the path which I in my lonely darkness had taken', Mayreder writes, referring to her early individualism (*MP*, p. 154). It is a spontaneous agreement based on disposition' (*MP*, p. 151) which binds her to Goethe, she insists. Yet it is hard to believe that her thought would have taken the form it did without these thinkers, for her work is shot through with their influence. Mayreder's feminism is surely a product not only of her adolescent rebellion against norms of femininity but also of her intellectual milieu. Her path to feminism is not (as she herself had claimed) that of the lonely outsider who propagates emancipatory ideas which have arisen spontaneously, but on the contrary is paved by active participation in the intellectual ferment of her day. Her own contribution is that she combined a largely unfocused account of her personal situation with that intellectual context to arrive at a critique of femininity which, above all, applies the individualism of these thinkers to the female personality. It seems that Mayreder's belief in the supremacy of the individual blinded her to the extent of her debt to these other thinkers who accompanied her on her journey to feminism.

In contrast to both Mayreder and Fickert, the path to feminism taken by Marie Lang (1858–1934) did not stretch back to adolescence but began in adulthood. It was prompted not by suppressed anger at personal limitation on account of gender, as theirs partly was, nor by material pressures, as Fickert's was, but by a charismatic experience. And the source of this experience was none other than Auguste Fickert herself. Lang describes how before attending a meeting of the AÖFV she had never been interested in women's rights but only in human rights in general.[12] In the winter probably of 1893, at the suggestion of Mayreder, at that time a cherished friend, she went to her first women's event. She was motivated more by a desire to meet the literary historian Emil Reich than by an interest in women's issues. And there she encountered Auguste Fickert:

> What beauty, this firm, clear, pure countenance [. . .] Pure, but forceful was her lightly curved brow, from which her silvery white hair was combed up quite straight. Large and slim, firm and strong her whole form. Tremendous!... She stood there, tall and upright, like an archangel with the fiery sword! Unforgettable!

The religious overtones in Lang's account are unmistakable. Fickert appears as a conquering, triumphant archangel with raised sword, 'almost cold', but of 'overpowering strength', and Lang as her converted disciple whose conscience is 'almost threatened' by Fickert's speech. An inner impulse to follow the word of Fickert takes possession of her, she records, referring to the celibacy regulations for women teachers: 'But what distress – and what a cry for help – it forces me to come to the side of this wonderful woman'.[13] Despite Mayreder's attempts to dissuade her, Lang offered her services to Fickert immediately, and an intense friendship with strong emotional and even erotic undercurrents developed between the two women.[14] Lang was a leading member of the AÖFV until early 1900, when severe tensions between her and Fickert came to a head and Lang left the Association.

Lang's impulsive enthusiasms were by no means confined to the women's movement. She threw herself into a variety of initiatives with panache and was always on the look-out for idols. This applies also to her interest in mysticism and the occult, phenomena which were *en vogue* in semi-bohemian artistic-intellectual circles in Vienna in the 1880s. Lang was at the centre of such a group, which counted amongst its members not only Rudolf Steiner, Friedrich Eckstein, and Franz Hartmann, but also Hugo Wolf and later Rosa Mayreder, who, however, maintained a distance from mystical, theosophical ideas. Eckstein interpreted Lang's interest in feminism as a rejection of mysticism and theosophy in favour of 'social problems and the practical tasks of modern life, in particular the struggle for women's rights'.[15]

In contrast to Eckstein, however, it is possible to see her feminist engagement as being in many ways a continuation of her interest in theosophy in another form rather than running counter to it. As becomes clear from Lang's speeches and written contributions to the debate on the 'woman question', she saw feminism as offering the possibility of uncovering the powers of nature latent in human beings and also its mysteries, two stated goals of the Theosophic Society.[16] For her, as for the theosophists, nature was an 'omnipresent and omnipotent creative potentiality'[17] which deserved worship and which feminism, above all in its critiques of governing sexual mores and motherhood, could restore to its full mystical and mythical splendour. It was not only Fickert's imposing presence which converted Lang, for a while at least, to feminist engagement but also the subject of Fickert's speech, for this appealed to precisely this creed based on nature. Thus Lang criticised the encroachment on women's freedom represented by the celibacy regulations not on grounds of women's rights to their own reproductive power but on grounds of the unnatural emotional deprivation this entailed for these women, denied the fulfilment of 'woman's most wonderful profession'.[18] And it was a profession she herself lived to the full. The mother of four, Lang revelled in her maternal role and impressed the sanctity and beauty of sexuality and procreation on her children. Thus, for example, she insisted that they should not 'desecrate' the parental bed by romping on it for it was the place of birth, love, and death.[19] For Lang, therefore, feminism was closely linked to spiritual and sensual fulfilment. She was inspired to join the women's movement by an experience similar to religious conversion centering on an adored leader (Fickert), reinforced by a belief in the holy mysteries of nature.

For all three of these radicals, feminist engagement was connected to a religious attitude. Both Fickert and Mayreder saw themselves as missionaries spreading the word of female freedom – Fickert through public performance, Mayreder by setting an example through the development of her own individuality – while Lang sought there the realisation of her religion of nature. This feature forms an immediate contrast to the leading moderate of the movement, Marianne Hainisch (1839–1936). For her, the wife of a cotton-factory owner, it was not a question of missionary zeal or spirituality but simply one of alleviating the plight of the well-bred, middle-class woman forced to fend for herself and her family. She records how she came to recognise the existence of the problem when a woman friend was thrown back on her own earning power and they both discovered that the typical woman of this social background was as good as helpless. 'As I saw her go,' Hainisch recounts, 'a beggar, condemned to beg for the rest of her life, in spite of her talents and so-called good education, an indescribable feeling overcame me. . . That very same day and in the following night I matured to become a self-aware woman. Suddenly it became clear to me that woman, too, must be independent'.[20] This revelation caused her to launch the campaign for girls' secondary education as a precondition of middle-class women's earning power – for it was also clear to her that 'of course it was a question of gainful employment which would guarantee a substantial wage and which corresponded to the social position of the husband'.[21] The initial impulse was, then, the fulfilment of a specific goal.

Yet Hainisch's account of her motives emphasises that they were not guided solely by a rational decision. 'It was as if my privileged lot drove me to help...'.

'Life had taken hold of me', she declares. She had had 'contact with a living reality' which 'seized' her, she maintains, expressly distancing herself from the majority of well-off women who through ignorance dismissed women's efforts at change as a 'sport'.[22] This emphasis on immediate experience over second-hand knowledge is, however, somewhat surprising coming from a woman who was, in fact, never in the position of the women she was trying to help and who, by her own account, came to support those efforts precisely through second-hand knowledge and, thus, intellectual insight. It is as though this emphasis on lived experience rather than insight is to exonerate her from any decision for which she could be held responsible; she is the tool of non-rational forces and in this way her feminist agitation is to be justified.

Accompanying this renunciation of responsibility is an implicit rejection of the erroneous popular image of the radical women's righter as hostile to men and motherhood. In her memoirs Hainisch constantly stresses the harmony of her family life, both as a child and as an adult. There is no hint of conflict, in sharp contrast to Fickert's account, which brims with repressed anger, and Mayreder's, which revels in anti-patriarchal rebellion. Moral conduct lessons at school, enjoining the girls to neighbourly love, fulfilment of one's duty, and self-improvement, are seen positively, and Hainisch's courtship and marriage – quite unlike Mayreder's – seem to have been conventional. Most conspicuous is the constant emphasis on the joys of motherhood. 'I had a child and desired nothing more,' she declares of the birth of her son, Michael, later the first President of the Austrian Republic.[23] And that she should experience no conflict between motherhood and public engagement is taken for granted: 'Of course my activities did not stop me from raising my children,' she asserts.[24] In this way Hainisch distances herself from the radicals and any hint of feminism as rebellion against the patriarchal status quo, usually seen to be most threatened by a feminist critique of motherhood. Feminism, for her, is limited to pragmatic considerations. It is not to entail any claims to a far-reaching emancipation. Nor is it to entail any religious attitude, as was the case for Fickert, Mayreder, and Lang. Although all came from Roman Catholic backgrounds (in contrast to many other progressive Viennese movements, where the Jewish element tended to predominate in the leadership), Hainisch remained the most orthodox and thus probably felt least need to find an alternative expression to her religiosity.

This enquiry into leading feminists' very different motives for joining the women's movement invites brief consideration of how these motives may have marked their feminist engagement. Fickert's adolescent search for a moral mission can be regarded as the foundation of her truly visionary conception of the feminist mission as it later emerges in her numerous speeches and articles. For her, it is not primarily a question of a struggle for women's rights but of initiating a new era of humanity which will have evolved beyond the age of barbarism, that is, the struggle for power, to reach higher, more moral forms of social existence. And these, Fickert maintains, are based on the rule of reason and, therefore, the removal of all relations of exploitation (but particularly those between the sexes), be these rooted in physical strength or one-sided intellectual development.[25] In this process of human evolution women are to play a leading role. Like Antigone, whom Fickert cites, so the new woman, the feminist, comes not to join her voice to those who hate, but to those who love.[26] And through this insight (amongst others) humanity will be led to freedom and happiness,[27] and will achieve full personal development.

Mayreder's feminism likewise hints at its origins. Corresponding to her own youthful emphasis on the intellect, Mayreder became the most distinguished theorist of the Austrian women's movement, writing the successful collection of essays *Zur Kritik der Weiblichkeit* (1905).[28] There she emphasises the primacy of the individual over the collective, a concern which can be traced back to her strong adolescent sense of her own exceptional personality; she stresses that it is the intellect which raises the individual above the mass of humanity, and above all that it is the intellectual woman, the feminist, who will whittle away the tyranny of ruling and repressive norms.

Feminism as the search for the spiritual led Lang in a rather different direction from both Fickert and Mayreder. She was concerned to liberate natural, divine forces rather than acknowledge the power relations of women's oppression (as Fickert did) or commit herself to a differentiated intellectual discussion of sex and gender (like Mayreder). Like a number of feminists, she called for sex education, but unlike them Lang does not touch on questions of ethics, let alone sexual politics, but stresses the revelation of the sacred mysteries of the reproduction of the species which, she asserts, lead to the most profound insights into existence and a sense of divinity.[29] Along similar lines she sees education, a common theme of feminists, as the cultivation of the 'primal being' of the child, the cultivation of the 'divinely beautiful' naked body as well as the mind and soul.[30] And, as Lang portentously asserts after experiencing a performance by the dancer Isadora Duncan at the Secession, 'the mystery of the Greeks is manifest to her, that is, that the secret of all majesty rests within us and that we can reveal it to ourselves.'[31] Thus Lang endows Mayreder's and also Fickert's similar claims for the development of human (and particularly female) potential with a further mythical, spiritual dimension.

In contrast to Fickert, Mayreder, and Lang, engagement in the women's movement was for Hainisch restricted in vision, as her goal-orientated motivation and adherence to feminine norms imply. In her first speech for the foundation of a girls' grammar school, she was, for example, careful to dissociate herself from claims for women's emancipation.[32] And although she later joined the chorus for female suffrage when such claims had lost their radical tinge, she was anxious never to overstep the boundaries of decorum on more delicate issues, such as sexual morality and the sanctity of the family. Indeed, the bolstering of the family as the bulwark of the state and society forms the basis of Hainisch's engagement; and it is to her that Austria owes the introduction of Mother's Day. Hainisch in this way became the respectable face of Austrian feminism for almost all groupings, proving that women could engage in social reform without losing their feminine identity, expressed above all in motherhood, in contrast to the popular negative image of the unfeminine feminist.

For all three radicals feminism was, therefore, not only – or even primarily – a question of solving the 'woman problem' in the sense most widely accepted by contemporaries of women's rights, employment, and educational opportunities, but one of much wider ranging and even more fundamental issues. This attitude found expression in the AÖFV's ambitious and diverse activities, which were seen to be means to these immeasurably higher ends. And for all three radicals, these issues are linked to a religious attitude; feminist engagement has a transcendental, spiritual dimension. For moderates such as Hainisch, on the other hand, feminism is reducible to practical goals, particularly in the sphere of education, and is devoid of this spiritual dimension.

Yet for all four, feminism is closely linked to an ideology of love. Not only Fickert, but also Mayreder and Lang stress the importance of love in their ideal, while Hainisch's motto was 'The happiness of my life was work and love.'[33] It also entailed for all, but particularly for Fickert and Hainisch, the two most active agitators, a significant change in their lives; it meant emerging from the private sphere to participate in a male-dominated public sphere of politics. This step was almost completely unfamiliar to women and was not without its dangers – symbolised by that embarrassing moment when Hainisch, accustomed to wearing a short dress at her country home, tripped over her long city dress just before making her public debut.[34] The decision to step into the public arena also demanded considerable courage, as Fickert was forced to discover when her forthright anti-clericalism led to public slander from Karl Lueger,[35] sharp reprimands from the Viennese school authorities, and wage cuts as a disciplinary measure.[36] Furthermore, it often entailed the loosening of family ties; Mayreder records how her family responded with horror to her first public speech opposing the state regulation of prostitution and tenaciously refused to acknowledge this side of Mayreder's life.[37] In spite of this, however, Fickert and Hainisch at least seem to have flourished in their new environment; Fickert found there the function and identity she had so eagerly sought as an adolescent, while Hainisch, having previously spent most of her days in the uneventful countryside south-west of Vienna, revelled in her discovery of 'life' and became an inveterate committee woman.

This probably explains why these two women remained active in feminist agitation up to their deaths. Mayreder and Lang, on the other hand, turned largely for personal reasons to other forms of self-expression – Mayreder to her writing and Lang to her family and the Settlement movement, an attempt to overcome class barriers. In feminist agitation, intelligent and active women could find the voice and public persona otherwise denied them. The satisfaction to be gained from public impact is, however, never admitted to be a reason for engagement. Instead, it is conspicuous that all perceive themselves to be driven exclusively by inner forces, a view which reinforces that perception of feminist engagement as stemming from a spiritual or, as for Hainisch, an at least deeply personal experience, rather than from a rational decision prompted by insights into the relations between gender and power. The personal is indeed political for these women.

Note on sources

There is a wealth of as yet largely untapped unpublished primary material relating to early middle-class Austrian feminists. The most important sources for the four dealt with in the present article are listed below.

AUGUSTE FICKERT. The Auguste Fickert *Nachlaß* is kept at the Manuscripts Department, Vienna City Library. One of the most revealing documents there is Fickert's diary, I.N. 70494. In addition, numerous letters to, and to a lesser extent from, Fickert are held by the Manuscripts Department, Vienna City Library.

ROSA MAYREDER. The Rosa Mayreder *Nachlaß* is also kept at the Manuscripts Department, Vienna City Library under the call mark 264/51–3. An important part of this are Mayreder's extensive diaries, extracts from which have been published as Rosa Mayreder, *Tagebücher 1873–1937*, ed. Harriet Anderson (Frankfurt, 1988). Numerous letters to and from Mayreder are also held by the Manuscripts Department, Vienna City Library. The manuscript of large parts of Mayreder's memoirs published as *Das Haus in der Landskrongasse*, ed. Käthe Braun-Prager (Vienna, 1948) and *Mein Pantheon*, ed. Susanne Kerkovius (Dornach, 1988) is kept at the Manuscripts and Rare Book Department of the Austrian National Library, Cod. Ser. 24.556.

MARIE LANG. In addition to letters to and from Lang in both the Manuscripts Department, Vienna City Library and the Manuscripts and Rare Book Department, Austrian National Library, a considerable amount of unpublished material is in private possession. For details see Irmgard Sparholz, 'Die Persönlichkeit Marie Lang und ihre Bedeutung für die Sozialreformen in Österreich im ausgehenden neunzehnten Jahrhundert' (unpublished MA thesis, University of Vienna, 1986).

MARIANNE HAINISCH. The extensive Marianne Hainisch *Nachlaß* is held by the Bund Österreichischer Frauenvereine, Wilhelm Exner-Gasse, Vienna. It relates largely to Hainisch's committee work in the Bund. A large amount of correspondence is kept at the Manuscripts Department, Vienna City Library. Hainisch's autobiographical 'Lebensgeschichte', a typescript, cited here, is in private possession. I am grateful to Dr Marianne Hainisch and Cornelia Hainisch for making this typescript available to me. My thanks also go to Dr Gertrude Jackson for establishing the connection. Further material, including Hainisch's diaries, is also in private possession, but was not available to me for the present article.

Notes

1. No comprehensive analytical studies of these three groupings have as yet been published. For a purely factual account of the middle-class movement see Elisabeth Guschlbauer, 'Der Beginn der politischen Emanzipation der Frau in Österreich 1848–1919' (unpublished Ph.D. thesis, University of Salzburg, 1974); further bibliographical details are given in Harriet Anderson, 'Beyond a Critique of Femininity. The Thought of Rosa Mayreder (1858–1938)' (unpublished Ph.D. thesis, University of London, 1985), p. 48. For the Social Democrats see Edith Prost (ed.), *'Die Partei hat mich nie enttäuscht.' Österreichische Sozialdemokratinnen* (Vienna, 1989). For the Catholics see Friedrich Steinkellner, 'Emanzipatorische Tendenzen im Christlichen Wiener Frauen-Bund und in der Katholischen Reichsfrauenorganisation Österreichs', in Rudolf G. Ardelt, Wolfgang J. A. Huber, and Anton Staudinger (eds), *Unterdrückung und Emanzipation. Festschrift für Erika Weinzierl* (Vienna, 1985), pp. 55–67. See also *Aufbruch ins Jahrhundert der Frau?* exhibition catalogue, Historisches Museum der Stadt Wien (Vienna, 1989).
2. An exception here are the works relating to Rosa Mayreder. For bibliographical details see Rosa Mayreder, *Oder wider die Tyrannei der Norm*, ed. Hanna Bubeniček

(Vienna, 1986), pp. 227–8.

3. A rare consideration of feminists' motives is offered by Olive Banks, *Becoming a Feminist. The Social Origins of 'First Wave' Feminism* (Brighton, 1986). Banks deals only with British feminists.

4. Auguste Fickert, 'Tagebuch', entry for 3 May 1874. See note on sources.

5. Ibid., entry for 14 December 1887.

6. Ibid., entry for 23 June 1888.

7. This forms part of the Auguste Fickert *Nachlaß* and has the call mark 71148/17. See note on sources.

8. Auguste Fickert, 'Tagebuch', entry for 1 January 1882.

9. For information on the situation of women teachers see Annetta Pfaff, 'Die Frau als Lehrerin', in Martha Stephanie Braun *et al.* (eds), *Frauenbewegung, Frauenbildung und Frauenarbeit in Österreich* (Vienna, 1930), pp. 283–94.

10. See Rosa Mayreder, *Mein Pantheon*, ed. Susanne Kerkovius (Dornach, 1988), p. 71. Subsequent references to this edition are abbreviated in the text as *MP*, followed by the page number.

11. See Rosa Mayreder, *Fabeleien über göttliche und menschliche Dinge* (Vienna, 1921), pp. 59–66.

12. See Marie Lang, 'Wie ich zur Arbeit an der Frauenbewegung kam', *Die Österreicherin* 3, iii (March 1930), pp. 3–4 (p. 4).

13. Ibid., p. 4.

14. For details of letters documenting this relationship see Irmgard Sparholz, 'Die Persönlichkeit Marie Lang. . .', pp. 41–6. See note on sources.

15. Friedrich Eckstein, 'Die erste Begegnung mit Marie Lang', in *Marie Lang. Gedenkblatt des Settlement* (Vienna, 1935), pp. 8–10 (p. 10).

16. See Helene Blavatsky, *The Key to Theosophy. Being a clear Exposition in the Form of Question and Answer of the Ethics, Science and Philosophy for the Study of which the Theosophical Society has been founded* (London, 1968), p. 39, first published in 1889.

17. Ibid., p. 64.

18. Marie Lang, 'Rede auf der ersten internat. Lehrerinnenversammlung in Berlin, Juni 1904', in *Marie Lang. Gedenkblatt*, p. 11.

19. See Irmgard Sparholz, 'Die Persönlichkeit Marie Lang. . .', p. 14.

20. Marianne Hainisch, 'Ein Mutterwort über die Frauenfrage', *Jahresbericht des Vereins für erweiterte Frauenbildung*, 6 (1892), pp. 21–32 (p. 25).

21. Marianne Hainisch, 'Zur Geschichte der österreichischen Frauenbewegung', in Martha Stephanie Braun *et al.* (eds), *Frauenbewegung*, pp. 13–24 (pp. 14–15).

22. Marianne Hainisch, 'Mutterwort', p. 25.

23. Marianne Hainisch, 'Lebensgeschichte', p. 14. See note on sources.

24. Ibid., p. 26.

25. See Auguste Fickert, 'Wohin die Frauenbewegung führt'. This is part of the Auguste Fickert *Nachlaß* and has the call mark 71148/57. See note on sources.

26. See *Stenographisches Protokoll über die Constituierende Versammlung des Allgemeinen Österreichischen Frauenvereins* (Vienna, 1893), p. 14.

27. 'Durch Erkenntnis zu Freiheit und Glück' was the motto of the AÖFV and probably devised by Fickert. See *Protokoll über die Constituierende Versammlung*, p. 14.

28. An English translation of this work appeared as *A Survey of the Woman Problem*, tr. Herman Scheffauer (London, 1913).

29. See *Die Volksstimme*, 10 December 1893, p. 8.

30. See Marie Lang, 'Über Erziehung', in *Die Zeit*, 21 May 1903, pp. 15–16.

31. Marie Lang, 'Offenbarung', *Dokumente der Frauen*, 6 (1902), pp. 636–8 (p. 637).

32. See Marianne Hainisch, *Zur Frage des Frauen-Unterrichts* (Vienna, 1870).

33. Cited by Marie Lang, 'Wie ich zur Arbeit an der Frauenbewegung kam', *Die Österreicherin*, 3, iii (March 1930), p. 4.

34. See Marianne Hainisch, 'Lebensgeschichte', p. 18.
35. See *Neue Freie Presse*, 5 June 1899, pp. 3–4.
36. See Auguste Fickert *Nachlaß*, documents 71182/2–8. See note on sources.
37. See Rosa Mayreder, *Mein Pantheon*, p. 185.

The 'Child-Woman':
Kraus, Freud, Wittels,
and Irma Karczewska

Edward Timms

Fritz Wittels (1880–1950) is best known as Freud's first biographer. In 1907 he became a member of the Vienna Psychoanalytic Society, but he was obliged to resign three years later for reasons which have never been fully explained.[1] During 1907–8 Wittels was also a member of Kraus's circle and a frequent contributor to *Die Fackel*. But his relationship with Kraus ended even more abruptly amid considerable acrimony. Previous accounts of these controversies have been inconclusive.[2] The actual sequence of events might have remained shrouded in mystery but for the discovery of Wittels's unpublished memoirs, written in English during his final years in New York. On the basis of these memoirs, which have been checked against other sources, it has now become possible to reconstruct the story in some detail.

It was in the spring of 1907 that Kraus and Wittels became acquainted. Born in Vienna in 1880, Wittels came from an assimilated Jewish family. At the time when he became a member of Kraus's circle, he was a medical student with literary ambitions. He was almost seven years younger than Kraus, but he made up in impudence for what he lacked in years. Out of the blue he sent Kraus one of his short stories, claiming that it was far superior to the work of Strindberg which had been appearing in *Die Fackel*. Kraus (as Wittels recalls) responded with a laconic note: 'Your self-assertion, to Strindberg's disadvantage, made a bad impression on me. I like your story and will print it' (p. 7).[3] The story, 'Ladislaus Posthumus', appeared in *Die Fackel* in February 1907 (F 218: 14–20).[4] It incorporates a dream motif with incestuous undertones, which indicates that Wittels was already familiar with the work of Freud.

Shortly afterwards Wittels sent Kraus an article arguing in favour of the legalisation of abortion. Published at the end of February under the pseudonym Avicenna, this outspoken article created a sensation. In Catholic Austria the prohibition against contraception resulted in many unwanted pregnancies; but a woman convicted of obtaining an abortion was liable to five years'

87

imprisonment with hard labour. Wittels argued that this law was itself a crime. The birth of unwanted children was causing terrible suffering, especially for families too impoverished to care for them. And the resulting high rate of child mortality was itself a form of 'murder in disguise', far more horrific than abortion. No woman, he concluded, should be forced to bear a child against her will (F 219–20: 1–22).

The publication of this article proved to be a turning point in Wittels's career. It won him not only the friendship of Kraus but also that of Freud. As a medical student, Wittels was already attending the lectures which Freud gave at the General Hospital in the Alserstrasse. But it was through the publication of this article that he became personally acquainted with the great man. Freud, who was a regular reader of *Die Fackel*, approached Wittels after his Saturday lecture and, pointing to the article, said: 'Did you write that? It is a regular legal brief, and I subscribe to every word of it' (p. 102). Shortly afterwards, on 27 March 1907, Wittels became a member of the Psychoanalytic Society. He was formally sponsored by Isidor Sadger, who was his uncle.

From March 1907 onwards (Wittels recalls in a suggestive phrase) he had 'two spiritual fathers' (p. 102) – Kraus and Freud. Wittels was one of the most active members of the Psychoanalytic Society, contributing no less than ten papers during the next three years. Between February 1907 and May 1908 he also published thirteen articles and stories in *Die Fackel*. Indeed, during those eighteen months he was Kraus's most important contributor and seems to have enjoyed his particular esteem. Five of the articles Wittels contributed to *Die Fackel* were also presented as papers at the Psychoanalytic Society, sometimes in a modified form.[5] And Wittels deserves credit for the cross-fertilisation which occurred between the two groups. It was almost certainly his encouragement which induced Kraus, in March 1907, to attend Freud's lectures. This enabled the satirist to obtain a first-hand impression of Freud's approach to the erotic significance of dreams.

For almost two years Wittels had the best of both worlds. He was valued by Freud for his wealth of ideas and by Kraus for his medical expertise. After completing his duties at the hospital, he would join Kraus and his friends in the evening at their favourite restaurant behind the Opera, 'Der rote Igel' ('The Red Hedgehog'). From there they would walk to the Café Pucher on the Kohlmarkt. Later they would go on to the Café Frohner, situated in the luxurious Hotel Imperial. Kraus was a heavy smoker, but never took a drop of alcohol. He was a gifted conversationalist and on good days, Wittels recalls, he enchanted everyone. All kinds of people – senior government officials as well as artists, actors, and attractive girls – would come to his table; and Kraus made them feel they were 'the centre of the universe'. Later, feeling the need to escape from the stifling atmosphere of bourgeois coffee houses, Kraus and his circle would move on to lower-class cafés patronised by prostitutes and bookies. And in the small hours of the morning he would go home to work at his desk until daybreak (pp. 8–10).

The Wednesday-evening meetings of the Psychoanalytic Society, patronised by writers and musicologists as well as by respectable medical men, were also intellectually stimulating. But Freud's circle was less glamorous than Kraus's bohemian entourage. When he qualified in January 1908, Wittels recalls, he left the General Hospital and opened a private practice in the Graben. He wanted to be at the centre of the district where the restaurants and coffee houses of Kraus's clique were situated. The stimulus provided by Kraus and his companions was more important to him than pursuing an orthodox medical career. Kraus had also drawn him into the whirl of his private life by introducing him to his mistress, Irma Karczewska.[6]

'The child-woman'

Irma, Wittels recalls, was the youngest daughter of a janitor living in a proletarian suburb of Vienna. She grew up in a petit-bourgeois Catholic milieu with little formal education. It may have been her aspirations as an actress that brought her to Kraus's attention. According to Wittels, Kraus's attachment to Irma was due to the fact that she reminded him of Annie Kalmar, the actress whose love he had tragically lost when she died in May 1901. Both women had 'the same dark hair, brown complexion, blue eyes' (pp. 107–8). But Irma was more petite than Annie (among the members of Kraus's circle she became known as 'die Kleine'–'the little one'). When, in May 1905, Kraus organised his pioneering production of Wedekind's *Die Büchse der Pandora* (*Pandora's Box*), Irma played a minor role as Bob the Groom. By that date she had evidently been Kraus's mistress for some time, although she had had other lovers before they met. He supported her financially and tried to launch her on a career in cabaret (F 203: 18–19).

When Wittels first joined Kraus's circle in the spring of 1907, Irma hardly ever appeared. But Kraus was eager to share his discovery with others:

> Kraus told me all about her, how lovely she was, what a pagan in the Hellenic sense, how free in sexual matters and how unhappy . . . She was a dream of beauty. He showed me photographs of her with grape leaves and clusters in her black hair and a radiant smile on her parted lips. In short, I was in love with her before I ever saw her. [pp. 12–13]

The intensity of Wittels's feelings can be gauged not only from his memoirs (written thirty-five years later) but also from the letters he wrote to 'Liebes Irmerl' between April and December 1907. It is clear that by the summer of that year he and Irma had embarked on a passionate love affair. In one ecstatic letter, dated 21 July 1907, he reminds her of the moment 'when I dragged you out of Kraus's bed'.[7]

Here we seem to have the makings of a classic erotic triangle, with Wittels as the ardent young lover competing for Irma's favours against Kraus, his friend and mentor. Since the relationship between Kraus and Wittels did erupt at the end of 1908 into a bruising public row, with bitter exchanges of insults in print which culminated in a legal action, one might suppose that this was a case of male erotic rivalry. This is the inference which has been drawn in previous accounts of this affair. But in the bohemian subculture of Vienna nothing was ever quite what it seemed.

Wittels's memoirs reveal that the row was not due to jealousy – at least not in the conventional sense. Kraus was not hostile towards the younger man for stealing Irma's affections. On the contrary, it turns out that, tiring of his relationship with Irma, Kraus actually wanted to pass her on to Wittels and even to persuade him to marry her. 'All would perhaps have ended better', Wittels writes in his account of the rupture, 'had I been capable of permanently freeing Kraus of Irma. He wished to get rid of her in good grace' (p. 118). Unbeknown to Wittels, Kraus was emotionally involved with another actress, Bertha Maria Denk. Thus it would have been very convenient for him to get Irma off his hands by marrying her off to a promising young physician. The situation is very reminiscent of the scene in Wedekind's play *Erdgeist* (*Earth Spirit*), where the respectable Dr Schön tries to marry his mistress Lulu off to a younger man, on the understanding that she will still be available for the occasional house call.

The tension which built up between Kraus and Wittels during the summer of 1908 was, therefore, jealousy *in reverse*. Kraus wanted Wittels to take Irma off his hands; Wittels resisted this pressure, although he certainly found Irma extremely attractive. He was pressed into the ambiguous role of lover and therapist. Irma was frequently ill. She seems to have suffered from a number of disorders, including a venereal infection. She needed medical care as well as amorous companionship. Wittels recalls that he would spend the evenings looking after Irma when she was confined to her apartment. Long after midnight, when she was finally asleep, he would join Kraus and his crowd in the coffee house. In this capacity he seems to have made himself 'indispensable' to Kraus (p. 14). In long conversations with Wittels, Irma proudly described the 'orgiastic nights' which she had spent with Kraus. But 'nobody could bear her long, although she looked more than charming and compensated her lovers in the night for a good deal of what she vexed them with in the daytime'. Kraus apparently 'could not stand her chattering and therefore introduced her to more and more men who were supposed to take her out' (p. 108).

This inverted erotic triangle had its humorous side. Wittels recalls an episode when the three of them met in Venice, probably in September 1907.[8] He had been left in charge of Irma while Kraus took a holiday in southern Italy, and he travelled to Venice with their protégée by train. They met Kraus in the Café Giacomuzzi. Wittels complains that throughout the weekend Irma gave them nothing but trouble. First she insisted on having her high-heeled shoe repaired, while they were supposed to be relaxing on the beach. While Wittels took the shoe to the cobbler, Kraus began to lecture Irma on how discreditable it was for an elegant woman to damage one of her shoes. When Wittels returned, he heard from quite some distance Kraus and Irma having a furious row. He had (he recalls) to rescue his friend from her 'clawing nails'.

The next morning they decided to take Irma on a tour of the museums and churches of Venice. This turned out to be a mistake. Irma, whose lack of cultural interests is repeatedly emphasised, was terribly bored. But in one art gallery she caught sight of a plaster cast of Hercules, larger than life. She began to examine the body of this Hercules so intimately that Wittels became very embarrassed and tried to pretend that he did not know her. 'You're just jealous,' she said, 'you're no match for this one'. On the journey back to Vienna by train, Wittels tried to make it clear to her that she had spoilt their vacation. He persuaded her to go and apologise to Kraus, who was sitting in the next compartment. She went like a lamb. But a few minutes later Kraus came storming into Wittels's compartment, shouting: 'Do you know what she wants? A mahogany baby-grand, and I'm to order it for her immediately!' (pp. 19–20).

In reconstructing a relationship of this kind, it is hard to separate fact from fiction. Irma seems from the start to have been cast by Kraus in a quasi-mythical role, as a 'Dionysian girl born several thousand years too late' (p. 13). Wittels recalls how Kraus groomed her for a life of love, encouraging her to develop erotic refinements reminiscent of the 'hetaera' – the glamorous concubine of ancient Greece as described by Lucian (p. 110). A German edition of Lucian published in 1907, embellished with erotic images of the hetaera by Gustav Klimt, must have given an additional impetus to this idea.[9] Irma felt attracted by the glamour of her role:

> She could not understand all the philosophical talk and praise of the hetaera with which *Die Fackel* overflowed, but she quickly realised that all she had clandestinely practised from early puberty on, to the deep dismay of her petty bourgeois family, was now supposed to represent the sublimest peak a girl could reach. When she took sick in the course of her orgiastic life, she was celebrated as a heroine honourably hurt in her struggle for love. [pp. 108–09]

Wittels contributed to this myth through an article in *Die Fackel* of 15 July 1907 entitled 'The Child-Woman' ('Das Kindweib'). This was directly inspired by his relationship with Irma.[10] He claims to be describing the phenomenon of the 'child-woman' realistically: her precocious beauty, her complete freedom from sexual inhibition, her ability to gain sensuous pleasure from any lover, whether male or female. Freud's theory of infantile auto-eroticism is cited as the key to her emotional disposition. The child-woman's ability to obtain pleasure from any sexual partner echoes the infant's uninhibited sucking of whatever object is to hand: a finger or a toe, a black dummy or a brown one. But Wittels also invokes the concept of the 'primal woman' ('Urweib'), which obviously derives not from psychoanalysis but from the erotic subculture of Kraus and Wedekind.

Wittels insists that the destiny of this 'primal woman' is not to be confused with prostitution. He does briefly address the more sordid aspects of her existence: alcoholism, tuberculosis, and venereal disease. But the ideal which Wittels celebrates has strong undertones of wishful thinking. He dreams of resurrecting a 'religion of beauty' centred on the Greek ideal of the 'hetaera' – the woman whose exceptional beauty could inspire her male admirers to works of genius. But he is tragically aware that the spontaneity of Hellenistic culture can never be regained. The destiny of the child-woman is, thus, to suffer and die young (F 230–1: 14–33).

This cult of the 'hetaera' is one of the most extravagant products of the erotic subculture at the turn of the century. Kraus's enthusiasm seems to have been kindled by Wedekind's *Büchse der Pandora*, identified in October 1903 as the 'tragedy of a hetaera' (F 143: 26). By 1906, however, he had become more sceptical, especially about the notion of the 'exceptional hetaera', endowed with intellectual as well as erotic genius (F 192: 13). Behind this cryptic footnote we may detect Kraus's perplexity about the two women with whom he was having simultaneous affairs: the disconcertingly intelligent Bertha Maria Denk, and the completely uneducated Irma Karczewska.

Freud's response to this erotic cult was decidedly critical, although he had his own doubts about women's intellectual endowments. One evening Wittels read an early draft of 'The Child-Woman' to Freud in private. At first Freud listened to the paper benevolently. However, his mood changed when he realised that his own methods and concepts were 'being abused to sponsor what he called an outright feminine ragamuffin [*Haderlump*]'. Wittels was persuaded to tone down the argument in an attempt to turn his paper into 'a solid contribution to feminine psychology' (pp. 15, 20). He presented a version of this 'Child-Woman' article to the Psychoanalytic Society on 29 May 1907 under the title 'Die große Hetäre' ('The Great Courtesan'). The record of the ensuing discussion has unfortunately not survived.[11] However, it is clear that, far from being a contribution to feminine psychology, 'The Child-Woman' is a male fantasy which disregards the social origins of prostitution.

In the absence of Irma's own testimony, it is impossible to arrive at a balanced picture of her personality. It seems that towards the end of her life she did record in a notebook her own side of the story, embellished with aphorisms in the style of Kraus.[12] Until this notebook becomes available, we have to rely on the glimpses of her which we gain from third parties. These tend to be either tendentious or tantalisingly inconclusive. Erich Mühsam shared Wittels's view of Irma as a person created for sexual pleasure (he crudely refers to her in his letters as 'das Tierchen' ['the little animal']). There are also frequent references to 'die Kleine' in the letters of Karl Hauer, but they give no sense of Irma's individuality.[13]

Some of Kraus's women friends were more sympathetic. The actress Kete Parsenow (a friend of Else Låsker-Schüler) repeatedly inquires after 'die Kleine' in a long sequence of letters and postcards. The allusions in her correspondence tend to confirm Wittels's story that Irma, although she more than once got married, remained dependent upon Kraus until the end of her life. In a letter of July 1918 Kete inquires: 'How is the little one getting on? Is her husband with her? I really feel sorry for her. Do you still see her often? And how is the Baroness?'[14] Kete, who was herself on intimate terms with Kraus, was well aware that his personal entourage included a number of other women, in addition to Irma and Sidonie Nadherny (the Baroness). Her letters frequently mention Helene Kann, who first met Kraus in 1904 and apparently remained 'a loyal companion' until the end of his life.[15]

Kraus had some difficulty in keeping all these relationships in equilibrium. A further emotional attachment involved Elisabeth Reitler, sister of Helene Kann. His letters to Sidonie contain cryptic references to 'Frau R.', which describe her as 'intelligent, humane and feminine'. This scarcely suggests a strong attachment. But the news that Elisabeth Reitler had committed suicide on 7 November 1917 is followed by a letter full of anguish and self-reproach. 'Next to you,' Kraus writes to Sidonie, 'she was the best person I knew.' He acknowledges that the complex causes of Elisabeth's despair included a sense that she was not in a position to compete with Sidonie for his affection.[16] An 'Epitaph for Elisabeth R.' was included in the third volume of *Worte in Versen*, published in 1918.[17]

There were also periods of estrangement from Sidonie Nadherny – in 1918–20 and again in 1923–7. But, on the whole, Kraus seems to have succeeded in ensuring that his enduring attachment to 'the Baroness' was kept separate from his entanglements in Vienna. Vienna and Janowitz formed different worlds. Thus, Irma is never mentioned in Kraus's letters to Sidonie. From Kete Parsenow's letters we may infer that for a number of years Helene Kann remained on amicable terms with Irma. Each woman seems to have been assigned a clearly defined role in Kraus's unorthodox domestic arrangements. Helene, who had initially herself been a celebrated courtesan, evidently came to play a more motherly role, ensuring that Kraus was never short of feminine company: it was she who later introduced Kraus to Gina Kaus.[18] Irma's position was more like that of a dependent child. A card which Kete Parsenow sent to Kraus in January 1924 sums the situation up suggestively: 'How are things going with you and your family? You know who I mean.'[19]

In the absence of more objective testimony, we have to rely on Wittels's memoirs to complete the outline of Irma's biography. He writes with engaging frankness, and where it has been possible to check his recollections against other sources, they have usually proved reliable. At some date between 1908 and 1910 Irma married (not perhaps for the first time) and moved to Berlin. But the relationship was short-lived, and she 'came back to Vienna after six months' (p. 115). By 1912 she had presumably remarried, since she had changed her name once again. Her ambition was to make a career in the Berlin theatre, with Kraus's support; but in this, too, she was unsuccessful (p. 119).

Irma appears to have married three times in all.[20] But (as Wittels puts it): 'Men sooner or later withdrew and she always came back to Kraus, her foster father . . . Moreover he felt responsible for the course she pursued; he had implanted ideas of grandeur in a hussy from the outskirts of the city' (p. 109). It is in this sense that Wittels (borrowing a phrase from Nestroy) describes Irma as Kraus's 'personal nemesis' ('Nemesiserl'). Kraus evidently accepted responsibility for her: 'he remained her protector – often against his will – for over twenty-five years until she died and I think he will be forgiven all his sins for that' (p. 12). Wittels's epitaph on Irma, however, is rather less generous: 'Finally the little simpleton became as fat as a stuffed goose, and about twenty-five years after the time of which I am speaking, she died a suicide' (p. 109).

It has not been possible to clarify the circumstances of Irma's suicide. Towards the end of her life she apparently became alienated from Kraus, partly as a result of a dispute with Helene Kann. The decision to take her own life seems to have been prompted by the fear that she was suffering from terminal cancer.[21] The story of her life and death (in so far as it can be reconstructed) reveals the more sombre side of the erotic subculture. Irma was clearly treated as a plaything for privileged males, who enjoyed social, educational, and financial advantages which she was denied. However enthusiastically Wittels may celebrate her genius as a 'hetaera', his summary of the relationship in his memoirs seems far more apt: 'I was in love with this most attractive misfit' (p. 116). What 'The Child-Woman' and other early writings reveal is the immaturity of Wittels's outlook. Retrospectively he concedes that Freud's attitude was far more responsible than that of Kraus and the erotic subculture. 'We knew from Freud that repressed sex instincts made men neurotic to such an extent that an entire era was poisoned. What we did not know was that former puritans running wild will not help either' (p. 113). It was many decades before Wittels, through his experience as a psychoanalyst in New York, arrived at a more differentiated view of female sexuality.[22]

Kraus's own attitude to Irma remains a mystery. She certainly helped to inspire the cult of oversexed and under-educated women which fills the pages of *Die Fackel* in the period 1905–14. But if the unhappy story of Irma's later life made any impact on his thinking, he never acknowledged it in print. His changing attitude towards women has to be construed from his silences. Kraus never explicitly revoked his pre-war cult of female sexuality. But this theme abruptly vanishes from the pages of *Die Fackel* during the First World War and finds only occasional echoes in his writings of the 1920s and 1930s. He accepted without protest the reforms of 1919, which gave women full suffrage and enhanced civil rights. The shift in attitude is unmistakable. Women cease to be portrayed in *Die Fackel* as if they were primarily sex objects. And where Kraus earlier derided female emancipation, he now acknowledges progressive women's organisations as allies in the campaign for peace (F 557–60: inside back cover). The sobriety of Kraus's writings of the 1920s may, however, not be entirely attributable to altered political circumstances. It also seems likely that his experience with Irma Karczewska taught him a salutary lesson.

Spiritual fathers

Wittels's memoirs are subtitled 'The Story of a Freudian'. In fact, however, his narrative assigns equal weight to each of his 'spiritual fathers' – Kraus and Freud. His account of the controversies of 1909–10 shows how intimate the connections were between the erotic subculture of Vienna and the scientific pursuits of the Psychoanalytic Society. Acknowledging with admirable frankness the mistakes and follies of his youth, he offers a Freudian model of his own immaturity.

The frustrated quest for a substitute father is identified as the key to his dilemma. It was in May 1908 that Wittels's own father died. 'After the death of my father,' Wittels observes, 'I should have closed the long drawn out interlude with Kraus and entered the temple of science without reserve. It did not work out this way. True, I did work with Freud but a good portion of my unsettled conflicts remained in Kraus's camp' (p. 123). May 1908 was the month in which Wittels's final contribution to *Die Fackel* appeared. His personal relations with Kraus 'deteriorated from day to day' (p. 124). The psychoanalytic movement, by contrast, became increasingly attractive. Wittels felt honoured to be able to attend the first International Psychoanalytic Congress, held at Salzburg in the spring of 1908.

Meanwhile, Wittels was preparing two books for publication: a collection of essays on psychological and sexual problems, entitled *Die sexuelle Not* (*Sexual Need* or *Sexual Deprivation*); and a volume of short stories entitled *Alte Liebeshändel* (*Love Affairs in Bygone Days*). A large proportion of these writings had first appeared in *Die Fackel*. Despite this, it was not Kraus but Freud whom Wittels approached during the summer of 1908, asking for permission to dedicate *Die sexuelle Not* to him. Freud consented, but only after pointing out to Wittels that Kraus, who was becoming increasingly critical of psychoanalysis, would see this as an insult and might take his revenge. The fulsome dedication to Freud forms an incongruous contrast to the contents of *Die sexuelle Not* (especially chapters like 'The Child-Woman'), which are far closer in spirit to Kraus. But the debt to Kraus is only mentioned in a brief aside.

Alte Liebeshändel was published first, towards the end of October 1908. Kraus evidently admired the way in which these stories reinterpret historical romances in terms of modern sexual psychology. He even arranged for the book to be brought out by his own publisher, Jahoda & Siegel. When it appeared, Wittels presented him with a copy inscribed with the handwritten dedication: 'To my dear Karl Kraus of 1907'. He also records Kraus's response: 'What does that mean? It sounds so feminine.' By this time Wittels had become almost obsessed with the need to break with his mentor, feeling that if he did not do so, Kraus would forestall him (p. 128).

Kraus's increasing ambivalence towards Wittels expressed itself in a dream:
> One evening Kraus related a dream of his to the round table . . . He was sitting – he said – in the midst of his friends. I was among them and all the enemies whom he had crushed by making fools of them had to pass by. We burst into derisive laughter at each one as he passed. But when Benedikt, the arch enemy, passed by and all the other friends pointed at him with jeers and sneers, I alone separated from the circle, approached Benedikt and bowed deeply. [p. 120]

Moriz Benedikt, editor of the *Neue Freie Presse*, had frequently been attacked in *Die Fackel*. Both Kraus and Wittels construed this dream as a significant omen.

'Finally,' Wittels recalls, 'the atmosphere became so thick that I had a kind of obsession to break with Kraus.' He therefore wrote him a letter, echoing the language used by Brutus in Shakespeare's *Julius Caesar* to justify Caesar's assassination: 'Because you are a great writer, I revere you. Because you were a friend, I love you. But because you – and here a gap must remain in Brutus's speech – I will come no more to the coffee house' (pp. 128-9). That was apparently the complete text of the letter (the German original has not survived). By inserting the phrase 'here a gap must remain in Brutus's speech', Wittels was evidently acknowledging his inability to explain the feelings which impelled him to make the break. Many years later, looking back, he concluded that the phrase should have read: 'Because you do not behave as my father' or

'As you can never substitute for my father.' Less profoundly, he might have written: 'As Irma is more important to you than I.' But such a remark (he wryly adds) 'would have been feminine indeed' (p. 129).

It must have been immediately after this that Kraus received a copy of *Die sexuelle Not*, with the provocative dedication to Freud. He did, indeed, take his revenge. Without mentioning Wittels by name, he published in *Die Fackel* of 30 November 1908 a fourteen-page sequence of aphorisms under the title 'Persönliches' ('Personal Matters'), which castigate an unidentified intellectual renegade who has betrayed Kraus's standards by writing journalistic articles about sex. The very first of these aphorisms recalls the prophetic dream in which one of Kraus's loyal followers defects to Benedikt. Concealed allusions to *Die sexuelle Not* make it clear that Wittels is the target. In this book Kraus saw a travesty of his own ideas: a reduction of subtle erotic insights into propaganda for sexual permissiveness. The author is obliquely condemned as deficient in both intellectual and ethical integrity. And Kraus scathingly glosses the Brutus motif from Wittels's letter (F 266: 14–28).

Wittels felt shattered. He 'would have been able to survive the blow of Kraus's fourteen pages of aphorisms', since (as he rightly observes) 'most of them could hardly be understood by anybody but myself'. Nor was he too perturbed by 'a second ejaculation of wrath' in *Die Fackel* a few months later (presumably F 279–80: 2–6). What shattered him was the fact that Kraus was prepared to drop him so quickly and completely. He had expected Kraus to reply to his note about not coming to the coffee house by saying: 'Nonsense! We will remain friends; come back!' Instead, he found himself completely ostracised, not only by Kraus and his circle but also by Irma: 'It was unimaginable and confused me for weeks.' Sitting alone in a coffee house in a remote quarter of the city, he brooded on his next move. He resolved to take his 'revenge' (pp. 130–3).

Wittels's retaliation took two forms: a psychoanalytic character assassination and a satirical novel. On 12 January 1910, over a year after the break, he presented a paper at the Psychoanalytic Society, which has subsequently become notorious: 'The "Fackel"-Neurosis'. This paper attempts to discredit Kraus's character and career by means of arguments which are a travesty of psychoanalysis. It is clear from the Minutes of the subsequent discussion that Freud found the paper methodologically unacceptable and disagreed with its main conclusions, although he refrained from explicitly condemning Wittels's approach. Other speakers were far more willing to endorse this attempted character assassination. Wittels's repudiation of his former friend was received with general enthusiasm, although members of the Society were clearly apprehensive about Kraus's powers of retaliation.[23]

Freud seems to have welcomed Wittels's break with Kraus, for he was aware that the two of them were rivals for Wittels's allegiance. His comments on *Die sexuelle Not* in December 1908 had explicitly used parental metaphors. He observed:

> Wittels's book stems from a paternal and a maternal source. The first one, represented by *Die Fackel*, goes part of the way with us in its assertion that the suppression of sexuality is the root of all evil. But we go further,

and say: we liberate sexuality through our treatment, but not in order that man may from now on be dominated by sexuality, but in order to make a suppression possible – a rejection of the instincts under the guidance of a 'higher agency'.[24]

A year later, Wittels had completely cut himself off from the 'paternal' environment of *Die Fackel*. His quest for a spiritual father seemed to have been resolved in favour of Freud. But even this relationship was put at risk by his controversy with Kraus.

Satirising the satirist

By January 1910 Wittels had completed his novel, *Ezechiel der Zugereiste* (*Ezechiel the Visitor from Abroad*). Even before the break with Kraus, he had already been planning 'a satirical review not unlike Voltaire's *Candide*' (p. 135). This satire on the literary scene is narrated by a modern reincarnation of Voltaire's *ingénu*: a naive American visitor named Ezechiel, who reacts with scandalised delight to all the decadence, malice, and intrigue he encounters in Vienna. Into this framework Wittels then inserted the figure of Benjamin Eckelhaft ('Benjamin Disgusting'), a caricature of Kraus. He recalls in his memoirs that he 'intentionally overlooked all the positive qualities of the man, derided his overgrown vanity, described his narcissistic infidelity and debunked the technique of his aphorisms . . . Benjamin Disgusting was an insult from start to finish' (pp. 134–5).

Other members of Kraus's circle, including his two closest companions Karl Hauer and Ludwig von Janikowski, are caricatured under suggestive names: Josef Windig, a sycophantic schoolteacher; and Stanislaw von Sinepopowski, a caricature of Polish intellectual pretentiousness. His female admirers are also ridiculed, together with the whole cult of the hetaera. The only member from Kraus's circle to be treated with any sympathy is Irma, thinly disguised under the name of Mizerl. However, the novel includes scurrilous allusions to her venereal infection. A whole chapter is devoted to the comic episode of her losing her heel during the ill-fated excursion to Venice. And, true to his theory that the 'child-woman' is destined to die young, Wittels adds a chapter of his own invention in which Mizerl meets her 'exemplary end'. Medically, she has been diagnosed as suffering from 'galloping consumption'. But Ezechiel has his own theory about the true cause of her death. For Mizerl's secret is that she is pregnant. And it is a law of nature that a 'child' like Mizerl can never become a mother.[25]

In 1911, at the height of the ensuing controversy, Wittels tried to justify these scurrilous anecdotes about former friends in two articles published in *Die Schaubühne*: 'I had a brilliant idea,' he writes, 'I wanted to satirize the satirists.' Why should Kraus be so sensitive, when his own life was dedicated to irony and ridicule? Wittels claims to have expected that his opponent would respond light-heartedly to what was intended as an entertaining novel.[26] In a sense Kraus had, indeed, been hoist with his own petard. But it is clear from Wittels's memoirs that his self-defence in *Die Schaubühne* was disingenuous. *Ezechiel* was not

97

conceived as a piece of fun. It was inspired by 'a lust for revenge' (p. 135).

Wittels's reconstruction of his motives in writing this novel culminates in the strangest episode in this whole affair:

> One night while hard at the work of writing this novel in which I flayed my former friend, a feeling of intense bitterness and revulsion came over me and, on impulse, I did something which I later completely forgot. This is what I did. I tore off a piece of the sheet on which I wrote and quickly scribbled a few lines to Kraus in which I suggested that we forget all the anger and misunderstanding which had grown up between us and renew our friendship . . . A short time later, the tenth anniversary of *Die Fackel* came around and again I wrote him in a friendly tone.

He was (as he puts it) in an 'ambivalent phase' of 'hate-love or love-hate' (pp. 135–6).

Kraus made no reply, but filed the letters away for future reference. So Wittels continued writing and in due course completed his novel, designed as a 'terrific blow' against his 'enemy'. He was unsure, however, whether it would be wise to publish it; so he showed the manuscript in confidence to a number of friends. The result was precisely what one might predict, given the network of communication which linked one coffee-house circle with the next. Kraus was soon informed about the 'bombshell' which lay in Wittels's drawer. Worse still, Wittels was induced by a young woman of his acquaintance to lend her the manuscript so that she could read it at home. Predictably, she took the text straight to Kraus, who was thus able to read the novel at least twelve months before it was published. 'It was years later,' Wittels adds, 'that I learned of this act of treason' (pp. 136–7).

Kraus soon set about the task of trying to prevent publication. One method was to threaten legal action; but this was a risk that Wittels and his Berlin publisher, Egon Fleischel & Co., were willing to run. A more insidious method was to exploit the coffee-house network of rumour and counter-rumour in an attempt to intimidate Wittels and break his nerve. Thus, a rumour was circulated that he had secretly been writing articles for the *Neue Freie Presse*, the newspaper which was anathema to Kraus and all members of his circle, including Wittels himself. Wittels immediately reassured Kraus – via an intermediary – that he had never written for that paper. Wittels subsequently heard that Kraus had responded with the comment: 'Of course not! I won't let him!' Such comments 'passed back and forth through the coffee houses, from him to me, from me to him, although we did not see each other. He arrogated to himself a magic power over me and my pen which annoyed me as I began to feel that there was some truth in it. I could not produce unless the damned book was published first' (p. 139). Before the book could be published, however, Wittels had to overcome an even more formidable obstacle – the authority of his second 'spiritual father', Sigmund Freud.

Freud was well aware of the split between Kraus and Wittels which had developed since the publication of *Die sexuelle Not*. He may well have been rather relieved at this development, since he felt that Kraus was having an unfortunate influence on one of his own protégés. Freud himself became drawn into the dispute when he received a request to intervene with Wittels and persuade him not to publish the novel. The request came from Kraus himself. Freud was approached through one of Wittels's relatives, a senior psychiatrist in Prague. It was also made clear to him by Kraus's lawyer that the publication of Wittels's novel would result in a legal action which would bring the whole Psychoanalytic Society into disrepute.

Kraus's most telling move was to arrange for Freud to be shown the two affectionate letters which Wittels had sent him at the very moment when he was composing his scurrilous novel. The letters seem not to have survived, but they must have been extremely cordial, perhaps even intimate, in tone. For Freud – incredible though this may seem – was later to describe them as 'love letters'. And Kraus himself, in a cryptic allusion eight years later, also refers to them as 'Liebesbriefe' (F 484–98: 140).

Freud was initially reluctant to intervene. But he must have remembered that in 1906 Kraus had come to his assistance in an affair which Freud himself had found equally embarrassing: his dispute with his former friend, Wilhelm Fliess (F 210: 26–7). Without revealing to Wittels that he had been shown the 'love letters', Freud contented himself with asking whether it was true that 'a lady' was vilified in the novel. This Wittels denied. And there for a time the matter rested.

During the spring of 1910 Wittels saw Freud almost every day, since he was assisting him with the treatment of a hospitalised patient. By this date the novel had been printed and was almost ready for publication. Kraus's intermediaries redoubled their efforts to persuade Freud to intervene:

> One day [Wittels recalls] Freud asked me pointblank to let him read the printed manuscript. He read it within twenty-four hours and brought it back and said to me: 'I shall summarise my verdict in one sentence. You lose nothing if you do not publish this book; you lose everything if you do. The novel is bad. There are a few good passages in it because the author could not completely deny himself – that is all. Moreover, you have not told me the truth; there is all kind of gossip over a girl in it.'

Wittels tried to defend the justice of his cause, but Freud 'grew impatient and said: "Never mind the woman. He was your friend. When a friendship is broken, regardless of the reason, one has to keep silence." ' And Freud referred to his own break with Fliess. Finally, Freud 'grew angry and said: "Psychoanalysis is more important than your silly controversies. Why should I allow it to be damaged by your inconsiderate book?"' Freud then – and this is an indication of the seriousness and generosity of his intervention – offered to reimburse Wittels for all the printing and publication costs he had incurred, if he agreed to withdraw the book (pp. 139–40).

In the event Wittels postponed the decision until the autumn of 1910, although Freud repeatedly admonished him to make up his mind. 'You still owe me a decision,' he said. Finally Freud declared: 'You are impossible in my circle if you publish this book.' These words, Wittels recalls, 'settled the question and made me definitely decide to publish. I was much too obstinate to let anyone threaten me' (pp. 140–1). He was obliged to resign from the Psychoanalytical

Society. And *Ezechiel* appeared in the autumn of 1910, with the mocking face of the picaro emblazoned on its cover.

It is difficult not to feel a certain admiration for Wittels at this juncture: for the sheer obstinacy with which he defied both of his 'spiritual fathers', published his wretched novel, and faced the consequences. He now found himself ostracised by the two most intellectually high-powered circles in Vienna. Given the tightly-knit network of patronage, both in literature and in medicine, how was he to survive? The answer is that these circles must not be pictured as a static system. Like organic cell structures, they were constantly being modified, replaced and renewed. Wittels might not have been able to defy Freud so recklessly if he had not, several months previously, been admitted to a new circle of patronage. In the summer of 1910 he was offered an appointment at the prestigious Cottage Sanatorium in Vienna by its Director, Rudolf von Urbantschitsch, a member of Freud's circle. For an ambitious young Jewish physician this was a tremendous step up the social ladder, since the Cottage Sanatorium was supported by members of the Habsburg dynasty, including Archduke Franz Ferdinand. The association with Urbantschitsch launched Wittels on his medical career.[27]

Wittels now had to face a fiercely contested legal action which Kraus initiated against him and his publisher in Berlin. Formally, this case was conducted not in Kraus's name, but on behalf of Irma Karczewska and Ludwig von Janikowski. The account Wittels gives of the court proceedings offers a further glimpse behind the scenes. Kraus arranged for the incriminating 'love letters' to be read in court, together with a detailed account of Wittels's deficiencies of character. When Wittels himself was in the witness-box, he tried to deny that any of the episodes in the novel could possibly be taken as applying to real persons. But the references to Irma, including the episode of the broken heel, were far too transparent, while the caricature of Janikowski (who was suffering from incipient mental illness) was particularly offensive. So Wittels lost the case and the novel had to be withdrawn, though by that date it had already run through four impressions.

Wittels was not a man to be easily intimidated. His response to the court decision was to make a series of cosmetic changes in order to disguise the personal references in the novel. Mizerl is renamed 'Dorl', and the episode with the broken heel becomes a quarrel about a torn dress. Sinepopowski is renamed Boris Popow and becomes a Bulgarian, with the result that the satire on Polish intellectual pretensions loses its point. But some of the most offensive passages, which had not been covered by the court action, remained unchanged: for example, a scene in which Eckelhaft is the victim of physical assault and anti-Semitic abuse. Wittels thus complied with the letter of the court order, but not its spirit. *Ezechiel* was completely reset (this time in Latin type) and republished in Vienna in 1911 by Huber & Lahme.[28]

Kraus did not retaliate after the republication of the novel. Nor, indeed, did he fulfil his promise that he would give an account of the court case in *Die Fackel* (F 311–12: 56). His explanation for this omission is that further attention would only have nourished his opponent's feelings of 'love-hatred' (F 484–98: 140).

But there were doubtless other reasons. Kraus could hardly have launched a full-scale polemic without the risk that Irma's reputation would be further compromised and her chances of a happy marriage impaired. Freud, too, might have been dragged into the controversy. But Wittels, through an intermediary, 'had let Kraus know that Freud had done all he could to prevent the publication of my book' (p. 140). Kraus's disgust at Wittels's deviousness must, therefore, have been counterbalanced by his respect for Freud's integrity. The fact that throughout his polemics against psychoanalysis Kraus never attacked the leader of the movement in person reflects his tacit appreciation of Freud's role in this controversy.

Freud and the love letters

The conflict between Kraus and Wittels had a postscript which shows how deeply it affected all concerned, not least Freud. After war service with an Austrian medical mission in Turkey, Wittels resumed his career in Vienna during the 1920s both as author and physician. A chance meeting with Wilhelm Stekel in 1920 rekindled his interest in psychoanalysis. Stekel, who had been expelled from the Psychoanalytic Society in 1912 after an acrimonious dispute with Freud, had his own flourishing school of Active Psychoanalysis. Wittels now underwent one of Stekel's unconventional analyses, conducted during long walks through the Vienna Woods. 'I had in this analysis,' he recalls, 'most shaking experiences and I made discoveries which surprised me greatly although I had practised analysis myself since 1908' (p. 161). Crucial to this process of self-assessment were the detailed discussions he had with Stekel about his novel *Ezechiel*.

The paradoxical product of this encounter with Stekel was that Wittels wrote a book about Freud. It was published in German in 1924 and reissued in English shortly afterwards under the title *Sigmund Freud: His Personality, His Teaching, & His School*. This first-hand account of Freud and his circle has considerable documentary value. It also contains a section on the 'hetaera' which can be read as a summing up of Wittels's triangular relationship with Kraus and Irma:

> The immense success of women who are ardently desired and greatly loved depends upon homosexual impulses in men. The hetaera–cult of our day is no less homosexual than was that of classical Greece. What a man loves in the hetaera is the other men who have lain and will lie in her arms. Since the homosexual impulse is unconscious, it cannot manifest itself in the form of direct love for another man.[29]

This is clearly a coded reflection on his own earlier attachments. His analysis with Stekel enabled him to recognise an unconscious homosexual component in his love-hate relationship with Kraus.

At the end of 1923 Wittels sent Freud an advance copy of the German edition of his book. Freud's reactions were ambivalent. He was particularly irritated by the fact that the book was written from a position sympathetic to Stekel. Freud's work is treated with great respect, but Wittels has some harsh things to say about his authoritarian personality. Freud's own copy of the book survives in the

Freud Museum in Hampstead, with marginal annotations which express his annoyance at being (as he believed) so maligned. He wrote Wittels a letter setting out some of his objections to the book, and enclosing a list of suggested emendations. The letter concluded with a grudging acknowledgement that he valued Wittels's work, even though he could not wholly approve of it. With Freud's permission, this letter was translated and published as a preface to the English edition of Wittels's book.

Freud acknowledges that the book is neither 'hostile' nor 'unduly indiscreet'. His central objection in this letter is that Wittels's adoption of Stekel's standpoint has inevitably impaired its accuracy. 'Unfortunately,' he continues, 'your relationship with Stekel precludes further attempts on my part to clear up the misunderstanding.' It is not surprising that Freud felt provoked. Wittels compares Freud's authoritarianism to that of Jehovah, implying that he suffers from a 'Jehovah complex'. Not only does he describe Freud's attitude to Stekel as 'spiteful', but suggests that his character suffers from a 'permanent twist' derived from childhood, which impels him repeatedly to repudiate his closest friends. Stekel's offence was that he challenged Freud's dogma of infallibility' on matters like homosexuality and masturbation. He is, thus, given credit for shaking off 'the hypnotic influence that had emanated from Freud's imposing personality'.[30]

At many points Wittels's chapter on the dispute between Stekel and Freud reads like a coded account of his own rupture with Kraus. Kraus's name does not occur in the book, although there is an allusion to his celebrated definition of psychoanalysis as 'the disease of which it purports to be the cure'.[31] Wittels's unpublished correspondence with Freud reveals, however, that he did originally write a chapter about his own expulsion from the Psychoanalytic Society (which must have dealt with Kraus, Irma, and *Ezechiel*). This chapter was omitted from the book for reasons of which Freud approved. Thus this book, too, is significant through its silence. Indeed, the ensuing correspondence between Freud and Wittels shows that it is the most emotionally charged experiences which tend most readily to be erased.

After reading the suppressed chapter about the events of 1910, Freud wrote Wittels a remarkable letter (dated Vienna, 24 December 1923) elucidating the Kraus controversy. The text of the letter is quoted as Wittels translates it in his memoirs (p. 148):

> Dear Doctor:
> You were right not to insert in your book the chapter which you sent me. It belongs to a different continuity. Reading it refreshed my memory of those events. Of course I cannot recall all I am supposed to have said or done, but I don't doubt in the least that your presentation is correct. One point, though, astonished me. Could it be possible that you have so completely forgotten the motive which was exclusively responsible for the severance of our relations and am I permitted to remind you of it? It is true that the 'scandal' with which the other side threatened us was very unpleasant to me – and that I would have sacrificed much to prevent. But

certainly not you, personally, whom I appreciated. To that I was compelled only when the lawyer told me that you had addressed a certain person with affectionate letters while you were occupied with writing your lampoon. I do not remember any more whether he showed me these letters or but promised to do so but my memory cannot fail me in the fact that when I asked you, you yourself did not deny these letters and claimed the right of acting that inconsistently because your feelings were ambivalent. Your insisting on this point, mixing up the real and analytical worlds, your refusal to correct this mistake – this was the thing that startled me in those days. I always considered Kraus's influence on you very disadvantageous and thought then that you had succumbed to it for good and were prejudiced forever. On this point your recent communication has reassured me; but you will admit that a presentation of your affaire, omitting this point, would have been unfair; on the other hand it is impossible to mention it.

With cordial greetings and best

Christmas wishes,

Yours,

Freud[32]

After receiving this letter, Wittels realised that he had indeed forgotten – repressed – the memory of those letters to Kraus. His explanation is that he was temporarily weakened by the death of his father and by 'the strange triangular world' in which he then lived. Retrospectively, he acknowledges his error:

> While I can see clearly that I should not have published my novel, I never blamed myself for the 'ambivalence' of the situation. I am exposing the matter in such length because of the weak spot in my case: I forgot the letters. The phenomenon of forgetting followed the mechanism made famous by Nietzsche: 'This is what you have done, says your memory. I cannot possibly have done it, says your pride. And by and by the memory gives in.' [p. 181]

Despite his reservations about Wittels's book, Freud seems to have forgiven him. For in 1925 Wittels was readmitted to the Vienna Psychoanalytic Society. This is perhaps the only occasion on which a disciple who had fallen into disfavour subsequently received Freud's pardon – a sign of the special affection in which Freud held him, despite his ambivalent conduct.

A few years later, in 1928, Wittels emigrated to New York to begin a new (and highly successful) phase in his career. His unpublished correspondence shows that Freud himself encouraged him to take this step.[33] Wittels was to become a leading figure in the New York psychoanalytic community – a defender of Freudian orthodoxy against heretics like Karen Horney.[34] His book on Freud, the first biographical study of its kind, had helped to establish his reputation in the English-speaking world; and he was soon asked by an American publisher to prepare a new edition. He wrote again to Freud for guidance. Should he publish a revised second edition or 'a totally new book?'

Freud replied in some detail in a letter (dated 8 January 1929) which throws further light on the earlier controversies. The letter is once again quoted in

Wittels's translation (p. 182):

> Dear Doctor:
>
> I am writing you immediately after receiving your letter of December 28th in which a passage is inexplicable to me and makes me apprehensive.
>
> This is your text: 'They are asking me here for a second edition of my sin of 1923 (the biography) and you can imagine my embarrassment. I think and think and cannot find the right way. Perhaps I had better let the book go out of print.'
>
> Well, I do not understand your embarrassment and I think that the right way cannot be missed. All the antecedents point to it. Let me present a short summary: In 1923, without asking me for authorization, you published a biography of me which, in many respects, drew a hateful caricature of my person. It had a great success in the public because of your gift of good presentation, because of the interest in your object and because it was a sop to the world's gossipy tendencies. It is true that you were then in no personal relation to me and were under no obligation. I was sorry that you had written this book. I had thought that a certain esteem of me had remained with you from previous contacts. I was not conscious of having done you an injustice. I had no idea that, under the influence of Stekel, you had succeeded in building up such a picture of injustice. For this aim you had to forget the real cause of our breach. It is odd enough that you were able to do that. Let me be cautious and remind you of it. During your brawl with Kraus you had simultaneously written lampoons against and friendly letters to him. When asked about this you answered defiantly that you had felt ambivalent and would not allow yourself to be deprived of the privilege of acting according to your feelings. To us, however, not only to myself, this refusal of a cultural correction of an impulsive attitude seemed to be incompatible with the duties of the analyst to the public.[35]

Even with this exchange of letters, the Kraus episode was still not closed. In the summer of 1933, with the Nazi storm clouds gathering over Austria, Wittels visited Freud in Vienna for the last time. They started talking once again about the passages in Wittels's biography which Freud had found objectionable. Suddenly (Wittels recalls) Freud changed the subject and, growing angry, said: ' "It wasn't the biography alone; there are those letters that you wrote to Kraus – regular 'love letters', while you were occupied in attacking him. That was very unfair of you, and not only that, it was an act of cowardice" '. 'I hardly trusted my ears', Wittels continues. ' "Professor," I said, "do you realise that this was twenty-five years ago?" He made a soothing gesture towards me. "I know," he said, "but you were close to me"' (p. 189).

This final conversation, at a time when Freud was approaching his eightieth birthday, shows how deep the emotions of that original erotic triangle must have run. Indeed, it suggests that Freud was not an impartial arbitrator, standing outside the controversy. He, too, was caught up in a complex web of emotions. They were 'love letters', Freud says, and 'you were close to me'. Freud was

evidently part of an all-male emotional triangle, in which both he and Kraus
– the two 'spiritual fathers' – were competing for the loyalty and affection of
their prodigal son.

What was it, after all, that held those intellectual circles together in the first
place? Obviously, not ideas alone. Libidinal energies of attraction and rivalry
also played their part in that explosion of creativity in the coffee-house culture
of Vienna. In this sense the erotic subculture was not really a separate dimension.
Erotic energies interfused the whole network of intellectual and artistic
endeavour. To understand these complex interactions, with their unconscious
homosexual undertones, it is necessary to square the circle, placing the principal
names one at each corner: Freud, Kraus, Wittels, Stekel. At the centre is a blank
space where we must insert a name which has tended to be erased from Viennese
cultural history: Irma Karczewska, the 'child-woman'.

Notes

1. *Minutes of the Vienna Psychoanalytic Society*, ed. Herman Nunberg and Ernst Federn,
tr. M. Nunberg, 4 vols (New York, 1962–75). I, p. xxxvii.
2. See Edward Timms, *Karl Kraus – Apocalyptic Satirist: Culture and Catastrophe in
Habsburg Vienna* (New Haven and London, 1986), pp. 97–103.
3. Page references given in brackets in this article identify quotations from Fritz Wittels,
'Wrestling with the Man: The Story of a Freudian' (typescript of his unpublished
memoirs).
4. References to Kraus's journal *Die Fackel* are identified by F, followed by number
and page.
5. 'Tatjana Leontief'(*Minutes*, 10 April 1907)/ 'Weibliche Attentäter' (F 246–7: 26–38);
'Female Physicians' (*Minutes*, 15 May 1907)/ 'Weibliche Ärzte' (F 225: 10–24); 'The
Great Courtesan' (*Minutes*, 29 May 1907)/ 'Das Kindweib' (F 230–1: 14–33);
'Venereal Disease' (*Minutes*, 13 November 1907)/ 'Die Lustseuche' (F 238: 1–24);
'The Natural Position of Women' (*Minutes*, 11 March 1908)/ 'Die Feministen' (F
248: 9–14).
6. In Wittels's memoirs Irma Karczewska is referred to throughout by the name of
Mizerl (the name that he used for her fictional reincarnation in the first edition of
Ezechiel der Zugereiste).
7. 'Und wie ich Dich aus dem Bett des Kraus herauszerrte . . .' Fritz Wittels,
unpublished letter to Irma Karczewska, 27 July 1907 (Vienna City Library,
Manuscript No. I.N.102.561).
8. Plans for a trip to meet Kraus in Venice are mentioned by Wittels in a letter to Irma
dated 9 September 1907 (I.N.102.557).
9. *Die Hetaerengespräche des Lukian*, with fifteen drawings by Gustav Klimt (Leipzig,
1907).
10. Fritz Wittels, letter to Irma Karczewska, 21 July 1907 (I.N.102.561).
11. *Minutes*, I, p. 195, footnote.
12. Oral communication by Sophie Schick.
13. The first reference to 'die Kleine' in the extensive unpublished correspondence from
Hauer to Kraus occurs in a letter dated 29 June [1906] (I.N.140.905). She is also
repeatedly referred to in the correspondence from Mühsam to Kraus, starting with
a postcard dated 5 May 1906 (I.N.138.043).
14. Kete Parsenow, postcard to Kraus dated 3 July 1918 (I.N.139.618): 'Wie geht es der
Kleinen? Ist ihr Mann bei ihr? Sie tut mir wirklich leid. Siehst du sie noch viel? Und

wie geht es der Baronin?'

15. Paul Schick, *Karl Kraus in Selbstzeugnissen und Bilddokumenten* (Reinbek bei Hamburg, 1965), p. 53.
16. Karl Kraus, *Briefe an Sidonie Nadherny von Borutin*, 2 vols (Munich, 1974), I, pp. 325, 422, 444–7.
17. Karl Kraus, *Worte in Versen*, III (Leipzig, 1918), p. 23.
18. Gina Kaus, *Und was für ein Leben* (Hamburg, 1979), p. 122.
19. Kete Parsenow, postcard to Kraus postmarked 25 January 1924 (I.N.139.649): 'Wie geht es dir u. deiner Familie? Du weißt wen ich meine.'
20. Oral communication by Sophie Schick.
21. Oral communication by Sophie Schick.
22. For a summary of Wittels's career and a list of his principal writings, see Philip R. Lehrman, 'Fritz Wittels 1880–1950', *Psychoanalytic Quarterly*, 20 (1951), 96–104. For his subsequent view of female sexuality, see his *Sex Habits of American Women* (posthumously published, New York, 1952).
23. *Minutes*, II, pp. 382–93 ('The "Fackel"-Neurosis') and 473–6 ('the Kraus affair'). For a critical account of this meeting of the Psychoanalytic Society, see Thomas Szasz, *Karl Kraus and the Soul Doctors* (London, 1977), pp. 31–8.
24. *Minutes*, II, p. 89.
25. Fritz Wittels, *Ezechiel der Zugereiste* (Berlin, 1910), especially pp. 162–8 (on venereal infection) and 228–33 (on Mizerl's death).
26. Fritz Wittels, 'Mein satirischer Versuch', *Die Schaubühne*, 7 (1911), 331–3, 356.
27. See Rudolf von Urban, *Myself Not Least: A Confessional Autobiography of a Psychoanalyst and Some Explanatory Case Histories* (London, 1958), especially pp. 102–15.
28. Fritz Wittels, *Ezechiel der Zugereiste*, Fünfte Auflage (Vienna, 1911).
29. Fritz Wittels, *Sigmund Freud: His Personality, His Teaching, and His School*, tr. Eden and Cedar Paul (London, 1924), p. 212.
30. Ibid., pp. 11–13 and 216–33. The Jehovah passage (p. 28) is one of those marked with an irate exclamation mark in Freud's own copy, *Sigmund Freud: Der Mann, die Lehre, die Schule* (Leipzig, 1924), p. 21. The phrase 'Jehovah complex' does not occur in this context, but Wittels explains in his memoirs (p. 186) that this is what he meant.
31. Wittels, *Sigmund Freud*, p. 223; cf. F 376–7: 21.
32. Wittels's translation of this letter has been checked against the original in the Library of Congress and found to be accurate. The only significant deviation is that Wittels uses the words 'affectionate letters' for Freud's more emotionally charged phrase 'zärtlich werbende Briefe'.
33. Sigmund Freud, letter of 20 April 1928 to Fritz Wittels (Library of Congress).
34. See Susan Quinn, *A Mind of her Own: The Life of Karen Horney* (London, 1987), pp. 337–40.
35. Quoted from the (incomplete) translation by Wittels in his memoirs. The letter concludes with comments on Stekel. The original unfortunately could not be traced in the Library of Congress. Wittels's letters to Freud were reportedly destroyed in 1938, when the Freud family was forced to leave Vienna. See Anna Freud, letter of 15 December 1951 to Wittels's widow, Poldi Goetz Wittels (collection of Gerhard Fichtner, Tübingen).

Acknowledgements

I am grateful to the New York Psychoanalytic Institute for allowing me access to the Wittels papers; to John R. Wittels for permission to quote from his father's unpublished writings; to the Library of Congress (Washington), the Vienna City

Library, the Freud Museum (London), and Gerhard Fichtner (Tübingen) for allowing me to consult unpublished correspondence and other sources; and to Sigmund Freud Copyrights for permission to quote from Freud's letters.

I would particularly like to thank Sophie Schick (Vienna) for her comments on an earlier draft of this article, and for generously contributing to my understanding of Kraus's complex relationships.

The tendentious reception of *Professor Bernhardi*
Documentation in Schnitzler's collection of press cuttings
W. E. Yates

Throughout his career Arthur Schnitzler subscribed to press-cutting agencies which supplied him with reviews and other items relating to his work. Principal among these was the 'Observer' agency in Vienna, which was founded in 1896. There is no record in Schnitzler's diary of when he first commissioned the supply of press reports;[1] but the earliest cuttings in his collection which still bear the firm's heading date from May 1898. The very earliest items in the collection go back, in fact, to 1891, and include several of the first reviews of *Anatol* mentioned eagerly in Schnitzler's diary between 19 November and 19 December 1892.[2] The collection was assiduously maintained, and is mentioned in his testamentary disposition of his literary remains, dated 16 August 1918, as being available for scholarly study from five years after his death and as being, 'especially in that part which rejects my work, not without interest as a document of literary or rather cultural history' ('[...] besonders in ihrem negirenden Theile dürfte sie [die Sammlung] eines gewissen literar- od[er] vielmehr culturhistorischen Interesses nicht entbehren').[3] After his death it was continued until 1937 and also includes items on his son, Heinrich Schnitzler, from that period.

Schnitzler's autograph manuscripts and original typescripts are now mainly in Cambridge and Vienna. The collection of press cuttings, however, was given by his widow to H. B. Garland, who moved to Exeter in 1947 and remained there as Professor of German until his retirement in 1972. After Garland's death in 1981, the collection was given in December 1982 by his widow, Dr Mary Garland, to the University of Exeter Library. Originally housed in purpose-built wooden cabinets, it contains some 21 000 cuttings. These are still, for the most part, not catalogued in detail, but a project to organise the material and produce a computerised catalogue is under way, supported initially by the Research Fund of the University of Exeter and by the Österreichische Akademie der Wissenschaften. Many of the items are only brief reports or announcements, even incidental mentions; a large number are reviews; and some of the most interesting items relate to controversies such as Schnitzler's cashiering after the publication of *Leutnant Gustl* (there are 120 cuttings relating to this story from June–July 1901 alone) or, after his death, the banning of his books in Nazi Germany. The material is in bundles for each work, but otherwise was originally unsorted; and there are also quite a number of miscellaneous items. As well as the press-cuttings, there are photographs, theatre-bills and programmes, and copies of early critical essays; but the importance of the collection lies chiefly in the cuttings, many of them bearing the marks of Schnitzler's underlinings and also occasional annotation.

The works for which the largest body of material has accumulated are *Liebelei* and *Reigen*. The material on *Reigen* was used in 1929 by Otto P. Schinnerer when he was preparing his account of the stormy history of the play's reception;[4] that on *Liebelei*, which includes over fifty reviews of the first production in the Burgtheater in 1895, is swollen by items connected with later film and opera versions. The material on two plays from the middle years of Schnitzler's career, *Fink und Fliederbusch* and *Professor Bernhardi*, which were performed in Vienna for the first time in 1917 and 1918 respectively, also amounts to over 1 100 items in all.

There is generally less material on the prose works than on the plays (for which reviews accumulated as performances spread through Germany and the provinces): thus for the early *Sterben* there are only some forty reviews; and even on *Der Weg ins Freie*, which received a lot of attention (not least in the international Jewish press), the number of cuttings amounts only to about 200, among them a set of fifty-five reviews supplied by the publisher, S. Fischer. There are rather more on *Leutnant Gustl*, beginning with the first printing in the *Neue Freie Presse* (under the title 'Lieutenant Gustl') on 25 December 1900 and the subsequent protest, defending the honour of Austrian officers, in the *Reichspost* three days later, so that one can follow the whole course of the scandal and its reverberations, down to accounts in American papers reporting the fate that had befallen 'Arthur Switchlock', as the Boston *Globe* had it on 29 June, or 'Arthur Snitchlock', as he had become in *Harper's Weekly* (New York) on 13 July. That Schinnerer also made use of the material on *Leutnant Gustl* in his account of the scandal seems to be clear: two of the passages he quotes, excerpts from pieces in the virulently anti-Semitic *Österreichische Volkspresse* of 30 June 1901 and in the *Deutsche Zeitung* of 12 July, coincide with what Schnitzler himself had highlighted in red crayon.[5]

The collection not only brings together what must be the most comprehensive body of evidence on the reception of Schnitzler's work; it is unique in documenting what he himself incontrovertibly knew about that reception. In that respect it has a distinct biographical importance. That he kept it so carefully is consistent with his preservation of his diaries: the reviews and the diary entries both amount to a cumulative documentation of his life and achievements. The detailed evidence of the reviews he received complements the diaries, providing a basis for evaluating his reactions as recorded in the day-by-day entries.

Professor Bernhardi centres on the Jewish director of a Viennese clinic who prevents a Catholic priest from administering the last rites to a patient unaware that she is dying after an abortion. The matter becomes a *cause célèbre*, fought out in the clinic, in the press, and in parliament. Bernhardi is found guilty of insulting religion and is sentenced to prison. He refuses to appeal, and serves his sentence; but the play ends with his moral victory and reinstatement as physician. It is a work which lends itself in more than one way to illustrating the documentary value of the material in the Exeter archive. In the first place, the banning of all productions by the Habsburg censorship in 1912 provoked a press debate which is revealing of the whole cultural atmosphere at the time.[6] Secondly, it is a work on which critical opinion has still not settled, and many points made in the early reviews relate to issues still recurrently raised in critical debate.[7] Because of the quantity of material – Schnitzler's collection contains some 850 cuttings on *Professor Bernhardi* alone – the following account can offer no more than a selective survey; but supporting excerpts from a selection of reviews are given in an Appendix, to which reference is made in the body of the article. The excerpts are set out there in the chronological order of their original appearance, so that they may be read as a sampling of the vagaries of the work's reception.

The history of the play's genesis has been analysed by Sol Liptzin,[8] and the later stages can also be followed in Schnitzler's diaries from October 1909 onwards. He was very concerned to dispel inaccurate accounts of the background. An article by Georg Brandes in *Der Merker* in February 1913 relating Bernhardi's position to that of Schnitzler's father in the Poliklinik was countered both by an open letter by Schnitzler in *Der Merker* – a cutting is preserved in the Exeter archive – and by a private letter to Brandes, written on 27 February.[9] On 5 January 1919 the *Volkszeitung* published an article by Julius Stern which reported that the play had been written out of gratitude to the Deutsches Volkstheater. Stern claimed that Schnitzler had originally been morally committed to offer his works first to the Burgtheater, and that he had chosen the theme of *Professor Bernhardi* (unsuitable for the court theatre) after a discussion with Heinrich Glücksmann, the *Dramaturg* of the Deutsches Volkstheater. Schnitzler's copy of this piece is marked with red crayon underlinings, indicating his dissent; and when the Deutsches Volkstheater mounted a new production towards the end of his life, and the programme included a piece by Glücksmann entitled 'Wie "Professor Bernhardi" entstand', rehearsing much the same material (except that the commitment to the Burgtheater was now described as a contractual one), his exasperation at this further inaccuracy is again shown in the copy in the Exeter archive, the offending passage having been underlined and a curt 'falsch' written in the margin.

The play first hit the headlines when the intended production at the Deutsches Volkstheater was banned in October 1912. The history of the ban as reflected in the press from 1912 onwards does much to explain the bitterness that Schnitzler felt about the critical reception of his plays – a bitterness that led him, for example, to record in his diary on 19 November 1917 (after the première of *Fink und Fliederbusch*) his feeling that no other writer had ever been so much abused in the course of his career ('daß wohl noch niemals ein Autor im Laufe seines Schaffens so viel beschimpft wurde als ich').

The main official reason for prohibiting performance of the play in Austria (a reason made explicit only in an unpublished memorandum to the police authorities in Berlin) was not the fact that it treated the religious question, but rather its allegedly 'distorted' depiction of Austrian public life.[10] An aggressively phrased written parliamentary question (*Interpellation*) addressed to the Minister of Internal Affairs suggested that, in effect, Schnitzler was being regarded as guilty of polemicising against an importunate proselytism increasingly prevalent in hospitals. The text of the question was reported in full in the Social Democratic *Arbeiter-Zeitung* on 30 October 1912 (Document 1). Polemically defended by anti-clericals, the play was all too easily assumed to be polemically anti-clerical itself. In *Der Morgen* for 23 December 1912, Friedrich Hertz defended Schnitzler against precisely such an interpretation, which he alleged was that adopted by the censors (as, indeed, was the case),[11] and praised the play explicitly for its lack of tendentiousness (Document 6).

The public controversy was kept going partly by argument along predictable ideological lines, and partly by attempts to circumvent the ban. The Christian Social *Reichspost* (pro-clerical and anti-Semitic)[12] published an account which wholly supported the censor and dismissed the work as a malicious, inartistic, and defamatory polemic (Document 5). The *Arbeiter-Zeitung* took the opposite view that it showed up the deficiencies of the system of censorship (Document 1). And in the most prestigious organ of bourgeois liberalism, the *Neue Freie Presse*, an anonymous academic lawyer accused the censor of trying to be 'more clerical than the church' and declared the play clear of any offence: it was indeed a model example of moral drama holding a mirror to the world (Document 9). The prominent bookseller Hugo Heller organised a reading; and plans were forged – the idea is, indeed, mentioned at the end of Hertz's article – to mount a production in Pressburg (Bratislava), just across the Hungarian border. At the end of April 1913 this production also was banned by the local authorities (the *Theaterausschuß*). *Der Morgen* ironically recorded the unique concord between the two halves of the Dual Monarchy ('Österreich und Ungarn so einig wie noch nie!!', 5 May 1913). The previous day's issue of the satirical Kikeriki (another anti-Semitic publication) had reproduced an advertisement for 'a still more spicy Pressburg drama' ('ein noch pikanteres Preßburger Schauspiel') – daily performances of *Reigen*. In its next-but-one issue, on 11 May, *Kikeriki* carried a cartoon showing a grotesquely long-nosed Schnitzler departing from Pressburg to the strains of the folksong 'Muß i denn, muß i denn zum Städtele 'naus' (see Fig. 15).

The affair also attracted extensive comment in other papers. In the *Neues Wiener Tagblatt* of 30 April, Robert Hirschfeld began by pointing ironically to the double-edged effect of censorship, whose bans ensured the fame of the plays proscribed and guaranteed their commercial success (Document 10). But the main body of his article gives a very critical account of the play, beginning with the statement that over and above any moral consideration it offended against aesthetic taste, which formed an 'inner censorship' far more powerful than any

Figure 15. Caricature of Arthur Schnitzler after the banning of *Professor Bernhardi*

formally imposed censorship. This article was extensively quoted the next day in the *Preßburger Tagblatt* under the triumphant headline 'Ein Jude über "Professor Bernhardi"'.

It had been taken for granted from the first that Schnitzler's treatment of the so-called 'Jewish question' must have been one factor behind the original ban in Vienna (e.g. Document 7). Now Berta Zuckerkandl, writing in the *Wiener Allgemeine Zeitung* and also quoting Hirschfeld, could argue that what the Pressburg affair showed was that far from being merely reminiscent of the anti-Semitism of the past (the play is set in 'Vienna around 1900'), it was all too up to date and actually dealt with the present ('Die Zeit des "Bernhardi" ist 1913'). Worse was to come over the years; a sample of the anti-Semitic abuse that would later be heaped on the play may be seen in a supposedly patriotic piece which appeared during the war in the *Österreichische Volkspresse*, decrying it as a betrayal of Austria, bearing no relation to historical reality, and a creation of Schnitzler's Jewish 'fantasy' (Document 11).

The ideological distortions of the debate in Austria become even clearer by contrast with the critical reception in Berlin, where the play received its first performance on 28 November 1912. Schnitzler noted in his diary on 29 November that the press reviews were mostly favourable, with the possible exception of the *Berliner Tageblatt* ('Die Kritik im ganzen gut; Berl Tgbl. (Engel) am schwächsten'). The first night was indeed well received, on the whole; yet even in these generally appreciative early reviews, certain doubts can be read between the lines as to whether the play had realised the true dramatic potential of the material. That the central figure lacks the courage to fight his corner is at least briefly suggested, for example, in a review in the *Berliner Local-Anzeiger*; and this same point is put more sharply in the review in the *Berliner Tageblatt* by Fritz Engel. The work may look like a tendentiously polemical play of ideas ('ein Tendenzdrama'), Engel argues, but Schnitzler has neither the strength to take up a strong position nor the stomach to show intolerance to the intolerant (Document 2). This critique must have been all the more disappointing because Engel had written appreciatively of Schnitzler in the past, and less than six months earlier had published a very warm tribute on the occasion of Schnitzler's fiftieth birthday (*Berliner Tageblatt*, 15 May 1912).

When the play eventually appeared in print, the *Neue Freie Presse*, which was generally sympathetic to Schnitzler's work, carried, on 4 January 1913, a long review by Paul Goldmann, an old but increasingly critical friend. Goldmann praises the dialogue and realistic characterisation (especially of some of the secondary figures). But the central character is seen as less convincing in his confidence in his own infallibility and as being too unworldly ('weltfremd'); and Goldmann concludes that Schnitzler has only skimmed the surface of the problem inherent in his material (Document 8). Three months later *Die Wage* published an article by A. Halbert which again accuses the dramatist of dodging the issue of general principle, so that, instead of his achieving a tragedy or a comedy, what he has composed amounts to no more than a play based on a theatrical role ('Rollenstück').[13]

Meanwhile an issue of Karl Kraus's journal *Die Fackel* appeared on 5

February including an essay entitled 'Fern sei es von mir, den "Professor Bernhardi" zu lesen' ('Far be it from me to read *Professor Bernhardi*').[14] And the next-but-one issue, dated 1 April, again made the point that the play falls short of being specific in its polemical or satiric thrust.[15] A regular reader of *Die Fackel*, Schnitzler recorded both of these attacks in his diary, dismissing the second as 'rather lame' ('etwas lahme Angriffe', 1 April 1913). His copies of both are also in the Exeter archive. In view of his dislike and mistrust of Kraus,[16] the hardest blow of all may have come ten years later, when Siegfried Jacobsohn's journal, *Die Weltbühne*, carried an article, prompted by a production in the Residenz-Theater in Berlin, similarly arguing that the weakness of the play was manifested in the weakness of its hero, a 'hero' only in the sense of being the title role (Document 18): the real sting came in the tail, in the charge that the lack of bite, weakening the play by substituting witty irony for satirical fire, was typical of Austria and that the one exception was none other than Kraus.

Schnitzler himself conceived the play as a 'comedy of character' ('eine Charakterkomödie') – he used the term both in his letter of 4 January 1913 to Charmatz and again on 22 February 1919 when writing to Ludwig Hirschfeld. This comic element met with a mixed response. In 1912, on the day after the première, Emil Faktor, writing in the *Berliner Börsen-Courier*, praised the skill with which Schnitzler had wrought a comic effect out of the complex political and confessional cross-currents he was treating (Document 3); and among later critics who would also admire the shaping of the material towards the lightness of the final act was Alfred Kerr, reviewing the 1923 Berlin production (Document 17).[17] From the first, however, other reviewers were unsettled by the difficulty of assigning the play to a clearly defined genre, and this uncertainty is also reflected in repeated airings of the question of its antecedents. The connection with Lessing's *Nathan der Weise* was raised, albeit rather dismissively, as early as 1912 by Engel in his review of the Berlin première (Document 2), and again, for example, by the academic lawyer writing the following January in the *Neue Freie Presse*. Another comparison which seemed apposite was that with Ibsen's *An Enemy of the People*: Berta Zuckerkandl was one who compared the two plays in 1912 (Document 4). Later, Marco Brociner was to pursue the same comparison, to Schnitzler's disadvantage, in the *Neues Wiener Tagblatt* (22 December 1918), as did Auernheimer (Document 15) and Alfred Kerr (Document 17). The fundamental problem was that far from accepting the play as a 'comedy', most critics assessed it in ideological terms. Looking through the reviews of the première, Schnitzler noted in his diary on 5 December 1912 that some complained because *Professor Bernhardi* was politically 'tendentious', others because it was not ('Die einen halten sich darüber auf – daß ich ein Tendenzstück geschrieben, die andern – daß ich keins geschrieben habe').

This debate was renewed when the play was finally performed in Vienna in 1918.[18] That it had taken a world war and the collapse of an empire to make the performance possible was not lost on those of an ironic turn of mind. Schnitzler made the point in his diary as soon as the censorship was lifted (31 October 1918); and so did Auernheimer in a long article in the *Neue Freie Presse* in 1918 (Document 15). Schnitzler's first reaction in his diary (22 December 1918) was that the press reception was 'very good' ('Presse sehr gut'). Two days later he noted that even the review in the *Reichspost* seemed 'more decent than usual' ('anständiger als sonst'); but all things are relative, and though the piece in the *Reichspost* that day, signed 'N.', praised the lively dialogue, it also reported that the play was written for Jews and was repulsive to anti-Semites ('Antisemiten finden sich durchaus abgestoßen, das Stück ist für Juden geschrieben'). It is a strident formulation, with its brash antithesis between 'anti-Semites' and 'Jews'. In its review of December 1912 (Document 5) the *Reichspost* had phrased the antagonism less openly ('das christliche Volk' / 'gewisse Leute'). But anti-Semitism had been a powerful undercurrent in Austria since the late nineteenth century (the very term 'Anti-Semite' had indeed long carried no pejorative overtones in the right-wing press); and it was now gathering still more force in the aftermath of defeat, amid the political and social upheaval of the end of the monarchy.

Even in the liberal press this first Viennese production of *Professor Bernhardi* was given a mixed reception. Oskar Maurus Fontana, writing in *Die Wage* on 10 January 1919, declared the play interesting only as an example of old-fashioned liberalism ('als Schauspiel ziemlich uninteressant and nur interessant als Type der liberalen Dramatik'). Some of the most prominent critics, including both Marco Brociner in the *Neues Wiener Tagblatt* (Document 13) and particularly Alfred Polgar in the *Wiener Allgemeine Zeitung* (Document 14), also struck a negative note, as they had done about *Fink und Fliederbusch* a year earlier.[14] What stung most sharply in Polgar's review was his remark that the play bore no relation to art ('Mit Kunst hat das Schnitzlersche Stück nichts zu tun'), which Schnitzler underlined in crayon in his cutting and also quoted in his diary on 24 December 1918, calling the review 'uncontrollably envy-ridden' ('unbeherrscht neiderfüllt'). In describing the play as essentially a 'debate', Polgar's notice connects with the long-running discussions of its genre and intention. Felix Salten, writing in the *Fremdenblatt* a day earlier, had referred to it as a 'Tendenzstück', identifying the very action as inherently 'tendentious' ('tendenziös'). Salten added that in the humanity with which it treated all the double dealing, it rose imaginatively above mere polemics (Document 12); but what Schnitzler noted in his diary for that day was that despite the praise Salten was still insisting that it was a *Tendenzstück* ('Salten [in hohem Lob] besteht auf dem "Tendenzstück"'). The following day, readers of *Der Morgen* were similarly informed in a review signed 'hl' that the play was neither a comedy nor a satire but precisely a *Tendenzstück*. Auernheimer, in the *Neue Freie Presse*, produced a different definition: the play did not generalise in the way inherent in the *Tendenzstück*, it was, on the contrary, a problem play, innovative in treating a problem new to the theatre, and developing it wittily and with sustained dramatic mastery (Document 15). A few days later, however, in the *Wiener Mittag* for 27 December, Max Mell again discussed it as essentially tendentious, classifying it under the heading of polemical social plays ('Zeit- und Thesenstücke').[20] In his diary that day, Schnitzler dismissed Mell's review as 'respectfully impudent' ('hochachtungsvoll frech'), blaming the tone on the influence of Hofmannsthal.

The reputation of *Professor Bernhardi* as a *Tendenzstück* was now firmly established. The term was widely used in the wake of the first Viennese production – recurring, for example, quite factually in a piece in the *Wiener Medizinische Wochenschrift* of which the author, Curt Kronfeld, sent Schnitzler a signed offprint.[21] Auernheimer argued in the *Neue Freie Presse* that it was a misapprehension not based on the play itself but created by the ban that had been imposed on it in Austria. He made the point first in a brief review which appeared on 22 December 1918, signed 'A'. ('Dieses Verbot machte aus dem Drama ein Tendenzstück, indem es ihm eine Absicht unterschob, die es gar nicht hatte'); and he expanded on it two days later (Document 15). The term occurs again dismissively in reviews in anti-liberal and anti-Semitic provincial newspapers, such as the *Volksfreund* in 1919 (Document 16). How much the play's supposed polemical tendentiousness was taken for granted down the years, seeming hardly to need further argument, can be seen, for example, from a review in the *Neues Wiener Tagblatt* in 1924 (Document 19). Schnitzler himself insisted, most notably in a letter of 4 January 1913 to the historian Richard Charmatz, that what he had written was not a *Tendenzstück*. But to the end of his life he continued to receive reviews – such as one in the *Wiener Allgemeine Zeitung* in 1928 (Document 20) – which, even while defending *Professor Bernhardi* against the charge of tendentiousness, still stressed that it was a play with a clear 'message'; or which echoed Polgar's assessment by designating it a play of debate ('ein Debattierstück'), as in Emil Faktor's review in the *Berliner Börsen-Courier* (Abend-Ausgabe) on 24 January 1930.

That the play also presented a (more or less realistic) miniature of Austrian society was widely observed by early commentators.[22] But was it a satire? Arthur Eloesser, in an article entitled 'Schnitzler und Sohn' which appeared in *Das Literarische Echo* on 1 January 1913, affirmed that it was, and indeed satire of a kind that was perhaps new in the German theatre ('eine Satire, wie sie Deutschland vielleicht noch nicht hatte'); three days later Paul Goldmann stressed the satirical force of the characterisation of Flint in his review in the *Neue Freie Presse* (Document 8). After the Viennese première in 1918, on the other hand, the reviewer in *Der Morgen* for 23 December ('hl'), insisting that the play was a *Tendenzstück*, stressed that it was not merely a Viennese comedy and not a satire ('Schnitzlers "Professor Bernhardi" ist natürlich ein Tendenzstück, nicht eine bloße Wienerische Komödie and nicht eine Satire'). The crayon underscorings in Schnitzler's cutting testify to his disagreement.

The element of 'debate' in the lay naturally focused attention on the role of the priest, whom those sympathetic to Schnitzler, such as Hertz and Goldmann, judged to be drawn as fairly as Bernhardi himself (Documents 6 and 8). The dialogue between physician and priest in Act Four received particular attention. This scene, drafted in September 1911 and completed in the spring of 1912, had been the most difficult in the play to compose, and Schnitzler even doubted at one stage whether the dramatic economy of the play required it at all (it was 'vielleicht in der Ökonomie des ganzen nicht einmal notwendig' – diary, 23 September 1911). *Die Wage* printed an article at the beginning of January 1913 suggesting that it was, on the contrary, the climax of the play, and that Schnitzler should, indeed, perhaps have ended it there, since the final act failed to maintain the same level of interest (Document 7). Polgar, on the other hand, while also perceiving that it was a key scene, judged that it failed to make the intended effect (Document 14). Further reviewers continued to reach divergent conclusions. In the 1924 production in the Deutsches Volkstheater, for example, it was found to be deficient in theatrical effect (Document 19).

One of the most admiring assessments of this scene was one that Schnitzler was not to live to see: Desmond MacCarthy, reviewing the 1936 London production in the *New Statesman*, found it 'the deepest scene in the play.'[23] MacCarthy's very favourable assessment of the play was unashamedly conditioned by the political climate of the mid-1930s: 'We are living in times in which integrity is at a discount, and ends are held to justify the most despicable and vile of means.' His view of *Professor Bernhardi* as 'a significant play, one of peculiar importance to-day' depends on his reading of Bernhardi himself as 'a man who puts his integrity before consequences, either to himself or to an institution to which he is devoted' and whose attitude is contrasted throughout 'with those of other characters who consider ends (whether selfish or unselfish) before means'.

Bernhardi's complex character – the very complexity praised from the first by Berta Zuckerkandl (Document 4) – was, as it has remained,[24] the chief bone of interpretative contention. Is he weak or a man of principle? There were even those, such as Goldmann and Robert Hirschfeld, who found him too overbearing (Documents 8 and 10). The question was all the more delicate because critics tended to equate Bernhardi with Schnitzler. It was an identification rejected by Engel (Document 2); but that was a review which Schnitzler disliked. In 1922, in a short study of Schnitzler's dramatic work, Theodor Kappstein associated the objectivity and irony of Bernhardi closely with the dramatist ('das ist von Schnitzlers eigenstem Geiste Spiegelung'). When Schnitzler wrote to Kappstein on 24 July, he picked out the chapter on *Professor Bernhardi*[25] as one of those that were particularly good; so it is reasonable to infer that he did not wholly reject the identification. Certainly, he considered Bernhardi wholly in the right in respect of his medical responsibilities: Emil Reich's doubts on this score were dismissed in the diary on 27 December 1918, and the letter of 10 April 1924 to Edith Werner reinforces the point.

The most dispiriting critiques of all were almost certainly those that did not take Bernhardi seriously, and in particular that by Marco Brociner (Document 13), who made amusing play with the idea that Bernhardi was no more than Anatol in another guise. (This is another passage angrily marked in crayon on the cutting in Schnitzler's collection, and quoted in his diary for 22 December 1918.) The success of Schnitzler's early plays about philandering men-about-town determined critical expectations. In 1913 he found it necessary to insist to Robert Roseeu that although *Professor Bernhardi* was different from *Anatol*, it was just as authentically 'Schnitzlerisch' (letter of 17 December 1913). Not even *Der Weg ins Freie* escaped reduction to the same cliché: Stefan Grossmann, writing in the *Arbeiter-Zeitung* on 16 July 1908, remarked that it might just as well be called *Liebelei* since it was only a more pretentious variation on Schnitzler's usual theme ('Mit mehr Recht könnte auch dieser Roman "Liebelei" heißen, denn er ist nur eine neue, anspruchsvollere Variation des alten Schnitzlerschen Themas'). In 1920 Schnitzler was still complaining that critics behaved as though he had never written anything except *Reigen* and *Anatol* ('[daß] die Recensenten sich anstellen, als existire außer Reigen and Anatol überhaupt kein Buch von mir' – letter to Dora Michaelis, 22 November 1920). What he was constantly expected to treat was erotic themes; and this is exactly what Marco Brociner, among others, wrote after the première of *Fink und Fliederbusch* in the Deutsches Volkstheater on 14 November 1917: it lacked that 'breath of eroticism' ('Kein Hauch jener Erotik [...]') with which Schnitzler created his most authentic effects.[26] And as 'a play without women' the work to which *Fink und Fliederbusch* was likened – by, for example, Salten, writing in the *Berliner Tageblatt* (Abend-Ausgabe, 15 November 1917) – was none other than *Professor Bernhardi* ([. . .] 'ein Männerstück wie sein "Professor Bernhardi"'). It is precisely the stereotyped expectation of 'eroticism', together with the repeated charge of polemicising, that Schnitzler picked out in his satirical summary of the critics' view of the play in the poem 'Meine Kritiker':

Bernhardi, pfui Teufel, ein Thesenstück
Und ohne Weiber! er geht zurück.[27]

[*Bernhardi* – ugh, a problem play!
No women, either – he's had his day.]

When considering the reception of the Berlin première of *Professor Bernhardi*, Schnitzler confided to his diary on 5 December 1912, aphoristically phrased, his resignation at the fact that critics inherently tend to misunderstand living writers ('Die Tendenz der Kritik heißt mißverstehen – wenigstens dem Lebenden gegenüber'). Yet the early reviewers included some distinguished and perceptive critics, and the issues they raised include several that have remained central to scholarly discussion of the play: Schnitzler's representation of anti-Semitism; the links with *Nathan der Weise* and *An Enemy of the People*; the role and character of the priest.[28] In this article I have tried to draw on characteristic examples from the great wealth of contemporary reviews available in the Exeter archive. It is an exercise which could be repeated for all his other works published during his lifetime, for the collection of press-cuttings provides an incomparable documentary source. Indeed, there is not even any serviceable bibliographical record of the reception of Schnitzler's works: of the reviews excerpted in the Appendix to this article, only two are listed in Richard H. Allen's bibliography of Schnitzler criticism.[29] On the first Viennese production in 1918 alone the collection has some fifty cuttings; the history of Schnitzler production in Vienna by Renate Wagner and Brigitte Vacha refers to only four reviews.[30]

In reading through the reviews of Schnitzler's earliest works from 1891 onwards one relives something of the excitement that he himself must have felt on receiving them. As the years went by and he repeatedly found himself typecast as the author of *Anatol* and the object of ever more strident anti-Semitic hostility, the reviews also help us to understand the souring disillusion of his later life. Schnitzler liked praise: the one review of the 1918 Viennese production of *Professor Bernhardi* that he singled out in his diary on 24 December 1918 as 'excellent' ('vortrefflich') was Auernheimer's long and very positive *feuilleton* (Document 15); Kappstein's chapter on *Professor Bernhardi*, which he also mentioned with approval, gives an uncritically effusive assessment of his characterisation. What he sought in the notices he received was continual confirmation of his artistic achievement; his careful preservation of them is part of his defence against his life-long uncertainty about his very identity as an artist, that same uncertainty which his diary both testifies and combats.[31] Hence his sensitivity to reviews which misrepresented his achievement. And no other work can have carried this biographical significance to a greater degree than *Professor Bernhardi*, for which he had a special affection: 'There are works of mine I like better,' he wrote in his diary on 27 March 1918, 'but nowhere do I like myself better than in *Bernhardi*' ('Es gibt Sachen von mir die ich lieber habe, – aber mich hab ich nirgends lieber als im Bernhardi').

Appendix: Documentation

1. Wegen des von uns schon besprochenen Verbotes der Schnitzlerschen Komödie 'Professor Bernhardi' haben die Abgeordneten Winter, Hanusch und Genossen gestern folgende Interpellation an den Minister des Innern eingebracht:
    ['. . .] Wie man hört, ist das Verbot deshalb erfolgt, weil Schnitzlers Drama an einen infolge der Verpfaffung der Krankenzimmer allmählich weiter verbreiteten Vorgang anknüpft, nämlich an jene widerwärtigen Behelligungen, denen ahnungslose Kranke so oft durch zudringliche Proselytenmacher ausgesetzt werden. Doch ist bei der künstlerischen Art dieses Dichters jede vulgäre Tendenzmache ausgeschlossen. [. . .']
    Dieser letzte beschämende Fall eines albernen Zensurverbotes wird nun jedem klar machen, daß selbst in dem rückständigen Oesterreich ein gesetzliches, mit Rechtgarantien umgebenes Zensurverfahren notwendig ist.
    ['Die Rechtlosigkeit der dramatischen Kunst in Oesterreich', *Arbeiter-Zeitung*, 30 October 1912]
2. Arthur Schnitzler hat den Stoff, den er seinem neuesten Bühnenwerk gegeben, nicht bewältigt. Er mag ihn ursprünglich stark empfunden haben, hat ihn dann aber abgeschwächt, aus Gründen des 'künstlerischen Intellekts', mehr noch aus Gründen seiner Weltanschauung, die sehr zart sein will, allzu zart, um den Mut einer Stellungnahme zu finden. Er gibt den Rahmen eines Tendenzdramas und beschwört uns zugleich, nur ja nicht an eine Tendenz zu glauben. [. . .] Er predigt, im Wien vom Jahre 1900, die alte Nathanweisheit von der Gleichberechtigung aller Menschen, hat aber nicht die Lust, gegen die Intoleranten etwas intolerant zu werden. [. . .]
    Dieser Bernhardi ist nicht Schnitzler selbst; er ist nur das Ideal, das der Dichter sein möchte.
    [Fritz Engel, 'Der unpolitische Politiker', *Berliner Tageblatt*, 29 November 1912]
3. Er schildert ein Stück Oesterreich, die Donauresidenz der Konfessionen und Parteien, der kleinen und großen politischen Händel. Und das gelang ihm so gut, daß sich der Grundton seiner aufregenden Komödie wandelte, daß seriöse Konflikte ihren Ausklang in sehr heiteren, sehr boshaften Situationen finden. Daß aus einer Erregung ein Gelächter entsteht über Verhältnisse und Menschlichkeiten.

[Emil Faktor, *Berliner Börsen-Courier*, Morgenausgabe, 29 November 1912]
4. Auch Ibsens 'Volksfeind' ist eine Abrechnung gewesen. [...] Mit ähnlicher Erbitterung nun schildert Schnitzler die Entwicklung eines Schicksals, das durch die Strömungen des hereinbrechenden antisemitisch-deutschnationalen und klerikalen Regims aus seiner geruhigen, harmonischen und geradgeleisigen Bahn gerissen wird. [...]
   Und die Figur Bernardis gehört ganz dem Geschlecht jener halben Helden an, in deren Seele Leidenschaft und Skepsis miteinander ringen. So liebevoll auch Schnitzler dieser tragenden Gestalt seiner Komödie gegenübersteht, er vermag es dennoch, mit der nachspürenden, gedankenvollen Kritik, welche ja die eigenste Methode seines Schaffens ist, die Problematik einer zwiespältigen Natur stark zu beleuchten.
   [B.Z. (= Berta Zuckerkandl), 'Professor Bernardi', *Wiener Allgemeine Zeitung*, 2 December 1912]
5. [...] Mit dem ersten Akte endet das Drama. Was nun kommt, ist ein so tendenziösgehässiger Feldzug, daß es schwer ist, kühl und rein sachlich darüber zu schreiben. [...]
   Die Zensur, die dieses Stück verbot, tat wahrlich wohl daran. Sie hielt ein Werk vom Theater fern, das nichts mit Kunst zu tun hat und nicht ins Theater gehört, sondern allenfalls zu Wahlzeiten in einen Versammlungssaal, vorausgesetzt, daß die Versammelten danach sind, es sich bieten zu lassen. Gewisse Leute mögen ja in dem Verbote der Zensur eine zu scharfe Maßregel erblicken. Das christliche Volk aber – dies hat die Behörde richtig erkannt – würde dieses Stück nicht ruhig hingenommen haben. Jedermann hätte es als das erkannt, was es ist: eine gehässige, verleumderische Abrechnung mit einem Gegner.
   Von derartigen Auswüchsen muß die Bühne rein gehalten werden.
   [H.B., *Reichspost*, 3 December 1912]
6. Schnitzler schließt mit aller Bestimmtheit die naheliegende Deutung aus, von der sich wohl auch die Zensurbehörde leiten ließ, daß sein Werk ein antiklerikales Tendenzstück sei. Der Gegensatz zwischen freier Menschlichkeit und Kirchenglaube verkörpert sich in den gleicherweise sympathischen Gestalten Bernhardis und des Pfarrers. [...]
   Schnitzler hat ein Bild Österreichs geschaffen, das in seiner schlichten Prägnanz und Tendenzlosigkeit erschüttert.
   [Friedrich Hertz, 'Der Fall Bernhardi. Politische Glossen zu Schnitzlers Stück', *Der Morgen*, 23 December 1912]
7. Man ahnt sofort, daß die Darstellung des Konfliktes zwischen Arzt und Priester, Wissenschaft und Kirche, eines Konfliktes, der noch dadurch verschärft wird, daß der Vertreter der ärztlichen Wissenschaft Jude ist, irgendwie das Zensurverbot herbeigeführt haben müsse. [...]
   In einer wunderschönen und tiefergreifenden Szene, die man wohl als den Angelpunkt des ganzen Stückes bezeichnen kann, stellt der Dichter den Verurteilten dem Urheber seines Unglücks, dem Pfarrer, wieder gegenüber. [...]
   Mit dieser Szene ist der Höhepunkt des Dramas erreicht, und der Dichter hätte vielleicht gut getan, mit ihr auch das Werk zu beschließen. Denn was nun folgt, zumal im fünften Akt, bietet wohl eine reiche Fülle geistvoller und funkelnd zugeschliffener Aperçus, vermag aber doch unser in den vorangegangenen Szenen so stark erregtes Interesse nicht mehr voll zu befriedigen.
   [–β–, 'Arzt und Priester', *Die Wage* 16, no. 1 (January 1913), pp. 24-8 (pp. 24 and 26)]
8. Mit schöner Unparteilichkeit hingegen hat der Dichter sich bemüht, dem Pfarrer gerecht zu werden [...] Die Szene, in der nach dem Prozesse der Pfarrer zu Professor Bernhardi kommt, um [...] sein Gewissen zu entlasten, ist sicherlich eine der schönsten des Stückes. [...]

Von allen den vielen Figuren des Dramas ist aber keine so prächtig geraten, keine so unfehlbar bühnenwirksam als die des Unterrichtsministers Dr. Flint. Hier ist, in packender Lebenswahrheit ausgeführt, von einer feinen und doch überaus treffenden Satire beleuchtet, das typische Bild des politischen Strebers geschaffen – typisch nicht für Oesterreich allein, so spezifisch österreichisch Exzellenz Flint auch sein mag. Es ist ein Meisterwerk satirischer Charakterzeichnung. [...]

Der Dichter hat es nur mit seinem Helden zu gut gemeint und hat aus ihm nicht allein einen Ehrenmann gemacht, sondern ganz einfach die Mensch gewordene Vollkommenheit. [...] Die Art, wie er in seinem Unfehlbarkeitsdünkel mit dem übrigen Menschenpack verkehrt, fällt unangenehm auf; und der Ton überlegener Ironie, den er jedem gegenüber anschlägt, geht auf die Nerven. [...]

Es ist also bedauerlich, daß Professor Bernhardi so gar nicht kämpfen will; und es ist bedauerlich, daß der Dichter das große Problem, das sein Stoff ihm darbot, eigentlich nur gestreift [...]

[Paul Goldmann, 'Berliner Theater', *Neue Freie Presse*, 4 January 1913]

9. Liest man das Stück genau, so muß man sagen, es gibt in neuester Zeit wenig Dramen mit so wenig anstößigen Stellen wie der Bernhardi, und Artur Schnitzler, dessen erotische Probleme bei aller Feinheit der Psychologie nicht immer Wohlgefallen ausgelöst haben, hat sich auf der Höhe ernster Behandlung gezeigt. [...]

Also weshalb diesmal eine so große Empfindlichkeit der Zensur, die kirchlicher sein will als die Kirche? [...]

Wenn das Drama eine moralische Anstalt sein soll und der Dichter der Welt einen Spiegel vorhalten soll, dann ist ein Drama wie dieses ein Musterstück [...].

['Das Zensurverbot gegen Schnitzlers "Professor Bernhardi". Von einem hervorragenden Rechtslehrer', *Neue Freie Presse*, 19 January 1913]

10. Die wundertätige Zensur schafft gerade den Stücken, die sie mit dem Bann belegt, eine mühelose Verbreitung. Sie beflügelt den Ruhm, den sie lähmen soll. Was sie zum Schaden berührt, verwandelt sich in Gold. Unter ihren Fäusten blühen Erfolge auf. [...]

Es gibt auch eine innere Zensur, die dem Gemüte die Teilnahme an einem Werke verbietet. Diese innere Zensur ist stärker als die gewaltsame äußere, weil sie aus dem ästhetischen Urteil fließt, das keinen Einspruch gestattet. [...] Von sittlichen Werten zunächst ganz abgesehen, gilt mir in der inneren Anschauung die Komödie 'Professor Bernhardi' als Verstoß gegen den künstlerischen Geschmack. [...]

Unter allen Starrköpfen und Rechthabern der Literatur verdient dieser Professor Bernhardi die geringste Sympathie. Sein anmaßender, immer überlegener Ton wird unerträglich wie sein Eigendünkel, seine Eigenliebe [...]

[Robert Hirschfeld, 'Innere Zensur', *Neues Wiener Tagblatt*, 30 April 1913]

11. Das *erbärmlichste, allergemeinste, das Österreichertum am tiefsten verletzende Theaterstück 'Professor Bernhardi'* wurde zwar nicht in Wien, aber zum Gaudium der Berliner Freiheitlichen aufgeführt. [...] Nun weiß aber die ganze Welt, daß der Aufbau des Stückes 'Professor Bernhardi' auf *gar keiner Basis* beruhen kann, weil sich derlei durch den Freimaurerautor niedergelegte Anschauungen in Oesterreich nie ereignet haben und nie ereignen konnten, sondern bloß der *Phantasie* des ∴ Bruders Arthur Schnitzler entsprungen sind. Jetzt ist die Sache natürlich anders. Oesterreich kämpft Schulter an Schulter heldenmütig mit seinem wackeren deutschen Bruder und dadurch wird auch die Jauche, die von dem Freimaurerdichter dem deutschen Volke eingeimpft wird, wirkungslos [...]

[*Österreichische Volkspresse*, 8 January 1915]

12. Die Handlung ist tendenziös. [...] Die Geschichte dieses Professors, der dann, nicht aus Frömmigkeit, sondern aus Haß, Neid und politischer Streberei verfolgt wird, ist sicherlich tendenziös. Und sie ist auch in mancher Beziehung anfechtbar. Aber die Abrechnung, die da mit der Lüge, dem Neid, der Inferiorität gehalten wird, ist

einfach meisterhaft, und das Stück hebt sich von Akt zu Akt hoch über alle Tendenz hinaus in eine dichterisch reine Menschlichkeit.

[f. s. (=Felix Salten), *Fremdenblatt*, 22 December 1918]

13. Das Werk ist im letzten Grunde das Erzeugnis einer scharfen Intellektualität, einer sehr feinen, aber an der Oberfläche hingleitenden ironischen Welt- und Menschenbetrachtung, ohne mitreißende innerliche Ergriffenheit und darum auch ohne dramatisches Rückgrat und ohne dramatischen Schwung. [...]

Will man übrigens Professor Bernhardi aus seinem Wesenskern heraus verstehen, so muß man an seine Vorgeschichte denken, die allerdings in der Komödie verschwiegen wird. Er hieß in seiner Jugend Anatol, der, nachdem er sich satt geliebt, mit heißem Bemühen medizinische Studien getrieben. Nun ist er – er hat es weit gebracht – eine Zierde der medizinischen Fakultät, ein vornehmer, gütiger Arzt und ein abgeklärter Familienvater. Aber wenn eine ernste Gewissensfrage an ihn herantritt, deren Lösung einen ganzen Mann fordert, dann erwacht der alte Anatol in ihm, und er denkt lächelnd an die Weisheit se[i]nes Rufes, den er in den Vorstädten, wo er einstmals geliebelt, gehört: 'Verkauft's mei G'wand, i fahr' in Himmel!'

[Marco Brociner, *Neues Wiener Tagblatt*, 22 December 1918]

14. Mit Kunst hat das Schnitzlersche Stück nichts zu tun. Es ist eine sauber geflochtene, breite, fadenreiche Debatte, hineingewirkt Figuren und Bildchen aus dem politischen Wien von 1900. Die Szene Bernhardi-Priester, in der das Stück sich vom Boden lösen und in kühlere, dunstlose Regionen aufschweben will, erfüllt nicht ganz ihren Zweck. Sie weht nur ein Düftchen besserer Schnitzlerscher Melancholie heran. [...] Die Zuhörer wurden der noblen Schnitzlerschen Art, empfindliche Stellen zu berühren, ohne daß die Berührung tief ginge oder weh täte, dankbarst froh.

[a. p. (= Alfred Polgar), *Wiener Allgemeine Zeitung*, 23 December 1918]

15. Reiche mußten bersten, Throne stürzen, Oesterreich in seine Bestandteile zerfallen, all das nicht metaphorisch, sondern buchstäblich genommen, damit das Natürliche geschehen konnte, daß das Werk eines hervorragenden und berühmten Wiener Dichters in Wien zur Aufführung gelangte [...]

Manche wollen in diesem Stücke ein Tendenzstück erblicken. Nun, mit ebensoviel Berechtigung könnte man auch Ibsens 'Volksfeind', der ein nordischer Vetter des Bernhardi ist, ein Tendenzstück nennen[...] Es gibt aber kein Tendenzstück ohne Verallgemeinerung und Schnitzlers 'Professor Bernhardi' ist auch keines. Es ist ein Problemstück, das, von einer auf dem Theater neuen Situation ausgehend, ein interessantes Problem auf eine geistreiche und dramatisch meisterhafte Art durch fünf Akte entfaltet. Erst das ungerechtfertigte, auch vom Standpunkt religiöser Empfindlichkeiten nicht zu rechtfertigende Verbot des Dramas hat einen tendenziösen Zug hineingetragen [...]]

[R. A. (= Raoul Auerheimer), 'Professor Bernhardi', *Neue Freie Presse*, 24 December 1918]

16. 'Professor Bernhardi', Komödie in fünf Akten von Arthur Schnitzler, ist ein Stück von so ausgeprägter Tendenz, daß es sich dadurch von dem eigentlichen Zweck des Theaters zu weit entfernt. Nicht die Kunst, sondern nur die Gesinnung ist es, die hier den Effekt erzielt und die Bühne zur Rednertribüne macht.

[*Volksfreund* (Brünn), 21 October 1919]

17. Schnitzler selbst zeigt sich ... als ein tapferer Kerl. Packt einen Stier treuherzig-unbeirrt an den Hörnern (es gibt zahlreiche Stiere). Meint jedoch, als Oesterreicher, nachgiebig am Schluß: ganz wahrheitsgerecht kann man eh' nicht handeln, also wozu. . . ?

(Vielleicht ist es nicht Nachgiebigkeit – sondern eine Seelenlüftung mehr; eine Ehrlichkeit mehr.)

Technisch gesehen, bauhaft gesehen: drei Akte Kampf, crescendo. Dann ein Akt Besinnlichkeit. Und ein Schlußakt komödisch; entlastend; abebbend. . . Sehr fein gebaut. Von einer hierorts recht seltenen Hand.

Ibsens 'Volksfeind' an der schönen blauen Donau? Das Werk hat weniger Grundsätzliches als derlei beim Ibsen; weniger Allgemeingeltendes: doch in jener feierlosen Ehrlichkeit am Schluß (die nur sekundenlang irrig wie Schwäche wirkt) – in diesem einen Zug überragt es den Ibsen. . . .

[Alfred Kerr, *Tageblatt-Abendzeitung,* 28 February 1923]

18. Dieser Bernhardi ist nur primitiv. Wir sehen, daß er Arzt und Jude und Wiener ist und zuerst protestiert, zuletzt resigniert. Das ist Alles. Der Mann hat seinen Beruf, seine Abstammung und seine Wahlheimat – aber wo sind seine Nerven? Er schreitet oder gleitet von einer schönen Würde zu einer schönen Wurschtigkeit – aber wo sind die Züge seines Wesens, durch die er uns trotzdem reizvoll würde? Was also ist er? Ein Titelheld [...] O, du mein Österreich! Du hast das Glück (oder das Unglück), daß deine Ankläger deine Opfer sind. Daß deine Satiriker statt grimmig zu lachen, ironisch lächeln. Daß sie witzig flackern, statt verzehrend zu flammen. Das sie statt aufschreckender Streitschriften beruhigende Theaterstücke verfassen. Immer, selbstverständlich, den einen Karl Kraus ausgenommen.

[*Die Weltbühne,* 19, no. 10, 8 March 1923, pp. 275–7 (pp. 276–7)]

19. Kühnheit altert schnell. Auch Schnitzlers 'Professor Bernhardi' hat in unsern Tagen viel von seiner literarischen Verwegenheit eingebüßt. Man sieht das gedankliche Skelett seiner Programm-Menschen zu genau, fühlt oft zu deutlich den Tendenzfaden seiner Lebens- und Theatertechnik [...] Auch Bernhardis Konflikt geht uns menschlich nicht mehr sehr nahe. Was aber auch in diesem Zeitstücke unverwüstlich lebendig bleibt, das sind die Schnitzlerschen Charakterzeichnungen, seine Typen, die er aus irgendeinem Kollegium gelangt und förmlich dampfend frisch auf die Bühne gestellt hat[...]Sie sind wahr, echt und in ihrer Tragik oder Komik köstlich amüsant, namentlich dann, wenn sie im Lichte des richtigen Schnitzlerdialogs stehen, der so wienerisch ist daß man darüber längst vergaß, wie sehr er sich am französischen Konversationsstück schulte. [...]] Auch diesmal empfand man, daß die theaterschwächste Szene, die Unterredung Bernhardis mit dem Pfarrer, dichterisch der Höhepunkt des Stückes ist, vielleicht, weil das Menschliche dort beginnt, wo die Technik versagt.

[H. T., *Neues Wiener Tagblatt,* 23 February 1924]

20. Das von der Zensur ehemals verbotene Stück hat [. . .] nichts von seiner aktuellen Schlagkraft eingebüßt. [...]Schnitzler hat dieses Thema, fern aller Empfindung, vor das Forum seines scharfen, klaren Verstandes gerückt und behandelt es in einer langen Reihe von Auseinandersetzungen und Debatten, abseits jeder Tendenz. Er rechtfertigt beide Teile, indem er sie vollkommen objektiv gelten läßt. Die Tendenz des Stückes besteht aber in seiner vermeinten Tendenzlosigkeit nur um so aufdringlicher.

[...]In den beiden großen Szenen zwischen Bernhardi und Unterrichtsminister und Bernhardi–Priester lösen sich die Probleme vom rein Stofflichen und erheben sich in die Welt des Allgemein-Menschlichen und Ewig-Gültigen.

[M. D., *Wiener Allgemeine Zeitung,* 11 September 1928]

Notes

Enquiries concerning use of the Exeter Schnitzler archive should be addressed to The Librarian, University Library, Stocker Road, Exeter EX4 4PT.

1. I am grateful for this and other information to Peter Michael Braunwarth (Österreichische Akademie der Wissenschaften, Kommission für literarische Gebrauchsformen).

2. References to Schnitzler's diaries are to the following volumes of the Österreichische Akademie der Wissenschaften edition, ed. Werner Welzig *et al.*: *Tagebuch 1879–1892*

(Vienna, 1987), *Tagebuch 1909–1912* (Vienna, 1981), and *Tagebuch 1917–1919* (Vienna, 1985). References are given to the date of the entries quoted.

3. Reproduced in Gerhard Neumann and Jutta Müller, *Der Nachlaß Arthur Schnitzlers* (Munich, 1969), pp. 23–31 (p. 31).

4. Otto P. Schinnerer, 'The History of Schnitzler's *Reigen*', *PMLA*, 46 (1931), 839–59. On Schinnerer's use of the cuttings, see Schnitzler's letter of 2 August 1929 to Olga Schnitzler. That Schnitzler himself also subsequently consulted them in answering queries from Schinnerer is shown by his letter of 6 February 1930 to Schinnerer.

5. Otto P. Schinnerer, 'Schnitzler and the military censorship: unpublished correspondence', *Germanic Review*, 5 (1930), 238–46 (p. 245).

6. The history of the censorship of *Professor Bernhardi* has been fully documented by Werner Wilhelm Schnabel, '"Professor Bernhardi" und die Wiener Zensur. Zur Rezeptionsgeschichte der Schnitzlerschen Komödie', *Jahrbuch der deutschen Schillergesellschaft*, 28 (1984), 349–83. But although Schnabel quite properly presents his account as contributing to the history of the play's 'reception', in fact its *critical* reception – even press reaction to the various stages of censorship – is marginal to his main concern.

7. A concise synthesis of recent interpretations is given by Michaela L. Perlmann, *Arthur Schnitzler* (Stuttgart, 1987), pp. 96–101.

8. Sol Liptzin, 'The Genesis of Schnitzler's *Professor Bernhardi*', *Philological Quarterly*, 10 (1931), 348–55. Schnitzler saw this article before it appeared, and expressed his approval in his letter to Liptzin of 13 May 1931. See also Sol Liptzin, *Arthur Schnitzler* (New York, 1932), pp. 175–89.

9. Quotations from Schnitzler's letters are from Arthur Schnitzler, *Briefe 1913–1931*, ed. Peter Michael Braunwarth *et al.* (Frankfurt, 1984). References are given to the date of the letters quoted.

10. 'Für das Verbot war nicht so sehr die in der Komödie diskutierte religiöse Frage entscheidend, als vielmehr die tendenziöse und entstellende Schilderung hierländischer öffentlicher Verhältnisse.' Quoted by Karl Glossy, *Vierzig Jahre Deutsches Volkstheater. Ein Beitrag zur deutschen Theatergeschichte* (Vienna, n.d. [1929]), p. 221. Glossy's account of the negotiations with the authorities (pp. 221–4) is also reprinted in Reinhard Urbach, *Schnitzler-Kommentar zu den erzählenden Schriften und dramatischen Werken* (Munich, 1974), pp. 186–8.

11. After renewed appeals to lift the ban in late 1913, the censor insisted that the play was 'ein pamphletistisches Werk von geringem literarischen Wert' (Glossy, *op. cit.*, p. 223).

12. The political colouring of the cultural reporting in the *Reichspost* is discussed by Ulrich Weinzierl, 'Die Kultur der "Reichspost"', in Franz Kadrnoska (ed.), *Aufbruch und Untergang: Österreichische Kultur zwischen 1918 und 1938* (Vienna, 1981), pp. 325–44.

13. A. Halbert, 'Die Tragikomödie des Starrsinns. Zu Arthur Schnitzlers *Professor Bernhardi*', *Die Wage*, 16, (16) [19 April 1913], 385–7: the play is described as 'Die Tragikomödie des Starrsinns, der nicht so recht den ganzen Mut hat, starren Sinns zu bleiben', and as being 'deshalb kein Kunstwerk, weil der Dichter nicht den guten Mut zur Tragödie und nicht die Laune zur Komödie hatte' (p. 386).

14. *Die Fackel*, 368–9, 5 February 1913, pp. 1–4.

15. 'Schnitzler ist kühn', *Die Fackel*, 372–3, 1 April 1913, p. 13.

16. See Reinhard Urbach, 'Karl Kraus und Arthur Schnitzler: Eine Dokumentation', *Literatur und Kritik*, 49 (1970), 513–30; Renate Wagner, '"Und dieser Kern ist Niedrigkeit". Dokumentarisches zur Beziehung Arthur Schnitzler/Karl Kraus, unter besonderer Berücksichtigung der *Fackel*', *Maske und Kothurn*, 27 (1981), 322–34.

17. In 1930, when Fritz Kortner played the title role in the Theater in der Königgrätzer-

straße, Faktor put it less kindly, observing that the struggle for justice fades away into the conventional happy ending of comedy ('Der Kampf ums Recht klingt in ein happy end aus' [*Berliner Börsen-Courier*, Abend-Ausgabe, 24 January 1930]). A debt to salon comedy in particular, especially in the dialogue, was perceived by a critic in the *Neues Wiener Tagblatt* in 1924 (Document 19).

18. Following its first performance in Berlin, *Professor Bernhardi* had also been performed in other cities, including Zürich, Berne, Budapest, Munich, and Hamburg, in 1912–13, and there had been productions in New York and Stockholm in 1914 – all these productions documented by reviews in the collection.

19. m. b. [= Marco Brociner], *Neues Wiener Tagblatt*, 15 November 1917; Alfred Polgar, *Prager Tagblatt*, 15 November 1917; a.p., *Wiener Allgemeine Zeitung*, 16 November 1917; Alfred Polgar, *Vossische Zeitung* (Berlin), Morgen-Ausgabe, 18 November 1917. Schnitzler's acute disappointment with the critical response to *Fink und Fliederbusch* is summed up in his letter of 24 December 1917 to Rudolph Lothar.

20. This review has been reprinted in *Max Mell als Theaterkritiker*, ed. Margret Dietrich (Vienna, 1983), pp. 61–2.

21. Ct. Kfd., 'Ärtztestücke', *Wiener Medizinische Wochenschrift* (1919) 9 (22 February).

22. For example, Emil Faktor (Document 3); Friedrich Hertz (Document 6); Arthur Eloesser, 'Schnitzler und Sohn', *Das Literarische Echo*, 15, cols 475–8 (col. 477) (1 January 1913); C[ur]t K[ron]f[el]d, 'Ärztestücke' ('mehr ein Stück Leben als Theater').

23. Desmond MacCarthy, 'Greatly to Find Quarrel in a Straw?', *New Statesman and Nation*, 22 August 1936, pp. 255–6. This is the only review quoted in this article which appears not to be in the Exeter archive.

24. On Bernhardi's 'moral ambivalence', see M. W. Swales, 'Arthur Schnitzler as a moralist', *Modern Language Review*, 62 (1967), 462–75. For a defence of Bernhardi's moral stature, see William H. Rey, *Arthur Schnitzler: 'Professor Bernhardi'* (Munich, 1971). See also the review by Peter Horwath, *Modern Austrian Literature*, 6 (1–2) (1973), 188–92.

25. Theodor Kappstein, *Arthur Schnitzler und seine besten Bühnenwerke* (Berlin and Leipzig, 1922), pp. 90–3 (p. 93).

26. m. b., *Neues Wiener Tagblatt*, 15 November 1917. See also: –co–, *Die Zeit* (Vienna), 15 November 1917; *Wiener Abendpost*, 12 November 1917; G., *Wiener Montagblatt*, 20 November 1917; Theodor Antropp, *Österreichische Rundschau*, 1 December 1917, pp. 234–5.

27. Schnitzler, *Aphorismen und Betrachtungen*, ed. Robert O. Weiss (Frankfurt, 1967), pp. 296–7 (p. 296).

28. E.g. Rolf-Peter Janz, 'Professor Bernhardi – "Eine Art medizinischer Dreyfus"'? Die Darstellung des Antisemitismus bei Arthur Schnitzler', *Jahrbuch für Internationale Germanistik*, Reihe A, 13 (1985), 108–17; Ernst L. Offermanns, *Arthur Schnitzler: Das Komödienwerk als Kritik des Impressionismus* (Munich, 1973), pp. 107–9; Jeffrey B. Berlin, 'The priest figure in Schnitzler's *Professor Bernhardi*', *Neophilologus*, 64 (1980), 433–8.

29. Richard H. Allen, *An Annotated Arthur Schnitzler Bibliography: Editions and Criticism in German, French and English 1879–1965* (Chapel Hill, N. Carolina, n.d. [1966]), pp. 68–9.

30. Renate Wagner and Brigitte Vacha, *Wiener Schnitzler-Aufführungen 1891–1970* (Munich, 1971), pp. 111–12 (notes p. 175).

31. See my article 'Erinnerung und Elegie in der Wiener Literatur 1890-1930', *Literatur und Kritik*, 223–4 (1988), 153–69, especially pp. 166–8.

Quo vadis, Austria?
Gustav Sieber's conundrum
Ian Foster

In August 1913 the second crisis in the Balkans in under six months came to a close with the Treaty of Bucharest. Serbia, Romania, and Greece had inflicted a crushing defeat on Bulgaria. As a result, Serbia gained most of northern Macedonia. Austro-Hungarian policy in the region, directed by Count Berchtold, was aimed at containing Serbian national and territorial ambitions. Yet for a second time, Austria–Hungary had proved unwilling or unable to commit itself to inhibiting Serbian claims. Already, in the First Balkan War of 1912–13, Austria–Hungary had only been able to prevent Serbia from gaining an Adriatic port by accepting the situation created by the victory of the Balkan League in driving Turkish troops to within thirty miles of Constantinople.

Internally, the Dual Monarchy also appeared weak. In June of the same year, the Redl case came to light. The news that a senior colonel in the Austro-Hungarian intelligence service had been selling military secrets to enemy powers was greeted with a mixture of shock and outrage by the spokesmen of the army in the pages of military newspapers like *Danzer's Armee-Zeitung*. As the summer wore on, the wider public was scandalised by the circumstances of Redl's suicide. Redl, it seemed, had been permitted to take his own life by an officer corps hoping to avoid a full investigation.[1] The faith of the Habsburg establishment in the reliability of the army was shaken. Confidence in the force of Austro-Hungarian arms and the Great Power status of the Dual Monarchy was at a low ebb.

At this moment of crisis an anonymous novel was published which seemed to the military authorities to capture the current demoralised mood and, hence, to pose a threat to the integrity of the army. The novel was entitled *Quo vadis, Austria?*, subtitled *Ein Roman der Resignation von einem österreichischen Offizier*.[2] It was published in Berlin and confiscated on arrival at the border. Its eye-catching cover showed the Habsburg double-headed eagle against a black and yellow background with the title question on a ribbon drawn across the bird's talons. The distribution of the novel was banned and the process of identifying and prosecuting its author set in motion.

The mythological preface

At the beginning of the novel is a dedication:

> Allen denen, die das geliebte Vaterland groß und herrlich wissen wollen, Allen österreichischen Offizieren, denen die Siege vergangener Tage der einzige Lichtschimmer im Dunkel des Daseins sind, Allen denen, die einst im Donner der Kanonen Österreichs Schicksal wenden wollen, in der Hoffnung auf stolzere Tage gewidmet vom Verfasser.

> [Dedicated by the author in expectation of prouder days to all those who wish to see our beloved Fatherland great and resplendent, to all Austrian officers for whom the victories of past days are the only glimmer of light in the darkness of their existence, and to all those who hope one day to transform Austria's fate amid the thunder of cannons.]

The 'message' of the novel is clearly directed at the officers of the Habsburg Army. The combination of 'einst', which can refer to past or future, and the reference to the 'victories of past days' makes it clear that the idea of a loyal officer corps fed on the memories of 'Old Austria' ('Altösterreich') is being invoked.

Following the dedication is a preface in which the narrator encounters a Cassandra figure. He interrogates the seer as to the fate of the Dual Monarchy. She prophesies the doom of 'proud Ilion': the state will be torn apart, its rulers forced into exile. She refers to Austria–Hungary variously as 'Österreich', 'Ilion', 'der alte Kaiserstaat'. The country is doomed because a unified state is possible only through blood: 'Und das geht nur durch Blut!' In the context of the rise of nationalism in nineteenth-century Europe, one might assume that this refers to the idea that the unity of a state is only assured if it is based upon a single linguistic, racial, or cultural community. However, Cassandra's prophecies imply something very different. She holds out a single chance that the Habsburg state can survive:

> Laß' die Toten auferstehen im Geiste.
> All' die, die für Habsburgs Erbe geblutet haben, all' die, die in besseren Zeiten die Steine zum Baue Österreichs fügten.
> Und gehe zum Herrscher deines Landes und künde ihm deinen Schmerz.
> Und künde ihm, was ich sage:
> Er soll mit eiserner Faust der Hydra den Kopf zerschmettern und die nicht vergessen, die seines Wortes harren.
> Und soll mit Blut und Feuer Ilions Wiedergeburt feiern – denn anders geht es nicht.
> Und soll auf seine Offiziere bauen und seine Armee! (pp. xi-xii)

> [Let the dead arise in spirit. All those who have shed their blood for the Habsburg inheritance, all those who in better times laid the stones for the

building of Austria. And go to the ruler of your country and tell him of
your pain. And tell him what I say: he must shatter the head of the Hydra
with an iron fist and not forget those who await his word. And with blood
and fire he must celebrate Ilion's rebirth – for there is no other way. And
he must build upon his officers and his army!]

Blood in this case means bloodshed. Cassandra's vision is of a Habsburg state
regenerated by war. The army is no longer the primary bond holding the
polyglot empire together, but its final hope of survival. Decisive action can come
only from the Emperor.

The envisaged war is, however, directed at a symbolic foe, the Hydra, an
empty signifier into which any potential enemy can be projected. This lack of
specificity in the use of mythological imagery characterises the whole preface.
Diverse mythological material is appropriated to deliver a pessimistic prophecy
couched in a sonorous language which nevertheless offers a final hope in military
force. The language is resonant with classical and biblical overtones, though
verbal echoes of specific texts are faint at best (see p. ix ll. 8–9, p. xi ll. 14–16,
l. 23). Like the choice of a Cassandra figure and reference to the Fall of Troy,
this heightened language creates a mythologically resonant backdrop for the
prophecy. Austria–Hungary's enemies 'pour down from the clouds', the new
state arising from the old becomes the Phoenix rising from its ashes. In this way,
the historical crisis of 1913 is conflated with mythological details to create an
ahistorical 'Altösterreich'.

The officer corps is to provide a bastion against these mythologised enemies.
Only in unity is there hope that disaster can be prevented. Cassandra's fatalism
is a rhetorical device. On the one hand, she says: 'Alles muß eins sein, das
drohende Verhängnis aufzuhalten – und das wird nie geschehen' (p. xi) ('All
must be one if the fate that threatens us is to be averted – and that will never
happen'). On the other hand, when the narrator asks her what will be the
outcome if, despite everything, unity is achieved and the Emperor deploys his
army, she replies with the 'ancient melody' ('uralte Melodie') of Austria's
greatness: 'O du mein Österreich!' (p. xii). The rhetorical strategy is similar to
that of the argument of the 'Zukunftskrieg' or 'future war' story, a kind of fiction
published in huge quantities in the period leading up to the First World War,
in which a projected military defeat was intended to drum up support for further
investment in military hardware or, as was the case in Britain, to support the
introduction of conscription.[3] The vision of disaster is intended as a warning.
Cassandra's 'ancient melody' returns throughout the novel. Each time, it points
up the contrast between the dismal state of the army as viewed by the narrator
and the faith that regeneration is possible through military action (see pp. 32,
53, 266, and 391).

The mythological preface prefigures the argument of the main text and is
linked to it by the use of epigraphs. These are drawn from two poems by
Schiller: 'Kassandra' (1802) and 'Der Graf von Habsburg' (1803), referring
respectively to the two mythological moments conflated in the preface. Lines
from 'Kassandra' invoke a sense of impending doom, while lines from the 'Graf

von Habsburg' refer to Rudolf I, the first Habsburg Emperor of the Holy Roman Empire, and so invoke an idealised tradition of imperial rule. The parallelism of Troy=Austria–Hungary is sustained, therefore, alongside a self-conscious idealisation of the role of the Emperor.

Love versus career: Uchatius as *raisonneur*

The main text of *Quo vadis, Austria?* tells the story of the growing disillusionment and ultimate resignation of a young officer, Lieutenant Uchatius. The novel is divided into two parts. In the first, Uchatius takes part in the withdrawal of Austro-Hungarian troops from the Sanjak of Novi-Bazar and is on active service during the ensuing emergency. The Sanjak was a narrow strip of territory separating Serbia and Montenegro. Under the Treaty of Berlin (1878) Austria–Hungary had been granted the right to govern Bosnia-Hercegovina and to garrison the adjacent Sanjak, though these lands were nominally under Turkish sovereignty. In July 1908, the Young Turk Revolution brought the threat of renewed Turkish nationalism and the possibility that Turkey might lay claim to what were, by then, regarded as Austro-Hungarian colonial possessions. Also, there was the threat that the destabilisation occasioned by a weakened Turkey would lead to a strengthening of the national aspirations of the Balkan states, Serbia in particular. The Austro-Hungarian Foreign Minister Aehrenthal decided, therefore, to annex Bosnia–Hercegovina, a move which had been planned for some time, and return the Sanjak to Turkish hands. For a while, a war with Serbia seemed unavoidable but was finally averted by the withdrawal of Russian support for Serbia under diplomatic pressure from Germany.[4]

The second part of the novel is set in the period 1911–13, giving the narrative a contemporary reference that is rare in Austrian fiction on the subject of the Habsburg Army. The Vienna riots of 1911, an event frequently glossed over by historians of the period, are described in detail in an eye-witness account from the soldier's viewpoint. Uchatius remains in Vienna to comment on Austria–Hungary's indecisive policy in the Balkan region during the crises of 1912–13. The novel ends with his decision to give up his career in early summer 1913.

If Uchatius's experience of professional life is one of growing disillusionment, his personal life moves in the opposite direction. He begins as a young man recently disappointed in love and cynical about the possibility of any relationship with a woman. Then, through the experience first of female friendship (in the shape of Esther Török, the wife of a fellow officer), and then love for his childhood sweetheart Evy, his personal life becomes more promising. In the fiction of the period the portrayal of the social life of officers frequently presented that social life in terms of a conflict between a career on the one hand and the possibility of marriage on the other. There is a historical basis for this conflict in the inordinately large sum of money which officers wishing to marry had to deposit in the form of a bond, known as the 'Kaution'. If the peripatetic life-style common to all soldiers on active service is also taken into consideration, it is not difficult to see why the issue of love versus career was a common theme. Typical fictional resolutions of the conflict would be a regretful resignation from the army or a marriage of convenience to a wealthy widow or the daughter of a well-to-do bourgeois family. In *Quo vadis, Austria?*, this topos of the officer caught between career and love is reversed. For Uchatius the prospect of marriage to Evy becomes a compensation for the frustrations of his career: a retreat into the private sphere in the face of a decadent public life. The career Uchatius leaves behind becomes the tragic theme.

This dichotomy between the pessimism of Uchatius's view of public events and his optimism regarding his private life also indicates the split between public and private in the structure of the novel itself. The hero Uchatius is a junior officer. He plays no real part in shaping the historical events he observes. He is always on the receiving end. At the same time, a large portion of the text is given over to his reflections and ideas about those events. The characterisation is somewhat colourless since the personal and the political are not sufficiently well integrated. One way of overcoming this problem is to make historical figures who did have a role in shaping events appear in the text. This was Bertha von Suttner's solution in her polemical anti-war novel *Die Waffen nieder!* (1889) – translated into English as *Lay Down Your Arms!* and read widely throughout Europe and America. Perhaps, also, the inertia of Austrian affairs made it difficult to envisage characters actively shaping events in the way earlier writers (Suttner is, again, a good example) were able to do.

Uchatius is the novel's chief *raisonneur*. His name is borrowed from one of the Habsburg Army's most celebrated figures – Major-General Uchatius was head of the Viennese Arsenal's gun manufacture in the 1870s and the inventor of gun barrels in use until the First World War. The narrator, who reminds the reader explicitly of this fact, does not, however, mention that the same Uchatius committed suicide after repeated failure to develop a heavier version of his design.[5] The choice of the name of Uchatius is ambivalent, conjuring up military tradition, technical innovation, and failure.

The Uchatius of *Quo vadis, Austria?* debates the Habsburg political dilemma with a series of other characters in the course of the novel. These arguments tend to become diatribes attacking current government policy. His most vocal sparring-partner in the early part of the novel is another officer, Lieutenant Helmers. Helmers is an adherent of the idea of that the officer is 'non-political' ('unpolitisch'), that politics and soldiering do not mix (p. 12). Uchatius takes up this naive conception of neutrality and reformulates it. Through repetition it acquires an ironic note and becomes a form of protest against current policy. The political situation has deteriorated so much, it is implied, that even the loyal, non-political soldier has to voice comment (see pp. 15, 46, 98). The theme of the non-political officer is referred to principally in the first part of the novel. It is less prominent in the second part, where Uchatius becomes ever more scornful of actual political debate as politicians repeatedly fail to implement what he considers to be the correct measures. The satirical device of ironically repeating the assertion that soldiers should not comment on politics, while at the same time commenting at length on political developments, is extremely effective. It expresses the historical paradox that the army, supposedly 'above politics' as one of the few 'dual' institutions of the Habsburg Monarchy, had become the most significant political force providing cohesion within the state. The novel aims at a combination of protest and propaganda. It gives an account of what it terms the 'unbearable conditions in the army' ('die unhaltbaren Zustände in der Armee') and seeks to persuade its readers that a particular response is the correct one (see p. 76).

The main subject of criticism in the novel is the state of the officer corps. Modern officers, it is claimed, lack the motivation of their predecessors. The narrator describes Helmers:

> Dieser moderne Offizier machte seinen Dienst zwar ebenso genau wie die meisten andern, aber damit glaubte er seiner Pflicht auch vollauf Genüge getan zu haben. Das überschwängliche, so leicht in Begeisterung oder tiefste Niedergeschlagenheit umschlagende Gefühl des echten Altöster-reichers für alles, was die Größe und Ehre der ruhmreichen Doppel-monarchie betraf, fehlte ihm. [p. 114]

> [This modern officer carried out his duties just as precisely as most others; however, in doing this much, he also believed that he had fulfilled his duty. He lacked the exuberant feeling of the genuine Old Austrian for everything that concerned the greatness and the honour of the Dual Monarchy, a feeling that could easily turn into enthusiasm or deepest depression.]

Uchatius, it is implied, does have the qualities of the genuine 'Altösterreicher'. He is the son of an officer. Helmers, on the other hand, is the illegitimate child of a sergeant and a chamber-maid. One can see clearly that the rejection of Helmers is based upon a conception of the 'right' sort of background for an officer. Uchatius is scathing about his fellow officers, who are completely lacking in chivalry and who frequent disreputable cafés. The officer corps has been undermined by the decline not only in aristocratic officer candidates, but also in candidates who are the sons of officials and officers.

Military education is condemned for failing to provide good officers. One officer comments: '[...] wir werden ja systematisch zur Unselbständigkeit erzogen' (p. 314, also p. 254) ('[...] we are systematically educated into a state of dependence'). Uchatius tells the story of an old army officer who gave his sons a civilian education at great cost to himself rather than taking advantage of the free military education open to them as the sons of an officer, which would oblige them to complete the same number of years in military service as they had spent in military schools. The old man explained his action by saying that he did not wish to see his sons become as embittered as he now was after twenty years as a soldier. In the present army officers are of lower class background than before. According to Uchatius, therefore, they are less suited to act in a manner in keeping with their station. Uchatius has in mind an ideal of the officer as aristocrat. He assumes that breakdowns in authority result from the change in the social composition of the officer corps – presumably soldiers are no longer able to recognise their social betters. He attributes the failure of those in command to restore the prestige of the army through decisive measures to a fear of bad publicity. The press is referred to as 'the seventh Great Power', a phrase that was already something of a cliché among conservative critics of the mass-circulation newspapers (see pp. 210–11).

What Uchatius's complaints about the public's lack of esteem for the army do not mention are the reasons why there should be such hostility. The novel itself provides the historical context. The use of troops to quell civil disturbances, euphemistically referred to in the language of Habsburg bureau-cracy as 'military co-operation' ('Militärassistenzen'), is described in detail. The relevant passage is one of the most vivid in the novel. An exact date is given: 16 September 1911. Uchatius joins his regiment in policing a demonstration by supporters of the Social Democratic Party. The civilian protestors, provoked by the military presence, hurl first insults, then stones, at the soldiers. News arrives that a school in the working-class district of Ottakring has been vandal-ised. In vain, a political official tries to restrain the officers from retaliating, but their patience is exhausted and their commander gives the order to open fire. Three demonstrators are killed and a number of others are wounded. Blame for the incident is laid at the door of those in government who have failed to order decisive military intervention at an earlier stage. The argument is that if the 'mob' ('der Pöbel', the word used to describe the demonstrators) knew that the army had orders to react forcibly without fear of the consequences, then such incidents would not occur (pp. 243–56).

Uchatius has nothing but contempt for nationalist or socialist dissent. While he accepts that his description of himself as 'ein Deutscher' might be interpreted as a declaration of pan-German sympathies, he insists that the German 'Nation' is the bearer of the culture of the polyglot empire (pp. 70–1). The insecurity of German-speaking officers is plain in Uchatius's description of the Slavs as 'the spoilt favourite children of the monarchy'. Concessions to Czech interests are seen as pandering to divisive and unstable elements (p. 381).

The decline in the army's public prestige is blamed on chronic underfunding. In particular, the lack of long-serving NCOs has increased the workload of junior officers to the point where the system is threatening to collapse (see pp. 73, 92, 206–7). Uchatius notes that Austria–Hungary was spending less per head of its population on its military budget than the other Great Powers. He describes the numbers of men at the army's disposal as a fire brigade level ('Feuerwehrstand') and makes an unfavourable comparison between the Dual Monarchy's 550 000 full-time bureaucrats and its 400 000 professional soldiers. Much of the blame is attributed to the Hungarian Parliament, whose obstruction of legislation has prevented investment. However, poor planning is also blamed. For example, troops withdrawing from the Sanjak are instructed to burn valuable supplies rather than sell them to the local population (see pp. 42, 102–7). Poor planning is also shown to have an adverse effect on morale, particularly during the long mobilisations of 1908–9 and 1912–13. Uchatius sums up the mood of the mobilised army after months of inaction in one word: vegetating ('Vegetieren').

The narrative framework is designed to make one point immediately clear: Uchatius's diagnosis will prove to be justified. He is justified in seeing events as a prologue ('Vorspiel') (p. 14). And he will be vindicated by history. The narrator frequently endorses his opinions; both he and Uchatius are advocates of the military solution. For example, the narrator refers to the final settlement of the Annexation Crisis in 1909 as 'a deeply humiliating period in the history of the Dual Monarchy' (p. 108). Aehrenthal's diplomatic solution is regarded with disdain by narrator and hero alike. Agreement between them becomes more pronounced as Uchatius's advocacy of force becomes more outspoken. For example, the emphatic approval that greets the hero's assertion that political authority should be maintained by force is comically blunt: 'Er hatte recht' (pp. 314–15). A less blatant example is provided by another narratorial comment:

> So flackerte in den österreichischen Offizierskreisen, die man so gerne Kriegspartei nennt, obwohl sie jede andere als diese Bezeichnung verdient, noch einmal die Hoffnung auf, bewaffnet einzuschreiten. . . [p. 371]

> [So it was that in Austrian officers' circles, which some like to refer to as the war party, although that is the last name they deserve, hopes of an armed intervention flickered into life once more.]

Into the description of the warlike mood among officers the narrator inserts a comment that betrays his sympathies.

The problem is one frequently encountered in novels and stories of the period about the army written by serving or former soldiers: the proximity of narrator and hero.[6] For the portrait of the army to be convincing, the narrative perspective has to imply that the narrator knows the world of his hero well. Often, they share the same assumptions. Those assumptions are defined by the officers' conception of honour. The theme of honour is first sounded in *Quo vadis, Austria?* in a speech given by a commanding colonel in the opening pages. Having outlined the deterioration of the situation in the Sanjak, he stresses that as the army of a foreign power they cannot interfere with local politics. However, they will at all costs preserve their honour: 'Ebenso gewiß ist aber, daß wir unsere Waffenehre auf jeden Fall wahren und nicht die geringste Verunglimpfung unseres glorreichen Kaiserstaates dulden werden' (p. 7) ('However, it is equally clear that we will preserve the honour of our arms in all cases and not allow the slightest defamation of our glorious empire'). The message is clear. While pursuing a policy of non-intervention, their hearts are elsewhere. Their vulnerability is self-evident. On the one hand, their presence is to secure peace; on the other, it is their profession to fight wars. A fragile sense of purpose is exposed in an overstated display of regimental pride. The compound noun 'Waffenehre' links the concrete weapon with the abstract honour and conveys the sense of force applied in a just cause.

Later, the commander of the local Turkish garrison asks for asylum and a military escort. The Austro-Hungarian general to whom this appeal is addressed realises that full-scale military action to rescue his Turkish counterpart may provoke a diplomatic incident. Therefore, he asks his assembled officers whether they will support him in taking action. They greet his words with one minute's silence. Then, a colonel replies 'for all' by saying that it is a simple matter of chivalrous duty ('Ritterpflicht') that they help when help is requested. The general replies that he knew that Habsburg officers could act in no other way (p. 64). The collective silence of the officers reflects their adherence to a norm of honourable behaviour. No conflict is possible, no debate required.

However, there are moments at which the narrator's account and that of the hero are in conflict. The living proof of the strength of the code of honour given in the previous example is at odds with Uchatius's assertion that the modern officer considers himself to be merely doing a job and has no inner motivation (see pp. 114–15). A similar ambiguity is evident in the theme of comradeship ('Kameradschaft'). On the one hand, Uchatius is sceptical: 'Österreichische Kameradschaft! Aber nicht mehr die alte aus Radetzkys Zeit! Beim Weine, da kam sie zum Ausdruck, und beim Anborgen feierte sie ihre größten Triumphe' (pp. 70–1) ('Austrian comradeship! But no longer the old kind from Radetzky's time! The new kind was found at the bottom of a glass [literally: 'over wine'] and celebrated its greatest triumphs when scrounging money'). And, on the other hand, the narrator describes the rescue of the Turkish commander as embodying the best of Austrian 'Kameradschaft': 'Mit echt österreichischer Kameradschaft und Liebenswürdigkeit reichte der Österreicher seinem türkischen Kamerade den Arm. . .' (p. 79) ('With truly Austrian comradeship and amiability the Austrian officer offered his arm to his Turkish comrade'). The structure is similar to that of Cassandra's rhetoric in the preface: Uchatius's damning judgement is counterbalanced by the narrator's implicit faith in the army's strength. The narrator is sympathetic to the hero's frustration and it is Uchatius's frustration which explains his pessimism. The narrator and Uchatius differ in their judgements about the spirit of the army, if not in their assessment of the material causes of its problems.

While the narrator's attitudes and the conception of honour among officers overtly shape the reader's receptiveness for Uchatius's account of the deficiencies of the army and ideas for possible reform, the hero's credibility is also enhanced in a number of other ways. He receives the wholesale approval of both major female characters. Esther Török's judgement of him contains the implicit suggestion that the army is not serving the best interests of the state if it cannot retain an officer like Uchatius (see p. 185). For her, Uchatius is the very model of a Habsburg officer with that lack of personal ambition which makes Habsburg officers so very different from their counterparts elsewhere (p. 183). Evy's reinforcement of Uchatius's views is more direct. Her conversation with him concerning the surrender of Skutari, for example, turns the satirical device of the naive eye to the purpose of supporting his interpretation of events when she asks how it is that a big country like Austria–Hungary allows its smaller neighbours to wage wars of conquest with impunity.

In this respect, Uchatius's relations with women deserve more careful examination. Through his conversations with Esther Török, the reader learns not only that Uchatius is one of the best kinds of officer but also that his personal life has been filled with disappointment. He had been a typical young officer who ran up debts and enjoyed a frivolous life-style. Typical, that is, except in one respect. He did not indulge in casual affairs. If ever he was tempted, he thought of his 'dear Mama'. When he first saw his future fiancée, Resi, she, of course, had the 'sweetest, angelic face'. The phrase he uses to describe his acquaintance with her is revealing: 'Ihr Bruder vermittelte sie mir endlich' ('Finally, her brother provided it [her] for me'). Grammatically, the pronoun 'sie' refers to 'Bekanntschaft' ('acquaintance'), but Uchatius's attitude is neatly summed up if one takes it to refer to Resi.[7] It is obvious that, as Uchatius puts it in the light of subsequent experience, for him Resi was 'too much a goddess and not enough of a woman for him to feel desire for her' (p. 145). Resi, for her part, was less interested in Uchatius than in the idea of a smart young officer as an admirer. When the prudish Uchatius realised this, he broke off their engagement and requested a transfer to the occupied zone.

Uchatius's first reunion with the adult Evy is described in terms which bring his attitudes to women into sharper focus. She touches him on the shoulder in order to attract his attention. He is shocked by her intimacy. As the narrator informs the reader, Uchatius would not allow even the best 'Kamerad' to make such an invasion of personal space (pp. 214–15). The presence of other males represents a threat to him (p. 228). The threat seems to extend to Evy herself. Uchatius' body is like 'iron' and 'steel', but unable to resist her. Other officers, who consort with prostitutes, are for Uchatius involuntary misogynists ('Frauenverächter wider Willen'). There may be some truth in this, but Uchatius hardly qualifies as a lover of women.

Evy, supposedly ten years younger than the hero, remains a girl. Her admiration for him is the unchanged admiration of the little girl who wondered at his sword and uniform at the time of his entry into the officer corps (see p. 216). She is sexually neutral and colourless as a character. She is a dancer, but, unlike other dancers, she is a virtuous 'Bürgermädel', who even sends money to her sick mother (p. 219). Two of her performances are described. On one occasion, she appears as a geisha, on the other, as a 'Pierette'. Her dancing embodies her subservient role and lack of individual identity. Evy correponds to a kind of woman born out of a patriarchal conception of an obedient, virgin wife. The true love of Uchatius and Evy consists in her devotion to his ideals. Political disillusionment and optimistic faith in love combine to prove him right, even if he resigns out of a conviction that being right is no longer enough.

'Altösterreich' – a solution?

Perhaps the most important support for Uchatius's views comes in an episode in the second half of the novel where the hero returns home to visit his dying father. His father still suffers from a disease contracted on the battlefields of Lombardy and a bullet he has carried in his stomach since Königgrätz. The symbolism is heavy-handed. Uchatius's father represents the 'old army'. According to him, the modern army is no longer the same loyal, imperial army since the abolition of the white infantry tunic (in 1868). He predicts that the era which began with the restructuring of the army after the defeat of 1866 will end in a bloody war. He adds the authority of the 'old army's' spirit to his son's vision of the army as a decaying institution and exhorts him to resign. The funeral of this old soldier is a lament to past glory. The funeral oration delivered by a general bemoans the fate of those who survived Königgrätz only to witness the present decline.

Throughout the novel it is stressed that Uchatius represents the 'old army'. In his debate with Helmers he rejects modern solutions. Helmers is enthusiastic about the benefits of technological progress:

> Wir leben nicht mehr in den Tagen, wo reiner Mut und Tollkühnheit die Schlachten entscheidet [*sic*]. . . Die moderne Kriegsweise verlangt ein ebenso modernes Aufgehen in die Folgerungen der Neuzeit, als es der Kampf ums tägliche Leben heischt. [p. 27]

> [We no longer live in the days when pure courage and devil-may-care boldness decide battles. . . Modern warfare demands as modern a devotion to the consequences of the new age as the struggle for daily existence.]

The individual or people that fails to keep up with the pace of change will be destroyed without mercy, according to Helmers. Uchatius's view is rather different:

> in diesem großem Kampfe wird derjenige siegen, der am meisten unverbrauchte Volkskraft hat, der nebst der Fähigkeit seine Waffen zu gebrauchen, auch genug Naturmensch ist, um nicht beim ersten Eindruck des modernen Kampfes mit seiner Willenskraft zu Ende zu sein. Denn in der heutigen Schlacht siegen neben anderen Faktoren auch die stärkeren Nerven. [p. 29]

> [in this great struggle he with the least dissipated popular strength will emerge victorious, he who, as well as having the ability to wield his weapons, also retains enough of the natural man not to lose his willpower at the first impression of modern conflict. For in today's battle, alongside other factors, it is strong nerves that are victorious.]

Both see nations as engaged in a Darwinian struggle for survival. However, where Helmers sees war as a technological competition, Uchatius views it as a spiritual matter of willpower, of the 'natural man'. There are similarities between the Social Darwinism of Uchatius and the ideas of Conrad von Hötzendorf, who saw war as part of a natural, biological struggle for survival.[8] The example Uchatius cites in support of his argument is that of the Ottoman Empire, whose current instability seems to him to be the natural consequence of the overthrow of the country's traditional means of government. He believes that Turkey's greatness relied upon religion, fanaticism, and fatalism. Without these, Turkey is doomed. For Uchatius, change brings destruction and progress away from a lost ideal (see p. 26).

Uchatius's reliance on the past has inescapable implications for the kind of solutions to Austria–Hungary's military and political problems advocated by the novel. Military force is seen as something to be welcomed, as a regenerating return to former decisiveness. Uchatius's attitude towards the rescue of the Turkish commander illustrates this. He says: 'Doch endlich einmal eine kleine Abwechslung, bei der es mich besonders freuen würde, wenn es ein wenig zum

Raufen käme' (p. 68). ('Now finally, for once a little change in routine in which I'd be especially pleased if it came to a bit of a scrap'). Force is also seen as the only means of dealing with civil disturbance. The narrator tells of a young lieutenant who punishes an insult to the Emperor made by a demonstrator. The punishment is death by the sword. Uchatius himself favours summary justice of this kind. He is swift to applaud a violent response, saying that in the past well-aimed sword blows and bullets were always the best remedy (pp. 314–15).

It is an important part of the novel's advocacy of force as a solution that force is sanctioned by those in command. The idea that decisive orders from above are necessary is the corollary of the novel's critique of those in command. Their fatalism is assessed by Uchatius in the phrase 'Après nous le déluge' (see pp. 152, 324, 384). The verdict reveals the soldier's dependence on authority: 'Bessermachen können es nur die droben...' ('Only those at the top can make things better'). And again: 'nicht wir sind schuld daran, sondern die dort oben...' (see pp. 98 and 254). (We're not to blame for it, it's those at the top...'). This, in turn, leads to the second part of the novel's solution: the call for a political strong man to take charge and wage a vigorous campaign against inner and outer enemies. Esther Törek first voices this idea when she expresses the hope that a new leader will take hold of the present situation with an 'iron fist' (see p. 184).

By the end of the novel, Uchatius despairs at a country that can no longer produce such a man:

> Und dieser Mann würde nie kommen, weil Österreich schon längst verlernt hatte, solche Naturen zur Geltung kommen zu lassen./Er würde nie kommen – nie./ Oder doch? [p. 378]

> [And that man would never come because Austria had long since forgotten how to allow natures like that to achieve their full potential. He would never come – never. Or maybe he would?]

He wonders for a moment whether Archduke Franz Ferdinand might be a candidate for the role as the supposed 'mysterious figure behind the so-called war-party' ('geheimnisvoller Lenker der sogenannten Kriegspartei'). Indeed, Franz Ferdinand has an obvious appeal as a candidate for the role of political strong man. As a loyal, patriotic officer Uchatius believes that solutions must be implemented by those in charge. Since those in charge seem unwilling to act in the way he imagines necessary, he is confronted with the double-bind of the patriot's complaint: on the one hand, if he voices his frustration, he will be seen as disloyal; on the other, he is disloyal to his own soldiering ideal if he remains silent. Franz Ferdinand provides the officially sanctioned solution. As future emperor, he is a figure to whom loyalty is due and a leader who plans to implement forceful reforms. For a whole generation of officers, Franz Ferdinand fulfilled a similar role. Franz Joseph's celebrated question as to whether a particular officer was a 'patriot for me' makes sense in this context. Adherence to Franz Ferdinand was an escape from an unbearable conflict for those officers who were loyal to the monarchy yet increasingly critical of its ageing head and the bureaucracy he represented. The contradictory structure of *Quo vadis, Austria?* well reflects the destructive tensions within the Habsburg

Army during the crises of 1912–13.

Uchatius's resignation is not the last line of the novel. Neither is his judgement upon Austro-Hungarian affairs: 'Unfrieden im Innern – allerwärts Feinde von außen – und ein schartiges, verrostetes Schwert', the final word. ('Discord at home – enemies everywhere abroad – and a jagged, rusty sword'). Having been awake all night, Uchatius falls into a deep sleep. As he sleeps, a regimental band passes by outside and strikes up the patriotic refrain 'O du mein Österreich!' (p. 391). Despite the personal pessimism of Uchatius, therefore, the novel's ending is a recapitulation of Cassandra's 'ancient melody': that the Dual Monarchy can be regenerated by military force – a return to 'Altösterreich'.

The trial of Gustav Sieber

Quo vadis, Austria? marks the culmination of the image of the Habsburg Army in Austrian fiction before 1914. It brings together many themes found in that fiction – the social status of officers, their training, and so on. Above all, it epitomises the retrospective orientation of predictive writing in the Dual Monarchy. In addition to its intrinsic interest, however, the controversies it aroused make it a landmark in the tradition of soldiering fiction.

The author of *Quo vadis, Austria?* was a lieutenant in the 54th Infantry Regiment named Gustav Sieber.[9] Born in 1885 in Mährisch-Trübau, Sieber was the son of a retired major. He had led an undistinguished career, having failed to complete a course at the Technical Military Academy. He joined the army as an officer cadet from the infantry officer cadet school in Marburg in 1905. He was promoted to lieutenant in 1908 and, like the hero of *Quo vadis, Austria?*, was stationed in Plevlje in the Sanjak of Novi-Bazar. His military record gives a picture of an irritable authoritarian officer frequently troubled by ill health. He was disciplined several times for ill-treating men in his charge and applied for leave on health grounds on a number of occasions.[10]

As he later told an enquiry, he first had the idea of writing a novel about the state of the army around Christmas 1912, while serving in Olmütz: 'Ich wollte durch diesen Roman die Aufmerksamkeit der maßgebenden Kreise auf verschiedene Zustände in der Armee lenken, die meiner Ansicht nach reformbedürftig waren' ('By means of this novel I wanted to bring to the attention of influential circles various conditions in the army which, in my opinion, were in need of reform').[11] He worked on the novel for three months, sometimes writing throughout the night, drinking large quantities of coffee and smoking heavily. A doctor had prescribed him laudanum to help him sleep, but this had proved ineffective against his increasing nervous stress. For the opinions expressed in the novel, he drew on conversations with fellow officers and various books and newspapers. *Danzer's Armee-Zeitung* is mentioned specifically; indeed, many of the novel's most serious criticisms are almost certainly based upon the polemics of Danzer and associates.

Around the beginning of April, he sent the manuscript to a Berlin publisher. He was later questioned repeatedly on this point, since publication in Germany was then a common ploy to avoid Austro-Hungarian censorship. He claimed, however, to have had no such intention. The title *Quo vadis, Austria?* was his own. However, the returned proofs bore a new subtitle: *Ein Roman der Resignation von einem österreichischen Offizier*. This was the publisher's invention. Sieber had originally wanted the novel to appear under his *nom de plume*, Gustav Holmes, under which name he had already published a number of *feuilletons* in the *Armeeblatt*.[12] Nevertheless, he raised no objection to the new subtitle, perhaps not fully aware that it misrepresented his intentions in writing a novel and that an anonymous work with such a title was more likely to attract the attention of the censors. He found himself unable to complete the correction of proofs and handed the task over to his publisher. Therefore he was able to disclaim final responsibility for the text. He claimed, for example, that the publisher had cut the final ten pages of the manuscript. Since he had burnt the original by the time of the trial, his claims have been viewed with some suspicion.

The novel appeared in August 1913. Confiscation and a ban on distributing were confirmed on 30 September. At the time, Sieber's ill health forced him to take six months' leave. While he had never denied authorship of the novel, it took some weeks for the authorities to identify him. On 20 December 1913, official proceedings against Sieber were begun. Officers of his regiment were questioned in secret. Only on 20 January 1914 was Sieber himself interviewed. The case then instituted by the divisional court ('Divisionsgericht') in Vienna was not, in fact, complete until 12 November 1914. After this, Sieber also had to face a 'court of honour', or 'Ehrenrat', a second, quasi-official trial by his fellow officers, which was to deal not so much with any crime that he had committed, but with whether that crime was dishonourable. It was a court of honour like this that had cashiered Schnitzler over the publication of *Leutnant Gustl* and the ensuing scandal in 1901. The proceedings of the court of honour in Sieber's case were not concluded until September 1915.

The whole sequence of events shows the Habsburg bureaucracy trapped by a historical paradox when one considers that *Quo vadis, Austria?*, for all its criticisms, was conceived and written in a spirit of patriotic zeal. In fact, the investigation recognised this from the outset: 'Es muß daher den Eindruck entscheiden, den die Schrift auf den unbefangenen Leser macht. Es sei nur kein Zweifel, daß der vorliegende Roman die Tendenz verfolgt, dem Vaterland einen Dienst zu erweisen'[13] ['Therefore, the impression which the book makes upon the naive reader has to be assessed. There is no doubt, however, that the novel in question has the aim of performing a service for the Fatherland']. The question the court was to resolve, therefore, was not whether Sieber's intentions were patriotic, but whether in the course of his arguments he might have exceeded the 'level of acceptable criticism' ('das Maß der zulässigen Kritik'). A clear distinction is drawn between the specialist and the naive reader, suggesting that works which would reach a civilian readership had to express their criticisms in a more guarded fashion than was customary in works which had a more restricted military audience. There was a perception, therefore, that Sieber was washing the army's dirty linen in public.

The court indicted Sieber on four separate counts referring to three paragraphs of the military penal code. A total of sixteen separate passages from the novel were cited in support of the prosecution case. Its Berlin publishers were subsequently able to capitalise on the censorship of specific passages by printing a special Austro-Hungarian edition containing the original text with the offending paragraphs left blank. In the spaces the publisher printed an assortment of literary quotations on the iniquities of censorship.[14]

The most serious charge against Sieber was that of 'Majestätsbeleidigung', or *lèse majesté*. The prosecution cited two passages from the novel as instances of this. The first was as follows.

> Wenn es wenigstens der Kaiser wüßte. Aber dem alten Herrn mit den weißen Haaren verschweigt man geflissentlich solche Dinge. Er glaubt die Armee wohl noch immer in dem Zustand, in dem sie ihre Siege von Custozza und Santa Lucia, Novara und Mortara erfocht. Er hat vielleicht gar keine Ahnung, daß dies längst vergangene, oft längst vergessene Zeiten sind.
>
> Der alte Kaiser träumt bei aller Arbeit und Pflichterfüllung, weil – man ihn träumen läßt.
>
> Nur eine Faust kann uns retten, ein Mann, der rücksichtslos, und wenn der Weg über Leichen geht, Ordnung schafft. Im Staate und in der Armee. (*Quo vadis, Austria?*, p. 230)

> [If only the Emperor knew. But they deliberately keep things like that secret from the white-haired old man. He probably thinks that the army is still in the state in which it fought victoriously at Custozza and Santa Lucia, Novara and Mortara. Perhaps he has no idea that those are long-forgotten times.
>
> The old Emperor is dreaming amidst all his work and fulfilment of duty because they let him dream.
>
> Only a strong hand can rescue us, a man who creates order without fear of the consequences, even if the way lies over corpses. In the state and in the army.]

The second passage cited expresses the idea that the Emperor might be against a war because of the threat of destruction and the desire to see out his reign in peace (see pp. 379–80). The prosecution argued that the very portrayal of the Emperor in such a novel was tantamount to an insult:

> Abgesehen davon, daß diese beiden beanstandeten Stellen des Werkes zweifellos die Ehrfurcht gegen den Kaiser verletzen, muß man schon an und für sich das Hineinziehen der Person seiner Majestät in einen Tendenzroman von der Qualität des vorliegenden. . . als zum Begriffe der Ehrfurchtsverletzung ausreichend ansehen.[15]

> [Apart from the fact that these two contested passages undoubtedly infringe respect for the Emperor, one has to consider the inclusion of the person of His Majesty in a tendentious novel of the quality of the one in question as already in itself a sufficient action to warrant the charge of infringing respect].

The Emperor was seldom portrayed in anything other than glowing terms in the fiction of the period. The portrayal in *Quo vadis, Austria?* might be compared with that in *Die Waffen nieder!* While Suttner's text showed Franz Joseph to be filled with compassion by the destruction of war, Sieber's novel portrays an Emperor who is the last resort of those who hope for military intervention, who would support action if he were presented with the full facts. The two passages cited by the court are a restatement in drastic terms of the theme of the preface, where the Emperor appears as the agent who can still offer a final hope of military regeneration. Since there were many other passages in the novel where 'deep admiration for the monarch' was expressed unambiguously, the court could not find Sieber guilty. A medical report on him was taken into account. He was diagnosed as suffering from nervous weakness to a high degree ('Nervenschwäche höheren Grades'), or 'Neurasthenie', as it was more commonly called at the time. The report concluded that while Sieber was ill and perhaps unaware of the full implications of what he was writing, he was not suffering from any form of delusion or serious mental illness. Indeed, as the doctor who examined him concluded, the logical structure of the novel testifies to a certain consistency of mind, though individual chapters bear the traces of having been written in extreme haste.

On the other charges against Sieber the court was not so lenient. These were referred to as offences against the integrity of honour ('Vergehen gegen die Sicherheit der Ehre') and prosecuted under paragraphs 764 and 765 of the military penal code ('Militärstrafgesetz') and Article V of the Law of 17 December 1862 (usually referred to as the 'Preßgesetz'). Sieber was accused of holding up to public ridicule the army in general, and its administration and the officer corps in particular, by attributing to them contemptible qualities and attitudes without producing any specific evidence.

An example will show the way in which the rhetorical strategy of *Quo vadis, Austria?* was interpreted by the court. At one point in the novel, a group of officers agrees with Uchatius's assessment of the apparent attitude of those in command ('Après nous le déluge'):

> Beifällig nickten die Kameraden. Hatten sie sich doch alle schon recht trübe Gedanken gemacht, wenn ihr Geist in die Zukunft schweifte und sie die alte ruhmreiche Armee in einem Zustand des Verfalles und der Auflösung sahen, der unausweichlich zum Ruin führen mußte, wenn man dem Übel nicht rechtzeitig steuerte und nicht ein eiserner Besen den Augiasstall von allem Kranken and Unreinen säuberte [*Quo vadis, Austria?*, p. 153].

> [His comrades nodded in approval. Had they not all had gloomy thoughts when their minds turned to the future and they saw the glorious old army in a state of decay and dissolution, which must inevitably lead to ruin if the problem was not taken under control in time and an iron broom used to clean all disease and impurity from the Augean stables.]

In passages like this, the negative judgement ('die alte ruhmreiche Armee in einem Zustand des Verfalles und der Auflösung') is contradicted by a final hope ('. . . wenn man dem Übel nicht rechtzeitig steuerte. . .'). The optimistic side of the equation is not always as clearly stated. Often, one has to consider the novel as a whole — as in the example concerning the discrepancy between the narrator's and Uchatius's views on modern 'Kameradschaft' discussed above. However, a despairing hope that the rebirth of Austria–Hungary's military fortunes may still be possible always counterbalances the most pessimistic statements.

In fact, Sieber repeatedly asked during questioning that the novel be read and interpreted as a whole. As he put it in a long, rambling letter to the investigating authority: 'Ich bitte deshalb. . ., mein Buch als Ganzes zu prüfen, nicht nur die einzigen Stellen.'[16] Sieber's defence also asserted that the statements of the novel concerning material deficiencies in the army were based on newspaper reports. He pleaded for clemency, conceding that though his intentions were good there were exaggerations in his negative account of the morale of the officer corps and the decisions of the army's leadership. In support of his case, he cited five reviews of the novel from a wide range of papers, all of which commented on its patriotic sentiments. In the *Armee-Zeitung*, Carl Maria Danzer wrote in Sieber's defence, praising his intentions, but criticising his methods: 'Das größte Übel, das uns heute bedroht, ist nicht eine Schädigung unseres Renommees, sondern die Indolenz in unseren eigenen Reihen. / Jene, die "Quo vadis?" stammeln, knirschen, wüten, die haben sich noch nicht dem erschlaffenden Gleichmut ergeben'.[17] ('The greatest evil that threatens us today is not damage to our reputation, but indolence in our own ranks. Those who stammer, gnash and rage "Quo vadis?" are those who have not yet surrendered to an enervating stoicism').

Despite Sieber's credentials as a patriot, the court decided that the negative side of the rhetorical structure outweighed the positive. The novel was, thus, likely to give the naive reader a false impression. The moment of the publication was also given considerable weight by the prosecution. It is referred to as having been at the time of a political crisis ('im Zeitpunkt einer politischen Krise'), that is, the end of the Second Balkan War mentioned in the introduction to this account.[18] Nevertheless, as a result of his evident patriotism, his ill health, and the fact that he had freely confessed to being the author of the novel, Sieber was lightly treated. He was sentenced to five weeks solitary confinement ('Profosenarrest'), a heavier penalty than the usual one or two weeks' imprisonment meted out for disciplinary offences, but considerably lighter than the penalty of being cashiered which the prosecution had demanded.

The investigation of the court of honour which followed in 1915 also dealt leniently with the author. Unlike the original investigation, it was initiated after the outbreak of the war which Sieber had so keenly anticipated. This gave a very different colouring to its final assessment:

> Der Roman war zweifellos geeignet, uneingeweihte Naturen über den Zustand der Armee zu desorientieren. Nunmehr aber, wo selbst der Krieg gesprochen, den Wert der Armee und ihrer einzelnen Teile dokumentiert, und sozusagen zu Siebers Buche Stellung genommen hat — will der ehrenrätl. Ausschuß die Handlungsweise des in Rede stehenden Offiziers . . . milder beurteilen.[19]

142

[The novel certainly was of a kind to mislead the uninitiated as to the state of the army. Now, however, that war itself has spoken and documented the value of the army and its individual elements and, as it were, expressed its view of Sieber's book, the panel of the court of honour wishes to judge the actions of the officer in question more indulgently.]

The panel of officers judging the case concluded that no further action was now necessary. Military pride, so fragile in August 1913 that the complaint of a patriot seemed to cast aspersions on the state of the army, was again unshakeable.

Rudolf Jeremias Kreutz and the commissioned reply

If the story of Sieber's prosecution was a logical sequel to the censorship of his novel, then another response inspired by *Quo vadis, Austria?* provides a bizarre epilogue. In December 1913, Rudolf Jeremias Kreutz (or Kriz), an army captain and contributor to numerous satirical publications, frequently under the pseudonym 'Jeremias', was transferred to the 'Kriegsarchiv' and ordered to write a 'Gegenroman' or counterblast to *Quo vadis, Austria?* The order came, according to Kreutz's subsequent report, from Archduke Franz Ferdinand himself. While there is no contemporary documentation to prove that this was the case, there is no reason to disbelieve this part of Kreutz's account, especially when one considers that the novel's rhetorical statements concerning Austria's inability to produce a great leader might be particularly galling to the man who expected to become Emperor. However, Kreutz's later versions of the story are unreliable.[20] Certainly, whoever commissioned Kreutz was unaware that he had at that point never written a novel. Kreutz also explains that it was his articles under the pseudonym 'spectator castrensis' in the *Armee-Zeitung* that led to his being chosen for the commission.

It now seems a curious idea to follow a critical novel with a counter-polemical work, but in the context of future war stories the project makes more sense. If one's country was shown to be vulnerable in a future war novel, the obvious reply was to write a work which put an opposing view. Patriotic replies to hostile future war stories were commonplace enough in the decades leading up to the First World War. However, the commissioning of a work by a state agency (the consent of the War Ministry had to be obtained in order to give Kreutz time to write) is an exceptional case.

Unfortunately for the would-be propagandists, the details of Kreutz's commission became public knowledge before his work was complete. In March 1914, the Hungarian newspaper *Pesti Napló* revealed to its readers that a captain named Kriz (Kreutz) had been ordered to write an official reply to the banned novel *Quo vadis, Austria?*[21] A few days later, the German-language newpapers also picked up the story. A letter from the officer-writer Rudolf Hans Bartsch to Kreutz reveals how this leak may have come about. He writes that Kreutz's task was an open secret among his associates: 'Ich selber hielt also die Sache für gar keine so reservate und sprach wirklich nur aus purem Zufall mit niemand darüber, als mit zwei Kameraden des Kriegsarchivs und mit Schönpflug. . .'[22] ('So I didn't myself consider the matter to be especially confidential and only

by pure coincidence did I speak with no-one about it other than with two com-
rades from the Kriegsarchiv and with Schönpflug [the military caricaturist]...').
It is not difficult to imagine how a supposed secret could fall into the hands of
a journalist in an atmosphere where all 'Kameraden' were automatically en-
trusted with it.

Karl Kraus delivered satirical comment on the affair by reprinting an article
concerning Kreutz's unusual military duties from the *Neues Wiener Journal* of
12 March 1914. Where the *Neues Wiener Journal* expresses its liberal indignation
about the fact that Kreutz was receiving the pay of an officer on active service
for a deskbound task, Kraus approved ironically of the idea of prosecuting
officers like Sieber for writing such bad novels, whatever their intentions, and
gave an acid summary of the significance of Kreutz's commission: 'Wenn wir
schon die Literatur durch die Tendenz herabziehen, so fügen wir zum Schaden
den Spott, indem wir die Tendenz durch die Schreiberei bloßstellen'[23] ('If we
are already dragging down literature by making it serve a purpose, then we add
insult to injury by unmasking its tendentiousness by means of endless
scribbling'). Newspaper reports of its literary enterprise did not deter the War
Ministry. Indeed, publication of the details of Kreutz's planned novel brought
an offer from a Berlin publisher to print the completed text.[24] Kreutz was
ordered to continue.

Despite his later claims that the text of the commissioned work was
completed before the outbreak of war, the surviving manuscript consists of only
three chapters, though there is a complete plan showing the author's intentions.
According to a note pencilled by Kreutz on the first page of this manuscript,
he was under orders to deliver two chapters each month to a coded address
('beurlaubt an den Caldamazzo See'). By the time of the assassination in Sarajevo, only two chapters had been delivered. The novel was to appear under the
pseudonym Jeremias and to be entitled 'Wir. Ein österreichischer Offiziersro-
man'. The opening chapter portrays the return of an infantry regiment from
Bosnia and the mood of its officers. Ironically, the propaganda message of
Kreutz's 'Gegenroman' is substantially the same as Sieber's original. For
example, Kreutz's *raisonneur* says at one point:

> Wenn das so weiter geht mit uns, wenn wir in Devotion vor einem
> Parlament ersticken, das keinen Schuß Pulver wert ist, und wenn der
> Schwung allemal in uns gebrochen wird, weil die oben glauben, man
> könne schon wieder befehlen, so geht's mit uns zu Ende. [Kreutz-
> Nachlaß, 'Wir', p. 13].

> [If things go on like this for us, if we suffocate in devotion before a
> parliament that isn't worth the candle, if our vitality is finally broken
> because those at the top believe they can command again, then that will
> be the end of us].

The criticism of 'die oben' is, if anything, more emphatic and more specific than
that in *Quo vadis, Austria?* The difference lies in Kreutz's avoidance of the theme
of the need for a political strong man and his fulsome praise of the average
Habsburg officer: 'Österreichers Eigenart: Er negiert des Reiches Zukunft mit

Stirnrunzeln, unkt von Verfall and Schwäche. . . Doch wenn es heilig wird und blutig, stirbt er fast ebenso gerne, als er gerne geschimpft hatte' (p. 14). ('The Austrian's special character: he wrinkles his brow and gives a negative view of the empire's future, he grumbles about decay and weakness ... yet when it is a holy matter of blood he dies almost as eagerly as he had cursed'). The fragmentary text of Kreutz's novel leaves little doubt that 'Wir' would have proved Kraus's judgement correct.[25]

Kreutz was not the only author to write a follow-up to *Quo vadis, Austria?* Sieber himself published a patriotic play entitled *Unter Halbmond und Doppeladler* in 1914.[26] He also planned and completed a novel with the title *Das Komplott*, which was intended to testify to his patriotism and repair any damage done to the army's image by his first novel. However, war intervened and the novel was never published. Despite illness, Sieber was keen to do his patriotic duty and volunteered for active service. In 1917, he was pardoned under a general amnesty and so never had to serve his prison sentence. The last year of the war found him working as a clerk in the press office of the War Ministry, the 'Kriegspressequartier', like so many other Austro-Hungarian writers. The author of one of Austria's most patriotic novels was finally permitted to write for his country.

Notes

1. For further details of the Redl case see Robert Asprey, *The Panther's Feast* (New York, 1959), and Georg Markus, *Der Fall Redl* (Vienna, 1984).
2. *Quo vadis, Austria? Ein Roman der Resignation von einem österreichischen Offizier* (Berlin, 1913).
3. See I. F.Clarke, *Voices Prophesying War, 1763–1984* (Oxford, 1966).
4. See Solomon Wank, 'Political versus military thinking in Austria–Hungary, 1908–1912', *Peace and Change. A Journal of Peace Research*, 7 (1 & 2) (1980), 4–5.
5. See Gunther Rothenberg, *The Army of Francis Joseph* (West Lafayette, Ind., 1976), p. 84.
6. Examples may be found in the fiction of Carl Baron Torresani and Ferdinand von Saar's *Leutenant Burda*.
7. *Quo vadis, Austria?* p. 144. Klaus Theweleit's comments on marriages to a friend's sister are of interest in this respect: see Klaus Theweleit, *Männerphantasien* (Frankfurt, 1976), I, 159–61.
8. See James Joll, *The Origins of the First World War* (London, 1984), pp. 185–6.
9. The following account is based on Sieber's statements as recorded in the papers of his trial. These may be consulted at the Austrian State Archive in Vienna (Kriegsarchiv). See KA K.u.K. Divisionsgericht Wien 1914, Faszikel Nr. 9046 (hereafter referred to as 'trial papers'). The papers of the 'Ehrenrätliche Verhandlung' against Sieber are also available in the 'Kriegsarchiv': KA KM 1915 Präs. 25-6/74, KA KM 1915 Präs. 25-6/74-2, KA KM 1915 Präs. 7-50/2-55. Also relevant is Sieber's service record or 'Qualifikationsliste', Fasz. 2723.
10. 'Qualifikationsliste', Fasz. 2723.
11. Trial papers, sheet no. 276 v.
12. Sieber's *feuilletons* were short, patriotic pieces which appeared in the following issues of the *Armeeblatt*: 3 October, 28 November 1912, 9 January, 27 March, 14 August 1913.

13. Trial papers, 'Gutächtlicher Antrag', 7 May 1914, sheet no. 156 r.
14. *Quo vadis, Austria? Ein Roman der Resignation von einem österreichischen Offizier. Nach der Konfiskation gereinigter Neudruck mit Fortlassung der beanstandeten Stellen* (Berlin, 1914).
15. Trial papers, sheet nos. 198 r. and v.
16. Trial papers, letter by Sieber to Majorauditor Kunz, received by K.u.K. ·Garnisonsgericht Wien, 27 January 1914, sheet no. 072 r.
17. *Danzer's Armee-Zeitung*, 28 October 1913.
18. Trial papers, 'Gutachtlicher Antrag', 7 May 1914, sheet no. 192 v.
19. KA KM 1915 Präs. 25-6/74-2, 'Bericht und Antrag', sheet no 29 r.
20. See *Die Presse*, 30 November 1946, *Die Furche*, 16 February 1957. The chronology of these later accounts is haphazard. Also, Kreutz's claim that the novel was complete before the outbreak of war seems suspect. I am grateful to Dr Eckart Früh for allowing me to consult Kreutz's 'Nachlaß' at the Kammer für Arbeiter und Angestellte in Vienna (Sozialwissenschaftliche Dokumentation, Tagblatt-Archiv), hereafter referred to as 'Kreutz-Nachlaß'.
21. See *Pesti Napló*, 3 March 1914, 'A patriotizmus szószólói — Großösterreich az irodalomban' ('The Advocates of Patriotism — Großösterreich in Literature'). I am grateful to Dr Attila Császár of Budapest for his assistance in translating this key article.
22. Kreutz-Nachlaß, letter from Rudolf Hans Bartsch to Kreutz, 14 March 1914.
23. *Die Fackel*, 395, 28 March 1914, p. 67.
24. Kreutz-Nachlaß, letter from F. Fontane & Co. to Kreutz, 26 March 1914.
25. Kreutz later wrote a play entitled *Der befohlene Roman* based on the story behind the commissioned novel. The text, completed in 1932, was never published and is available in Kreutz-Nachlaß. See also *Neues Wiener Tagblatt*, 24 October 1931.
26. Gustav Sieber, *Unter Halbmond und Doppeladler* (Berlin, 1914).

Part Two
Review Articles

Wittgenstein in Context

J. P. Stern

Brian McGuinness, *Wittgenstein: A Life*, I: *Young Ludwig (1889–1921)* (London: Duckworth, 1988), xiv + 322pp. £15.95.

Brian McGuinness, *Wittgensteins frühe Jahre*, tr. Joachim Schulte (Frankfurt: Suhrkamp, 1988), 492pp. DM 78.

J. C. Nyíri, *Am Rande Europas: Studien zur österreichisch-ungarischen Philosophiegeschichte* (Vienna, Graz, Cologne: Böhlau, 1988), 236pp. 280 Sch.

David Pears, *The False Prison: A Study of the Development of Wittgenstein's Philosophy*, I (Oxford: Clarendon Press, 1987), xii + 202pp. £6.95.

I

To place Ludwig Wittgenstein's philosophical writings in the history of European thought is an undertaking beset by difficulties. The first and most obvious of these derives from the fact that Wittgenstein himself published only one book, *Logisch-philosophische Abhandlung* (1921), better known as the *Tractatus Logico-Philosophicus*, the title G. E. Moore gave the book when it appeared in London in 1922, with an introduction by Bertrand Russell and a parallel English translation by C. K. Ogden. After his death in Cambridge in 1951, all his other works, beginning with *Philosophical Investigations* (Oxford, 1953), the manuscript of which is said to be lost, were published from a *Nachlaß* of some 13 000 pages of brief notes, reflections, and diary entries.[1] In the posthumous editions, these reflections are arranged in accordance with the philosopher's own intentions when these intentions are known; at other times the editors have had to rely on their own sense of the work, their task being made difficult by Wittgenstein's own doubts about the usefulness of any conventional arrangement:

> If I am thinking about a topic just for myself and not with a view to writing a book, I jump about all round it; that is the only way of thinking that comes naturally to me. Forcing my thoughts into an ordered sequence is a torment to me. Is it even worth attempting?
>
> I *squander* an unspeakable amount of effort making an arrangement of my thoughts, which may have no value at all.[2]

To complicate matters further, there are several volumes of lecture notes taken by Wittgenstein's students, in one of which (1933–4) the question of a systematic approach is raised:

> There is a truth in Schopenhauer's view that philosophy is an organism, and that a book on philosophy, with a beginning and an end, is a sort of contradiction. One difficulty with philosophy is that we lack a synoptic view. We encounter the kind of difficulty we should have with the

geography of a country for which we had no map, or else a map of isolated bits. The country we are talking about is language, and the geography is grammar. We can walk about the country quite well, but when forced to make a map, we go wrong. A map will show different roads through the same country, any one of which we can take, though not two, just as in philosophy we must take up problems one by one, though in fact each problem leads to a multitude of others. We must wait until we come round to the starting point before we can proceed to another section, that is, before we can either treat the problem we first attacked or proceed to another. In philosophy matters are not simple enough for us to say, 'Let's get a rough idea', for we do not know the country except by knowing the connections between the roads. So I suggest repetition as a means of surveying the connections.[3]

Overlaps, repetitions, and rearrangements are, thus, integral parts of 'a new conception of the way to do philosophy', whereas *a book* (such as the *Tractatus*) is, in David Pears's words:

an artificial break in a continuous development, like a still excerpted from a film. It must be remembered that [Wittgenstein] always found great difficulty in putting his thoughts in linear order to make the kind of treatise that is expected from a philosopher. They are interrelated in too many ways for the usual two-dimensional linear arrangement. That is one reason why he always had to struggle to make a book the natural expression of his thoughts. But there is also another, connected reason: his thoughts live in his notebooks, and form their relations with one another slowly over many years. A work published by him is, therefore, an artificial cut in a continuous process of growth, and, instead of treating either of his two great books [i.e. the *Tractatus* and *Philosophical Investigations*] as a definitive revelation, we ought to trace their ideas back to their points of germination and then move forward again, following the gradual process of growth in their own ecosystem [p. 192].

Similar considerations apply to Nietzsche's large posthumously published *oeuvre*: its fate demonstrates not only the need to make connections between disconnected notes, but also the danger of getting some of these connections wrong. In spite of some recent problematic editing of Wittgenstein's *Nachlaß*, one fervently hopes that the scandalous editorial practices which Nietzsche's work suffered for more than half a century will not be repeated.

A second difficulty relates to the dual 'background' of Wittgenstein's thinking. For many years we were presented with two Wittgensteins: a rigorously 'scientific' Anglo-Saxon logician, and an Austrian or Continental philosopher with 'mystical' leanings. Of the 'Cambridge' or 'scientific' philosopher, it was said that he was concerned with questions involving the relationship between facts and ideas and their representation in everyday language, with enquiries into the rules according to which we form pictures of the world, and with the difference between 'saying' things and 'showing' them or 'making them manifest'. This procedure involved above all determinations of the *logical* limits of language, for at the centre of the *Tractatus* lies the view that 'language cannot contain an analysis of the conditions of its own application,' (Pears, *op.cit.* p. 11). The 'mystical' thinker was said to be concerned with how to live the good life, what to do in the face of temptation and sin, how to endure solitude and (more difficult) how to endure company; what it is to have faith in God, and what it is to lack such faith. In this version much was made of the *ineffable* limits of language. Such questions are not actually discussed in the two books which Wittgenstein himself prepared for publication, but, of course, once you concentrate your reading entirely on 'mysticism' and ignore the rest, anything goes. It is one of the great merits of Brian McGuinness's biography that it disposes of this particular modish quandary; and so, in a different way, does J. C. Nyíri's study; in Pears's meticulous analysis of the *Tractatus* the question doesn't arise.

But there is a third difficulty. Wittgenstein wrote within a highly history-conscious culture, and in a massively politicised age. Yet the very few political reflections he confided to his letters and diaries are quirky rather than illuminating, and, compared with everything else he wrote, unremarkable. And what he says about history (again mainly in the diaries, and in the prefaces to some of his works) are little more than expressions of a heartfelt regret for the passing of more dignified and more *decent* ages. Professor Nyíri is right to call these views conservative, Viennese, and Austrian, but this does not make them original or profound. Both original and profound, however, are Wittgenstein's methodological observations, which, without necessarily mentioning history, are relevant to cultural enquiries of every kind.

What I have in mind is, above all, the method of family resemblances which Wittgenstein devised in order to do away with Procrustean generalisations (those which rely on the lowest common denominator or an invariable set of defining qualities). He replaces such generalisations by what has recently been called 'sporadic resemblances',[4] or again by the 'polythetic method', a method which shares 'a number of common characteristics, without any of these being essential for membership of the group or class in question'.[5] Wittgenstein offers several models of classification by family resemblances: in the lectures which came to be known as *The Blue Book* (1933–4), he speaks of our ability to recognise the members of one family because 'some of them have the same nose, others the same eyebrows, and others again the same way of walking', and others again (we may add) bear the same name — 'and these likenesses overlap'.[6] A second version of the same principle occurs in *Philosophical Investigations*, §67:[7] 'the strength of [a] thread does not reside in the fact that some one fibre runs through its whole length, but in the overlapping of many fibres,' and a third in §71 of the same book, where Wittgenstein writes of the advantages, *for a specific purpose*, of 'a concept with blurred edges' and then asks, 'Is it even always an advantage to replace an indistinct picture by a sharp one? Isn't the indistinct one often exactly what we need?'

These are some of the models Wittgenstein uses in applying his discovery to a variety of problems which had previously been dealt with by 'categorical' or 'monothetic' definitions. The method has been traced back to eighteenth-century taxonomy,[8] and examples of it may be found in Nietzsche, Benedetto

Croce, and, no doubt, in many others. Yet the convincing way Wittgenstein sets out the advantages of this procedure, along 'different roads through the same country' of language, the detailed way we can trace its development in his reflections, and the significance it has for his entire later philosophy – all these make me think that it will always, and justly, be associated with his name. Surprisingly, Professor Nyíri virtually ignores it. Its importance for every kind of synchronic or diachronic enquiry is obvious: it alone offers the means of preserving the significance of the single phenomenon. Avoiding what Wittgenstein calls 'the contemptuous attitude towards the particular case',[9] it gives the particular case its meaning as an element in a coherent and perspicuous, surveyable ('übersichtlich') picture.[10] In other words: the method offers a remedy against avoidable abstraction; which is what 'Geistesgeschichte' – a history of ideas constructed from trends and movements and 'isms' – so often fails to do.

II

The first aim of Professor Kristóf Nyíri's book is to describe, document, and illustrate the Austrian or Central European alternative to German (or Prussian, or Kantian) Idealism. This alternative arises at the end of the Enlightenment because (as Nyíri observes in the first of the five essays which make up his book) 'for the Austrian citizen the very abstract form of Kantian Idealism does not represent a natural direction of his thinking' (p. 178); and from this perception Nyíri proceeds to a confrontation of an Austrian Catholicism of good works with Luther's 'solifidianist' Protestantism. Abstraction is an important aspect of categorical or 'monothetic' generalisations. At this point Nyíri offers an outstandingly clear example of an argument conducted along 'polythetic' lines in a quotation from one of his heroes, the 'progressive Conservative' Graf Stephan Széchenyi, who discusses four different kinds of 'understanding' which overlap and are perfectly compatible with each other.[11] However, seeing that the quotation is tucked away in a footnote (p. 180), one cannot be sure whether Nyíri appreciates its relevance to Wittgenstein's method – or its philosophical importance as an example of *concrete* thinking.

However that may be, no other method is likely to do justice to what he is concerned with, to wit, the structure of a tradition: consciously or not, he shows the time and place in which the method provides the structure of richly variegated 'anthropological conservatism'. Founded in hallowed custom and a religious order of things, this is an inherently anti-ideological, Burkean tradition. And — this is the second aim of Nyíri's book – it is in this tradition that Wittgenstein's writings are to be placed, even though (as I have suggested) Wittgenstein himself is never directly concerned with either politics or history.

Professor Nyíri teaches the history of philosophy in the University of Budapest; he has edited some of Georg Lukács's writings, and has worked extensively in the Wittgenstein archives in Trinity College, Cambridge. He is thus singularly well placed to undertake the double task I have mentioned, but his study does not make for easy reading.[12] Nevertheless, given the rich variety of the material and its relative inaccessibility, its blemishes do not finally impair the book's considerable originality and interest.

Nyíri's first chapter outlines a brief history of 'Austrian conservative thinking' about man in society from the end of the eighteenth century through five generations to the second half of Wittgenstein's work, and to the writings of his cousin, F. A. Hayek (said by some to be Mrs Thatcher's guru). This, not counting an unconvincing attempt to make Freud an honorary member of a Viennese Primrose League, is one of the best chapters in the book. It includes an illuminating outline of the differences between Western and Eastern European feudalism, of the economic and social consequences of different forms of land tenure, and of the different political functions of religious reformers; and in his succinct accounts of the writings of two eminent Hungarian social critics, Graf Stephan Széchenyi (1791–1860) and Joseph Eötvös (1813–71), Nyíri presents Central European political thinking at its best. The following chapter is less convincing. One of its main subjects is an improbable compound of Wagnerian dramatist, Professor of Philosophy, and prophet of a new 'Eastern' Protestantism, called Christian von Ehrenfels (1859–1932): a figure somewhat dwarfed by being provided with a background of a thousand years of socio-economic and political history. Next, T. G. Masaryk's first study, on suicide in the modern world (1879), is convincingly related to his speculations on 'the spirit of Russia' and 'the spirit of the Czech nation', and Nyíri justly criticises the moralising and normative purpose of these speculations. The chapter on Ludwig Wittgenstein's father, presented as the most influential figure in the history of heavy industry in Central Europe, seems to belong to the unattractive history of *laissez-faire* capitalism, but it provides a family background for the topic of the next (fourth) chapter, the philosopher's 'conservative anthropology', to which I shall return. The working notes towards a book on Dostoevsky which the young Georg (still: von) Lukács sent to Paul Ernst (*c.* 1914) form the subject of Nyíri's last chapter; Lukács's book was never written, and the notes illustrate the rigidity and aridness of his literary criticism as well as the perceptiveness of his political understanding, even before he placed both in the service of Marxism. Through these chapters, nationalism tends to be seen in economic terms; its uneasy relationship with conservatism is not mentioned.

It will be readily seen from this sketchy outline that whatever went by the name of 'philosophy' in *this* Austrian tradition has very little in common with what Wittgenstein wrote. The genre called 'philosophy of history' which came into being in Central Europe in the wake of Herder (and of which the Czech historian, Frantisek Palacky (1798–1876) and Masaryk are the most famous practitioners) makes for tendentious history and unsubstantiated speculative philosophy alike. (Nyíri quotes [p. 24] a spirited attack by the young Franz Grillparzer on Hegelianism, which ends with a lament for the loss of philosophical sobriety and wit: 'O Lichtenberg, Lichtenberg, why wert thou reft so early from our native land?') Wittgenstein's programme is very different: 'In philosophy it is always a question of applying a series of extremely simple principles which are known to every child, and the only – albeit enormous – difficulty is to apply them amidst the confusion created by our language.'[13] This, too, is the way Bernard Bolzano (1781–1848), the first and only important

'Austrian' philosopher of the age, saw his task: 'to discover the objective ground of that which we already know with the greatest certainty and concreteness'.[14] But Bolzano is not mentioned in Nyíri's book.

III

Brian McGuinness's first volume contains the most detailed and by far the most reliable portrayal we have of Ludwig Wittgenstein's life up to the publication of the *Tractatus* in 1921, the only work of his to appear during his lifetime. It is a pleasure to note that the German translation, *Wittgensteins frühe Jahre*, by Joachim Schulte, is both elegant and accurate; it also contains a number of quotations from Wittgenstein's diaries and letters not included in the book's English version.

The greatest merit of Brian McGuinness's long-awaited book is that it firmly focuses on the connection between Wittgenstein's early philosophy and his life. Instead of the lurid gossip purveyed by at least one of his predecessors, McGuinness has written a philosopher's biography, at the centre of which lies the cardinal achievement of the first half of Wittgenstein's life, the *Tractatus*: mentioned only briefly by Nyíri, it is seen by McGuinness as the answer to its author's philosophical and existential problems. The 'logic' of that work is presented as the form and content of a philosophy. Abstract, schematic, and aphoristic it may be but, for the reader who learns how to read it (and even for one who skips the middle mathematical sections), it is rich in insight, and comprehensive. Though the style of McGuinness's remarkable book is that of a searching and abundantly documented biography, it has a polemical vein. This was a difficult life (the biographer is saying), it was difficult to live and it is difficult to describe, but there is nothing scurrilous about it.

It is, indeed, difficult to present convincingly a life cast in superlatives. The Wittgensteins, German and three-quarters Jewish by origin but Protestant by declared allegiance, were among the three or four wealthiest families in the Austro-Hungarian Monarchy. Karl Wittgenstein, the philosopher's father, was outstandingly successful both as an engineer and entrepreneur. The family houses in Vienna and Lower Austria were among the most lavishly appointed and fashionably designed of *fin-de-siècle* Vienna. Here Brahms and the Joachim Quartet 'made music', and some of Vienna's greatest artists were frequent guests. The acquisition of the vast family fortune (described also by Nyíri) was as dramatic as the philosopher's repeated renunciations of his share of it, his periods of ascetic withdrawal as untoward as his generosity to friends and his anonymous gifts. Momentous family conflicts, assertions of independence, and suicides abound. His father's choice of the Technische Hochschule in Berlin–Charlottenburg and of the University of Manchester for young Wittgenstein's engineering studies is as unusual as the student's approach to Gottlob Frege (1848–1925), then a largely unknown professor of mathematical logic at the University of Jena, whose posthumous fame places him among the greatest logicians since Aristotle; and the willingness of the old and reclusive Frege to discuss his own work with a young man 'whose mathematical education and sophistication barely qualified him to discuss mathematics' (p. 76) is as surprising as Frege's readiness to recommend that young man to Bertrand Russell at Cambridge. There is something superlative, too, about the bravery Wittgenstein showed and the deprivations he endured throughout four years of the First World War, and the subsequent months as a prisoner of war in Northern Italy and at Monte Cassino. Among the most moving passages in the book are McGuinness's descriptions of the hardships Wittgenstein bore on the Russian front, which 'gave him the sunken face that was to mark him for the rest of his life'; at the age of twenty-six he appeared 'no longer as a serious young man but as one who had suffered deeply' (p. 238). His mental suffering during that war was heightened by his awareness that most of the troops among whom he served were recruited from the Slavonic parts of the Empire, and, therefore, hostile to the cause for which they were supposed to be ready to lay down their lives; and his deep unhappiness was further increased by his early conviction, born of his knowledge of England, that the Austrians were fighting a war they could not win. Wittgenstein's war diaries, in which he records some of the horrendous events around him side by side with his philosophical ideas, reflect the greatest exaction of all: these years of mortal danger and all but annihilating doubt are the years, too, when the notes for the *Tractatus* and parts of the book itself were written.

In all this – Wittgenstein is thirty-two at the end of this first volume – are there no scandalous love affairs, no homosexual liaisons, no occasions for Freudian disclosures, not even a night out in a Viennese brothel? The answer to the prurient question is that, since McGuinness does not choose to entertain us with unfounded conjectures, we do not know; he is, as things go, an unfashionable biographer. He acknowledges much help from friends and members of the Wittgenstein family, and tells us that he has had full access to documents of every kind. As with two other recent outstanding biographies of the same time and place, Peter Gay's *Freud* and Edward Timms's *Karl Kraus*, we come away with the impression that the material that is still kept under lock and key by relations or archivists is not likely to alter the picture we form from what has been made available.

IV

To return to the two Wittgensteins – the severe logician and the 'mystic'. It is a part of McGuinness's argument that such a dichotomy is bound to be misleading, but we can think of instances where it may be justified. Detaching the philosophy from the life, we can picture a logician whose biography has nothing to do with his professional achievement. Gottlob Frege's is one of the two most powerful influences the young Wittgenstein encountered in his search for a meaningful vocation. Yet Frege's paramount discovery of a reliable common notation for logic and mathematics, together with his later work on the foundation of both, seem to be wholly unrelated to what we know of his biography; his immense achievements receive no added illumination from a knowledge of his sad and dispiriting personal circumstances, or frcm his anti-Catholic and anti-Semitic prejudices. Bertrand Russell (the other major influence on Wittgenstein) wrote a number of popular books which reflect his pacifist stand in the First World War, his marital problems, his experiments as an educator, and his politics; in a 'Reply to My Critics' of 1944 Russell writes that he sees 'no necessary connection between my views on social questions and my views on logic and epistemology'[15]: the work which formed the basis of Russell's close friendship with Wittgenstein and which made him think of Wittgenstein as his successor is unrelated to what he called 'my shilling shockers' (McGuinness, p. 107). Much has recently been written about Martin Heidegger's wholly reprehensible involvement in, and compromises with, National Socialism, and his subsequent refusal to retract or to give a truthful account of them, and there is a very obvious sense in which one may say that his political views and his personal actions in the twelve years of the Third Reich are both wholly unbecoming his calling as a philosopher.[16] Yet Heidegger's philosophy contains profound (and it may be unparalleled) insights into the impasse to which our technology is leading us, and the validity of these insights is unaffected not only by his personal conduct but also by those of his philosophical views which must now be read as attempts at justifying his own peculiar version of National Socialism.

The dichotomy is plausible in another sense, too. Focusing our attention on the life, we shall find that detaching it from the philosophical work is a way of making it available to literature. Thus, the sheer *interest* of Wittgenstein's strenuous life, with its rejections and self-imposed severities, resembling in so many ways the life of Adrian Leverkühn, the hero of Thomas Mann's *Doctor Faustus*, may constitute the narrative of a novel that need not take issue with the philosopher's 'professional' work. (At least two such fictions of the life have, in fact, been written; and the late Thomas Bernhard has written a weird play, *Ritter, Dene, Voss* (1986), which conveys not a single philosophical idea of Wittgenstein's while presenting his passionate commitment as a form of certified insanity.) There is a literariness about Wittgenstein's philosophical undertaking which McGuinness notes but does not fully explore.

To speak of Wittgenstein's philosophical passion is only another way of saying that he was not a 'professional' philosopher in this restricted sense of the word; of this sort of professionalism he was deeply contemptuous. The act of will by which he committed his life to the work is manifest on almost every page of McGuinness's book, which is guided throughout by the recognition that the biographer cannot be content to present the man as distinct from the philosopher. Without recourse to fiction or scandal, though not of course without reasonable conjectures clearly marked as such, McGuinness pursues his argument to the points where the two meet, and where he can show that such a division goes, not indeed against the arguments of the *Tractatus*, but against the spirit and ultimate intention of Wittgenstein himself. The biographer's intention is to take the writing of the *Tractatus* out of the realm of contingency at least to the extent of demonstrating that this man with this life was uniquely fitted to write this book.

Does McGuinness succeed? In a general sense he does. Working hard not to lose the reader who is not a philosopher, he shows how the *Tractatus* really fulfils the promise implied in its first sentence, by being about 'everything that is the case' – that is, the world seen in the mode of its logical relations. And this 'everything' will, of course, include the logical structure of the propositions of 'factual language' (the phrase is David Pears's) made in, and constituting, the life of the author of the *Tractatus*. But to acknowledge this general sense in which McGuinness is successful is not the same as acknowledging that there is a necessary relationship between the life and the work. If we ask the pertinent question at this point – what is there in the *Tractatus* by way of specific detail, which only this man, at home in this particular life and world, could have written? – we can see some areas where the biography offers specific answers to that question, and others which are less directly related to it. (I mean answers over and above the obvious one, that only a man of genius could have attempted the task undertaken in the *Tractatus*.)

Did Wittgenstein want his biography to be written? McGuinness conjectures – convincingly, I think – that he did, and my guess is that he might have approved of McGuinness as its author. But what is also clear, beyond conjecture, are the serious obstacles the author of the *Tractatus* puts in any biographer's way. For, of course, one of the things the *Tractatus* is about, especially in its second half, are the limits of our language: Wittgenstein's book reflects his abundantly reasoned insistence that the kind of language whose logical relations it explores is not available for the discussion of the problems of our existence whenever these are formulated as ethical, aesthetic, or religious problems; is not, therefore, available for substantial parts of McGuinness's undertaking. And this insistence on the limits of what can be clearly said, which is argued ever more strongly as the *Tractatus* moves towards its concluding negations, issues in the claim that, apart from the kind of language examined in the book, there is no other – there is only waffle (in his diaries Wittgenstein uses the homely Austrian term, 'Schwefeln') or silence. McGuinness neither waffles nor is he silent. But in his endeavour to connect the life and the work, and to be as accurate as possible about both, he is bound to write against the grain of the *Tractatus*.

V

Thinking about the limits of language – as opposed to the rigorous logical grounding of such thinking – is not original to Wittgenstein. Philosophy in Austria (I have suggested) begins almost precisely at the time of the dissolution of the Holy Roman Empire, with the work of the Bohemian priest, Bernard Bolzano. In this first phase it is (as Nyíri observes, p. 178) a reaction against German idealism in general and the Kantian critique in particular. Bolzano's effort (in his *Wissenschaftslehre* of 1825) had been directed towards replacing Kant's concept of an unknowable 'Ding an sich' by arguing for our ability to conceive of 'truths-in-themselves'.[17] But in many of his popular writings and sermons Bolzano was concerned with language – language seen not as an abstract philosophical problem, but as a social and political phenomenon. After Bolzano, philosophy as written, taught, and discussed in Vienna becomes increasingly an enquiry into what German idealism had ignored – it becomes a philosophical enquiry into the role played by language in experience. At much the same time, however, this enquiry, in *fin-de-siècle* Vienna and only there, ceases to be confined to philosophy and theoretical thinking about the natural sciences and technology, and is taken up in journalism, fiction, and polemical writings on the borderline between the two. This is the background which offers a partial but very specific answer to one of the questions asked in McGuinness's book: the question, 'Why should this man write a philosophical treatise, the central claim of which is that philosophy is nothing other than a critique of language?' Because at some point he comes to feel the need to make all this talk (some of it mere chatter) about language and its limits more precise. McGuinness is right to distinguish (pp. 251 ff) between contemporary Viennese polemics against the abuses of language conducted by the literati and politicians, and Wittgenstein's fundamental critique of it. The difference is, roughly, between seeing language as the source of evil and seeing it as the source of nonsense. But there is a family resemblance between these different kinds of critical language consciousness.

What I have called McGuinness's partial but specific answer to the question of Viennese language consciousness is one way of converting contingent biographical facts into necessary aspects of the philosophy. Still, the broader question remains: if, for Wittgenstein, *logic* is such a fundamental and all-embracing preoccupation as it is here claimed to be (not only a formal concern, but the content of the philosophy), can biography account for that? The short answer is that in Wittgenstein's preoccupation with logic a personal passion and a sense of duty are combined. The fuller answer which McGuinness's account of the first half of Wittgenstein's life suggests goes something like this:

(I) Here is a thinker who is at *almost* every point in his life visited by a sense of duties imposed on him, accepted and (judged by his own uncompromising standards) inadequately discharged. It is this sense which dominates McGuinness's account of Wittgenstein's relations with his family and friends, and especially his portrait of the philosopher's energetic, unconventional, and ambitious father. Such a portrait, in our day and age, can hardly be drawn without some help from Freud, but it is mercifully free from Freudian stereotype, jargon, and theory.

(II) Closely connected with this sense of a moral duty perceived and accepted are several extended references, based on his diaries and letters, to Wittgenstein's religious sense, which was perhaps awakened and certainly intensified by the war experience. And just as Wittgenstein's acknowledgement of moral duties is almost always accompanied by a sense of moral inadequacy, so the religious sense is almost always accompanied by a consciousness of sin. Though Wittgenstein rejected any institutional religious framework (remaining a stranger to institutions of any kind), his reading of Tolstoy and, perhaps more directly, of Dostoevsky and Kierkegaard, leaves one in no doubt that this religious sense was Christian.

(III) At some point, probably during his time as a student at the Technische Hochschule in Berlin (October 1906–May 1908), certainly during his time as a research engineer at Manchester (1908, with interruptions, until 1911), a

powerful philosophical ambition is awakened. Exactly how this happened is not clear. All McGuinness can say is that the move away from engineering was not caused by mathematical difficulties Wittgenstein encountered while experimenting (somewhat haphazardly, it appears) with kites and aeroplanes (p. 76). The interest in the connections between mathematics and logic was perhaps kindled, and certainly intensified, first by Frege and then by Russell, and it was this interest that took Wittgenstein, in the autumn of 1911, to Cambridge. These influences are not presented as sufficient reasons for his finding of a vocation, yet without them the philosophical achievement of a lifetime is unthinkable.

These three aspects of the young Wittgenstein's life and mind, including the religious, all point in the same direction. They offer different reasons why he conceived of his duty as a philosopher – his duty towards logic – 'religiously', that is, in the most rigorous and exacting manner. That this view of the philosopher's task did not change is confirmed by what Wittgenstein wrote in the 1940 Preface to *Philosophical Remarks* (not, it will be noted, in the book itself): 'I would like to say that "this book was written in honour of God"', but then he adds, with the bitterness with which he came to view Western civilisation, that 'this would nowadays be an infamy, i.e. it would not be understood correctly'.[18]

(IV) But a further aspect of this mind, mentioned by Mr McGuinness only in passing, must be considered. To some readers, especially to those who, like the present reviewer, are not philosophers, the most admirable and stimulating aspect of Wittgenstein's work is his capacity to muster a rich array of analogies and images, to see one set of ideas under the aspect of another: 'What I invent are new *metaphors [Gleichnisse]*.' [19] Often such images are not merely illustrations, but form the coda of the argument. (This capacity for lateral thinking he shared with the philosophical aphorist Georg Christoph Lichtenberg, though he gave one little thanks for pointing this out;[20] and it is a matter of regret that McGuinness's remarks on Lichtenberg are perfunctory.) This gift, which is one of the main sources of Wittgenstein's philosophical achievement, was fully developed by the time the *Tractatus* received its final shape. After all, the core of the book is formed by the insight (or, to use Lichtenberg's word, 'Einfall') that sentences are pictures; that the relationship between language and the world becomes clearer and ceases to be mystifying as soon as we see language as having a structure in some significant ways similar to the structure of the world; as soon as we see propositions in the same light as facts: 'A gramophone record, the musical idea, the written notes, and the sound-waves, all stand to one another in the same internal relation of depicting that holds between language and the world. They are all constructed according to a common logical plan.' The criticism of this view, as well as of the book as a whole, the biographer leaves for his second volume.

VI

If that gift for metaphor and analogy was as central to Wittgenstein's genius as I am suggesting, the question arises how it is related to the moral and religious elements in his thinking. And the answer must surely be that it is not, at least not in any determinable way; that the imagination (the gift for metaphor and analogy) is, in all of us, a free-floating, *wertfrei*, amoral gift. Its origin is akin to the origin of poetry: to paraphrase T. S. Eliot's famous formulation, it lies in a tradition disrupted *and* enriched by an individual talent. It can be placed in the service of ethical thinking and need not be indifferent to it, but it is unpredictable and indeterminable in its effects on it. Some pictures which the imagination conjures up mislead, others do not; beauty and ugliness and truth and lies are permutable. This may well be a truth about life and ourselves to which Wittgenstein felt incapable of reconciling himself, which he felt it his *duty* to deny.

Such a view of the imagination and of the aesthetic, its product, seems to run counter to Wittgenstein's philosophy of 'social contextualism'. This is Professor Nyíri's term (p. 131) to indicate Wittgenstein's central insight that 'language games' of all kinds are to be understood neither as mainly, or purely, mental acts, nor again as mainly, or purely, physical events, but as events which belong to the rich and varied whole contexts of socially embedded and institutionalised individual lives. (This insight, incidentally, is not all that distant from Heidegger's anti-mentalist phenomenology of skills and crafts and work.)[22] But why (one might object to this notion of a value-indifferent and in a sense free-floating nature of metaphors) should the imagination be exempt from this 'social contextualism'? Because metaphors are by their nature only tenuously connected with common situations. They are minute sorties which the imagination conducts against accepted rules, traditions, and social contexts and their laws, in order to illuminate these rules and contexts and laws, or in order to modify them and make them more precise: metaphors help our understanding by illuminating all 'forms of life', of which language is one ('Die Analogie . . .', says Wittgenstein, 'steckt uns ein Licht auf.' *Philosophische Untersuchungen*, § 83). They may fail to do this, or again they may succeed only much later, for another generation of readers or spectators; today's surrealism may become tomorrow's realism, a promise unredeemed is still a promise. The delight metaphors and the imagination yield is immediate, but this does not exempt them *finally* from the order of the contexts in which they appear, and which their appearance disrupts and may eventually alter. Hence, Wittgenstein's unease with Shakespeare: the reluctant admirer seems to trust neither the moments of instant delight nor the achievement of order deferred (least of all when these are described by 'a thousand professors of literature').[23] Any help from literary criticism – that is, from a discursive, non-aphoristic account of what happens when we read a text – is dismissed.

This mention of the imagination takes our argument to the frontier between philosophy and literature. It places in the foreground the figure of Karl Kraus, the Viennese satirist whose entire *oeuvre* constantly reiterates its author's conviction that the imagination is an absolute value in itself; that it is inseparably bound up with morality; or, in terms of the *Tractatus*, that 'ethics and aesthetics are one and the same' (6.421), or would be one and the same if there were a meaningful way of discussing them.

McGuinness mentions Wittgenstein's pre-war reading of Kraus's satirical periodical, *Die Fackel (The Torch)*, and his disastrous meeting with the satirist himself (p. 281). In the course of that meeting – there was probably only one, and it probably took place in 1919, after Wittgenstein's return from Italian captivity – Wittgenstein is reported as having accused Kraus of 'repulsive vanity', while Kraus is said to have taken Wittgenstein for a madman. Kraus certainly had no inkling of Wittgenstein's philosophical undertaking, and little understanding for the distaste Wittgenstein felt towards the coterie around the embattled satirist. As for Wittgenstein, what had changed his favourable pre-war view of Kraus's writing – his admiration of 'the man and his style' (McGuinness, p. 37) that is, the unity of 'ethics and aesthetics' – was his own traumatic war experience. Did he now feel that Kraus's 'repulsive vanity' was proof that he (Kraus) had not suffered as much? This was the kind of accusation Kraus was all too ready to launch against others. Embarrassingly, the post-war years in Austria and Germany abound with flauntings of suffering and self-sacrifice. It is a period in which many (like Joseph Roth) could not reconcile themselves to the new Central Europe that arose on the ruins of the defeated Empire, while others (like Kraus in the aftermath of the war) looked back on that Empire as a rotten state and its defeat as the deserved outcome of its history of iniquities and ineptitudes. It is very unlikely that Wittgenstein shared either of these views, and it is certain that he would have found the appeal to 'the supreme sacrifice' and to 'das Fronterlebnis' (the main plank of Hitler's and his contemporaries' political platform) morally *and* aesthetically repulsive; something it would not be proper to talk about: 'If you make a sacrifice and pride yourself on it, then both you and your sacrifice will be damned.'[24]

McGuinness sees Kraus's satirical undertaking as 'something very Austrian, and something, we can now see, very Wittgensteinian – to achieve a kind of moral reform of life and thought without attempting to alter the conditions of life' (pp. 205f). Too little troubled by what he calls its 'unworldliness', McGuinness describes this attempt at reform as 'an important discovery that the revolution needed (however impossible it might be) was not one in institutions but in the thinking and sensibility – Kraus would say in the language – of men'. I doubt whether this is really 'an important discovery', it looks more like a chimera. Distrust of institutions and lack of positive interest in them are a feature of Kraus's *and* Wittgenstein's thinking for the rest of their lives. This means that the 'social contextualism' which Nyíri sets up as the central insight of Wittgenstein's later philosophy needs to be qualified: Wittgenstein is more often concerned with emphasising the need for setting up such contexts beyond the reach of all psycho-physical dualisms than with working them out in concrete detail. To this lack of interest, however, there is an important exception: the discovery of language as an institution (recognised as such by Bolzano, but not by Frege)[25], a discovery which will not become a philosophical issue until the second half of Wittgenstein's *oeuvre*. Kraus's satire is built from the converse of the 'truth–beauty' equation. The cliché – the main butt of Kraus's satire – is seen not merely as ugly, but as the unfailing linguistic indication of moral turpitude; the satirist need do no more than show up the cliché for what it is, deconstruct it, to reveal the truth – always the ugly truth – about its author-perpetrator. Paul Engelmann, Wittgenstein's closest wartime friend, saw Wittgenstein's analysis of language as the philosophical analogue of Kraus's satirical sorties (McGuinness, p. 251). However that may be, by the time Wittgenstein returned from the war, Kraus's procedure had ceased to be of interest to him; in later years he thought it tediously repetitious.

VII

The belief in the inadequacy of language and the search for the unsayable, 'the mystical', was fashionable in the literature of the time. We find it in Rilke's poetry, in Hofmannsthal, and in Robert Musil's prose. The paradox of Rilke's poetic variations on 'das Unsägliche' (in the 'Ninth Duino Elegy') is adumbrated in a comment of Wittgenstein's on a very different poem, by Ludwig Uhland (1787-1862): 'If only you do not try to utter what is unutterable, then *nothing* gets lost. But the unutterable will be – unutterably – *contained* in what has been uttered.'[26] McGuinness relates this statement directly to the concept of 'showing' in the *Tractatus*:

> 4.12 Propositions can represent the whole of reality, but they cannot represent what they must have in common with reality in order to be able to represent it – logical form . . .
> 4.121 Propositions cannot represent logical form: it is mirrored in them. What finds its reflection in language, language cannot represent. What expresses *itself* in language, *we* cannot express by means of language. Propositions *show* the logical form of reality. They display it.

Now McGuinness's point, supported by quotations from the diaries and letters, is that these central passages of the *Tractatus* are 'wedded' to Wittgenstein's feeling for literature (p. 251); and this may well be true in a general sense. But the concern with the limits of language expressed in this quotation is surely of a very different kind, and it is not at all clear how it might be related to a 'feeling for literature'.

Uhland's ballad, 'Count Eberhard's Hawthorn' (the poem Wittgenstein loved well enough to recite thirty years later) tells the story of a German knight who, on his pilgrimage to the Holy Land, cut a spray of hawthorn and stuck it in his helmet. On his return he planted the spray in the soil of his native Württemberg and watched it grow into a majestic tree. Sitting beneath the tree, the old man would dream and remember his pilgrimage of long ago.

True, my prosy retelling of the story does little to recreate the charm of Uhland's poem. Attempting to indicate what is 'unutterably contained' in the poem, one would wish to say something about the way the life of the tree retraces and encompasses the passage of years, symbolises a lifetime. In such an analysis, too, something would be lost, though the loss would be diminished by one's pointing to that part of the poem which shows that the old count himself is reminded by the tree's arching branches of the past ('Die Wölbung, hoch und breit, /Mit sanftem Rauschen mahnt / Ihn an die alte Zeit / Und an das ferne Land'); in other words, the critical account would show that the poem itself

162

explicitly initiates its symbolic interpretation by using a part of its narrative to hint at what we would call the interpreter's 'meta-language'. And still the loss entailed by the prosy version would remain, yet a renewed reading of the poem would be enriched by what has been said about its symbolic meaning. I am not suggesting that critical analysis can replace the poem; but in the course of it 'the unutterable' becomes *relative* – relative to the skill and tact of the analysis – and therefore what remains unsaid is quite different from what remains unsaid because it is impossible for propositions to represent 'the logical form that is mirrored in them'.

What is involved, then, are two very different kinds of 'the unutterable', two different concerns with the limits of language. One has its grounds in the logic of the *Tractatus*; and the notion of a philosophical 'meta-language', considered but not named at the end of Bertrand Russell's 1921 introduction to the book, that will eventually serve as a refutation of that part of its logic. Whereas the second concern – this alone we may call literary – though ruled out of court in the *Tractatus*, is not subject to the same refutation.

An observation of Nietzsche's will help us to see more clearly what is involved in this 'literary' concern. Placing his argument on that borderline between ethics and aesthetics on which Wittgenstein will place Kraus's pre-war satire, Nietzsche writes:

> We no longer esteem ourselves sufficiently when we communicate ourselves. Our real experiences [*unsere eigentlichen Erlebnisse*] are not at all garrulous. They could not communicate themselves even if they tried. That is because they lack the right word. Whatever we have words for, we have already outgrown. In all talk [*in allem Reden*] there is a grain of contempt. Language, it seems, was invented only for the average, for the middling and communicable. With language the speaker *vulgarizes* himself.[27]

Nietzsche's reflection illuminates some of the ground of the aphoristic – that is, elegant *and* peremptory – style of the *Tractatus* (and of Wittgenstein's later writings). This style is not a matter of deliberate choice but reflects a necessity, it derives its force from the sheer abundance and magnitude of a philosophic vision which its author feels cannot be presented in a more discursive fashion. This vision is reflected in the style in many ways. It is a part of David Pears's argument that the aphoristic style reflects the author's concession to the necessity of that linear, *nacheinander* presentation that goes with printed language.[28] But what the style also shows is something more than impatience and less than arrogance – impatience with the reader who expects to be spoon-fed, but should either work out and supply by him or herself the connections that are not provided by the author, or else stay away. (All these remarks apply, *mutatis mutandis*, to those of Nietzsche's own writings which are cast in a similar mode, but that is another story.)

But (it will be objected) what has this to do with 'what cannot be said', with Wittgenstein's concern with the limits of language? Beyond the impatience, and connected with what may appear as arrogance, the style is governed by something like a personal categorical imperative. I mean Wittgenstein's deep (and surprisingly English) conviction that it is neither right nor proper, that it is not *decent*, to talk of the 'last', the most important and fundamental things in life; or perhaps it is right to *talk* about them, with a friend, or rather *to* a friend, but not to *write* about them, and by writing to 'vulgarise them', to make them available to any Tom, Dick, or Harry, because . . .? Because. (There is something like an aesthetic limit to explanation: challenging the view that 'God wills the good because it is the good' is more profound than 'the good is good because God wills it', Wittgenstein commends the latter view because 'it cuts short every explanation "why" it is good, whereas [the former] is the shallow, rationalist view, which proceeds "as if" that which is good could be given a further reason.')[29]

Thus, the limits of language are set not only by what David Pears calls 'the mystery of the world beneath the surface skimmed by factual language' (p. 5) but also by the rules of what is done and what is not done. Or rather: if the rules of what is done and what is not are what we call ethics and aesthetics, and if they are traced deeply enough, then they, too, belong to 'the mystery of the world beneath the surface'.

To speak of a personal categorical imperative is to use the sort of language the *Tractatus* is designed to proscribe (McGuinness, for one, does not use the term). It is to speak of an oxymoron, at least in the sense that this is an imperative which is not explicitly generalised. The term is convenient because it describes at least approximately the strength and seriousness of that conviction from which one of the two strands of the investigation into the limits of language proceeds – the strand which legitimates the biographer's work on the portrait of the author of the *Tractatus*.

In this imperative, the unity of ethics and aesthetics reappears in the implied claim that what is in bad taste is morally wrong, too. True, this imperative renders the idea of the limits of languge contingent upon the person of the philosopher; makes it contingent upon what McGuinness calls 'the helpless and hopeless situation of an Austrian officer' at the end of a war which brought with it the end of his world (p. 313). When the *Tractatus* at last found a publisher and made its appearance before a wholly incurious public, Wittgenstein saw nothing that would take the place of the ruins around him. But the contingency receives its philosophical sanction in the view of the world towards which the logic of the book has been advancing: 'The limits of my language mean the limits of my world' (5.6).

As the *Tractatus* nears its end, it turns repeatedly to the problems of 'life', of 'God, freedom and mortality' (the phrase is McGuinness's) – towards the things that, we were told, cannot be said. These sanctions contain 'the real message of the book' (p. 312). The message that (as Wittgenstein would have it) there is no message? Surely not. Truth, in this biography, is achieved against the grain. If one relates the *Tractatus* and its writing as closely to the life and personality of its author as McGuinness does, one's conclusion is bound to be different from the conclusion explicitly argued and then transcended by Wittgenstein himself. Setting out to show the limits of language, his book shows neither the non-existence of the problems raised by 'life . . . God, freedom and mortality' nor does it show them to be inexpressible. McGuinness concludes his first volume by anticipating very briefly the second. We shall no longer be able to presuppose that there is a procedure 'for the whole of logic', he writes, 'a logic [for the whole] of language, a logic of all thought' (p. 313). Or, as Franz Kafka puts it at the end of *his* book, *The Trial*, 'Logic is doubtless unshakeable, but it does not resist a man who wants to live.'

VIII

There is at least one major point of agreement between Nyíri's and McGuinness's views: for both, the end of the world in which Wittgenstein grew up – the dissolution of the Empire at the end of the last and most disastrous of the many wars in which Francis Joseph led his country to defeat – is also the end of Wittgenstein's systematic metaphysics. This is where Nyíri's Wittgenstein chapter begins and McGuinness's first volume ends, but Nyíri's interpretation proceeds very differently. His aim – to place Wittgenstein's later philosophy in a Conservative tradition – is supported in several ways: by extended references to Wittgenstein's love of such writers as Grillparzer, Dostoevsky, Paul Ernst, and Oswald Spengler; by quoting numerous examples of his hostility to 'the classical bourgeois image of man' generally (p. 107), and to the liberal ideal of Progress in particular; and by arguing that Wittgenstein's analyses of 'ordinary language', and his many objections to theoretical speculations unrelated to 'actual usage' (*Philosophical Investigations*, §124), are all signs of an 'essentially' Conservative attitude. Even though none of the definitions of Conservatism quoted comes from Wittgenstein's own writings, Nyíri does not hesitate to press an unequivocally party-political claim. It is not merely that concepts such as 'following' or 'obeying' a rule of our actual language (p. 199), or again Wittgenstein's (disastrous) pedagogic views, connote a vaguely conservative attitude – the Conservatism Nyíri has in mind is a fully-fledged political attitude, too.

The main interest of Nyíri's chapter lies in the many previously unpublished reflections he quotes from the Wittgenstein archives, but some of them strike me as only biographically interesting; showing, quite simply, that though the passion and the intensity are always there, they are sometimes misapplied. In saying this I am not proposing that any of the *Nachlaß* should be suppressed, merely that it should not all be treated in oracular fashion. Anyway, none of Wittgenstein's 'political' observations can be adduced to support more than a distaste for revolution and an air of tetchiness in respect of reforms individually initiated. ('The sickness of a time is cured by an alteration in the mode of life of human beings . . ., not through a medicine invented by a single person.'[30]) Some of these remarks are strikingly similar to Michael Oakeshott's writings on 'rationalism in politics',[31] but seen in this perspective they are merely casual: they lack the understanding that comes from a historian's extended consideration of social and political contexts. The only apparent exception are the well-known observations on *The Decline of the West*, a book which interested Wittgenstein not for its nationalist politics but for its comparative method.

Apart from Spengler, no evidence is offered to suggest that Wittgenstein showed any interest in the German 'Conservative Revolution', that he read any of the writings from which Nyíri quotes in support of his claim that Wittgenstein '*must have been deeply interested in*' the neo-Conservative views and literature of the 1920s (Nyíri, p. 115). The tell-tale phrase I have italicised indicates how little the chronicler and analyst of Wittgenstein's philosophy seems to have taken to heart its cardinal injunction to avoid all *must have beens*, and instead *to look* for what was the case (*Investigations*, §66).

As a result of all this, Wittgenstein's *oeuvre* is given the one kind of historical dimension it doesn't possess. To resume an earlier argument: his philosophy has of course its place in history; it contains profound insights into the structure of historical situations (the remark about 'the sickness of a time' is not one of them) as well as into reports on such structures; and it is especially original and illuminating about the relationship between the two, and between deeds and words generally. But it takes no issue with historical structures as such, as (say) Locke's, or Hegel's, or Marx's philosophies do.[32] 'Existentialists' are frequently scandalised by this omission, others think it regrettable – it may be that Nyíri did, and then constructed the 'Conservative' argument to supply it. However that may be, if Wittgenstein's philosophy is to be placed in a tradition, then the one summed up in the old story of the Austrian railway line – from Bolzano to Brentano, Meinong, and Husserl, to *Endstation* Wittgenstein – is undoubtedly more relevant than any other.

There are no signs that Wittgenstein was *au fait* either with the day-to-day events of the 1930s, or with its ideologies and practices, new and old. It is one of the truisms of the monstrous history of that age that the 'neo-Conservative circles' Nyíri mentions helped to bring about the dissolution of the Weimar Republic and the rise of National Socialism: again, we are offered no evidence that Wittgenstein paid any significant attention to this process. Such glimpses as one gets of his concern with politics – above all his summary condemnation of '. . . the fascism and socialism of our time'[33] – suggests that in such matters he was ready to let himself be seduced by 'the terminology in common currency'[34] – that is, by contemporary clichés. And this, I take it, must also apply to Wittgenstein's anti-Jewish remarks, many of them made in connection with Otto Weininger's *Sex and Character* (a book which, to me, reads in parts like a high-class edition of *Der Stürmer*). Nyíri sees these observations in a different light, and makes a valiant but, I think, vain effort to give them some sort of respectable meaning. McGuinness's comment seems a little more convincing: 'Today, after Hitler, most families with Jewish blood have a different attitude towards their origin and see it as the source of their energy and intelligence, but Ludwig belonged to an earlier way of thinking' (p. 2). At least, McGuinness follows the Wittgensteinian paradigm: to understand what was said at another time you have to understand more than – that is, the context of – what was said.

Nyíri hopes to show (pp. 129-30) that one of the cliché claims of the anti-Semites, to the effect that Judaism is a religion of words and letters and other-worldly bookishness, is misconceived. From an article by Rabbi Leo Baeck of 1930 he quotes the view that Judaism is really a religion of deeds and sacred ritual, and therefore a religion of *activity*; and he hopes to add substance to this well-intentioned apologia by contending that, in its activism, Judaism has the strongest possible affinities with Catholicism and its insistence on the activism of good works. As against these two, he declares Protestantism, and in particular Lutheran Protestantism with its emphasis on 'faith alone', to be incompatible with Wittgenstein's 'conservative anthropology'. Forgetting that it took Catholic Vienna some fifty years longer than Broad Church Cambridge to begin paying attention to Wittgenstein's work, Nyíri writes: 'Descended from a Protestant father but brought up in the Catholic faith, Wittgenstein really shows [*zeigt indessen eigentlich*] that the Protestant and particularly the Lutheran conception [of faith] must be *false* because one cannot speak meaningfully of designs and intentions, of willing and having opinions, except in the context of deeds, customs and practices' (p. 130). However honourable its intention, this entire argument is another *must have been*. It is based on a preconceived decision to ignore the non-active, mystical elements in some forms of Catholicism, to identify the ritual of worship in Judaism (but not, for instance, John Hus's Utraquism) with 'deeds' and 'works', and to ignore the role of good works in Luther's doctrine. To speak of the 'false' world picture of Protestantism would be a gross and unwarranted inference, even if it were supported by Wittgenstein's *obiter dicta* (which it is not). Cast in such terms as 'Judaism is. . .', 'Catholicism is. . .', Nyíri's argument here is informed by that 'contempt for the individual case' and its significant detail which Wittgenstein has taught us to avoid. (And Wittgenstein's injunction remains valid even though he himself occasionally ignores it, as when he, too, writes in his diaries that 'The Jew is' this, that, or the other.)

IX

Is Nyíri saying that a philosopher of a different political persuasion would have produced a different philosophy? Or that Wittgenstein's philosophy invalidates, say, socialism and its reformist ideology? If he comes close to implying such a conclusion, this is because at the centre of his argument there is something like an inadvertent metonymy.

The 'conservative' attitude that is basic to the philosophy is exemplified by Wittgenstein's insistence that certainty, understanding, agreement *and* disagreement among human beings are possible only within a shared institutional framework; not that reforms are impossible, or undesirable, but that what is being reformed (the status quo) is bound to be reflected in the outcome, for 'I cannot start from anywhere except where I happen to be'.[35] In support of Wittgenstein's Conservatism, Nyíri quotes (p. 107) from *Philosophical Investigations*, §18: 'Our language can be seen as an ancient city: a maze of little streets and squares, of old and new houses, and of houses with additions from various periods; and this surrounded by a multitude of new suburbs with straight regular streets and uniform houses.' But the metaphor says more than Nyíri takes from it: comparing our language to an ancient city, it 'speaks of the straight new avenues in the suburbs as well as of the twisted streets in the old centre'.[36]

People's disagreement about what should be left as it is and what should be changed and made straight, which is a disagreement in their *opinions*, is possible not in spite of but because of their agreement on the language they have in common, that is in their 'form of life' (§241). In setting out the implications of this seminal view of the way things actually are, Nyíri's argument is at its best: here, to one side of its *kaisertreu* apologia, lies its great value. But this 'conservative' disposition has nothing to do with party politics – seen in *that* perspective the argument, indeed the philosophy itself, turn out to be non-political, whereas the Conservative attitude that Nyíri also attributes to Wittgenstein is concerned with affirming one particular arrangement within a shared institutional framework, and denying not just the value but the possibility of other arrangements within the same framework. The misprision here is between a whole and one of its parts, or again between the *language* people use and the *opinions* they express in that language. At this point Wittgenstein's map of our language resembles Saussure's: the difference between the two meanings of 'c/Conservative' resembles the difference between '*langue*' and '*parole*'.[37]

If, then, Wittgenstein was not a conservative philosopher in the sense claimed here, his place as an 'Austrian' philosopher is equally problematic. As we have seen, the name may help to pinpoint certain aspects of his philosophy, but it offers no fundamental or final insight; it is not as though one could say, 'He has learned from, and argued with, Frege and Russell, he has taught and thought in Cambridge, in his writings Western critical philosophy reaches its summit, but *really*, you know, he is an Austrian at heart.'

Reflecting on 'the good Austrian' element in Grillparzer, Lenau, Anton Bruckner, and the composer Josef Labor (a friend of the family), Wittgenstein says that it – 'das gute Österreichische' – is 'particularly hard to understand. There is a sense in which it is *subtler* than anything else, and the truth it expresses never inclines towards plausibility [seine Wahrheit ist nie auf seiten der Wahrscheinlichkeit].'[38] In this sense, his name must be added to the list. But other things are Austrian, too, chief among them a propensity for myth which readily turns into chatter, and which, for more than a century, has been a mainstay of the country's search for a national identity. Indeed the concept of 'Public Relations', of *Kulturpolitik* as the chief agency of modern mythopoeia, is an Austrian invention. After years when his very name was ignored, a 'Wittgenstein myth' is now in the making. But for that he is not responsible.

Notes

1. This is Nyíri's estimate, see *Am Rande Europas*, p. 206.
2. Ludwig Wittgenstein (LW), *Culture and Value*, ed. G. H. von Wright, with parallel translations by Peter Winch (Oxford, 1980), p. 28; LW's italics. Selected – at random? – by the editor in collaboration with Heikki Nyman from LW's manuscript notes, these reflections are identical with, and leave uncorrected, the misreadings and misprints of *Vermischte Bemerkungen* (Frankfurt, 1977). Neither title is LW's. Whether or not the author wished these reflections to be published, it is certain that he could not have wished them to be torn out of their contexts.
3. *Wittgenstein's Lectures: Cambridge, 1932–1935*, ed. Alice Ambrose (Totowa, NJ, 1979), p. 43.

4. Rodney Needham, *Against the Tranquility of Axioms* (Berkeley, 1983), p. 38.
5. *OED*, 1982 supplement; and Needham, *op. cit.*, chapter 3.
6. LW, *The Blue and Brown Books* (Oxford, 1964), p. 17.
7. LW, *Philosophische Untersuchungen*, Part 1 of which was completed in 1945, and published posthumously as *Philosophical Investigations*, tr. G. E. M. Anscombe (Oxford, 1953).
8. Needham, *op. cit.*, p. 43, mentions the French botanist Jean Adanson (1727–1806), see also p. 37 and Friedrich Nietzsche, *Jenseits von Gut and Böse* (1886), § 20: 'Die Familien-Ähnlichkeit alles indischen, griechischen, deutschen Philosophierens. . .'; Benedetto Croce, on the other hand, in *Aesthetic as Science and General Linguistic* (London, 1967), p. 73, deplores the fact that 'family likenesses. . .derived from the historical conditions in which the various works [of literature] arise and from the relationship of souls among artists. . . . . can never be rendered with abstract determinations.'
9. LW, *The Blue Book*, p. 18.
10. LW, *Remarks on the Foundations of Mathematics*, ed. G. H. von Wright, Rush Rhees, G. E. M. Anscombe (Oxford, 1967), p. 65.
11. Nyíri, op. cit., p. 180, quotes Széchenyi listing four different uses of 'the understanding', and accepts each as 'rational' because each meaning 'corresponds to its [appropriate] circumstances'.
12. For one thing, the publishers have obviously been niggardly in the assistance they have provided in the making of the book, allowing it to appear with misprints and in a German which is occasionally awkward and rough. Equally unsettling, the author does not seem to have made up his mind whether he is offering a collection of five essays or a continuous historical account.
13 Nyíri, *op. cit.*, p. 110, and LW, *Philosophische Bemerkungen*, ed. Rush Rhees (Frankfurt, 1964) p.153, § 133.
14. '. . . . auf das Gewisseste und Anschaulichste. . .' in Bernard Bolzano, *Vermischte philosophische und physikalische Schriften, 1832–1848*, ed. Jan Berg and Jaromír Louzil, (Stuttgart – Bad Canstatt, 1978), pp. iii, 83–5.
15. *The Philosophy of Bertrand Russell*, ed. Arthur Schilpp (Evanston and Chicago, 1944), p. 727.
16. See my review of Hugo Ott, *Heidegger: unterwegs zu seiner Biographie* (Frankfurt, 1988), in *London Review of Books*, 20 April 1989, 7–9.
17. See the introduction to Bernard Bolzano, *Theory of Science*, ed. and tr. Rolf George (Oxford, 1972); also my 'Nationalism and language consciousness in the age of Bernard Bolzano', *Journal of European Studies*, 19 (1989), 169-89.
18. For a later version of this Introduction, see note 33 below.
19. LW, *Culture and Value*, p. 19.
20. For accounts of the family resemblances between LW and GCL, see G. H. von Wright, 'Lichtenberg als Philosoph', in *Theoria*, 8 (3) (Gøteborg, 1942), pp. 201ff; and J. P. Stern, *G. C. Lichtenberg: a Doctrine of Scattered Occasions* (Bloomington, 1959), *passim*.
21. *Tractatus*, 4.014, tr. D. F. Pears and Brian McGuinness (London, 1961).
22. See Martin Heidegger, *Sein und Zeit*; erste Hälfte [1927] (Halle an der Saale, 1941), § 15, 'Hermeneutik der Faktizität'.
23. See *Culture and Value*, pp. 93, 49.
24. Op. cit., p. 36.
25. See Michael Dummett, *Ursprünge der analytischen Philosophie*, tr. Joachim Schulte (Frankfurt, 1988), p. 22.
26. LW's letter to Engelmann, 9 April 1917, quoted by McGuinness, op. cit., p. 251.
27. Friedrich Nietzsche, *Götzendämmerung* (1888), 'Streifzüge eines Unzeitgemäßen', §26.

28. See above, p. 150.
29. Friedrich Waismann, *Wittgenstein und der Wiener Kreis,* ed. B. F. McGuinness (Frankfurt, 1967), p. 115. The same kind of argument is used by Kant in defence of Job, in 'Über das Mißlingen aller philosophischen Versuche in der Theodicee' of 1791.
30. LW, *Remarks on the Foundations of Mathematics,* p. 57.
31. See Michael Oakeshott, *Rationalism in Politics* (London, 1962); though LW and Oakeshott were Cambridge contemporaries, they do not seem to have met.
32. Nyíri doesn't mention Marx's (and Engels's) anti-metaphysical remarks (mainly in *Deutsche Ideologie* of 1845-6), which several writers have compared with LW's; see A. R. Manser, *The End of Philosophy: Marx and Wittgenstein* (Southampton, 1973); and David Rubinstein, *Marx and Wittgenstein: Social Praxis and Social Explanation* (London, 1981), especially chapter 9. My point is not that the parallels are close, but that they bring out the 'revolutionary' aspect of LW's thinking.
33. LW, *Culture and Value,* p. 6, from the Introduction mentioned in note 18, above.
34. *Op. cit.,* p. 74.
35. Renford Bambrough, 'Roots and branches', *The Listener,* January 1966, p. 126.
36. Renford Bambrough, 'Conflict and the scope of reason', *Ratio,* 20 (2) (1978), 86.
37. See J. P. Stern, 'Literature and Ideology', in *Comparative Criticism,* ed. E. S. Shaffer, 3 (1981), 51–70.
38. *Culture and Value,* p. 3, LW's italics.

Herzl and Zionism

Robert Wistrich

Klaus Dethloff (ed.), *Theodor Herzl oder Der Moses des Fin de siècle* (Vienna, Graz, Cologne: Böhlau, 1986), 300 pp., 296 Sch.

Norbert Leser (ed.), *Theodor Herzl und das Wien des Fin de siècle,* Schriftenreihe des Ludwig-Boltzmann-Instituts für neuere österreichische Geistesgeschichte, Band 5 (Vienna, Graz, Cologne: Böhlau, 1987), 200 pp., 340 Sch.

Adolf Gaisbauer, *Davidstern und Doppeladler: Zionismus und jüdischer Nationalismus in Österreich, 1882-1918* (Vienna, Graz, Cologne: Böhlau, 1988), 554 pp., 980 Sch.

Shortly after the publication of Theodor Herzl's *Der Judenstaat* in 1896, the Austrian-Jewish poet and dramatist Richard Beer-Hofmann wrote to him: 'At last we have a man who does not bear his Judaism resignedly as a burden or a tragedy, but is proud to be among the legitimate heirs of an ancient culture.' What attracted Beer-Hofmann to Herzl was less the political content of his programme than his reassertion of tarnished Jewish pride and dignity and its link with the historical legacy of the Jews. Beer-Hofmann, like Herzl himself, was, of course, an exception among the writers of the Austrian *fin de siècle,* most of whom were either sceptical, indifferent, or openly hostile to Zionism. It is this *exceptionality* and the charismatic quality in Herzl's personality (rarely has a political movement been so swiftly and dramatically transformed by an individual) which doubtless accounts in part for the perennial interest in the life of the founder of political Zionism. To this day, the deeper personal motivations and historical processes through which a thoroughly assimilated Viennese playwright and *feuilleton* editor of the *Neue Freie Presse* emerged as the visionary prophet of the modern Jewish state are a matter of conjecture and controversy among historians. What remains beyond dispute is the dominant role which Herzl came to play in the early formative years of the world Zionist movement.

Klaus Dethloff, a researcher at the Philosophy Institute of the University of Vienna, does not attempt to resolve the psychological enigma in his fifty-page introduction to an anthology of Herzl's writings between 1894 and 1898. He does, however, provide a reliable account of Herzl's development against the background of Austrian cultural history, notable mainly for emphasising two points that are sometimes overlooked in the standard accounts: the importance of Herzl's legal training in the conceptualisation of the practical arrangements which he envisaged for organising the exodus of the Jews; and his ambivalent identification with Moses and the false Messiah Sabbatai Zvi — a subject which raises the difficult and complex question of the relation between Zionism and Jewish Messianism. (This syndrome is handled in much greater depth by Jacob Allerhand in an article included in the Leser book.)

Dethloff's selection of texts closely reflects the main themes of his introduction. The anthology begins with Herzl's autobiographically revealing one-act comedy *Die Glosse* (written in 1894), which is set in the thirteenth century and has as its unlikely subject the *Corpus iuris civilis* and its commentaries. This is followed by the well-known four-act play *Das neue Ghetto*, which explores the 'Jewish question', and a perceptive essay on the French writer and parliamentarian Maurice Barrès — also written in 1894. Herzl's parting essay on ending his four-year stint as Paris correspondent of the *Neue Freie Presse*, 'Die Schule des Journalisten' (1895), is a minor masterpiece of observations concerning the relation between journalism and politics seen through the prism of an increasingly decadent French parliamentary democracy. It is succeeded by a *feuilleton* that Herzl published in the *Neue Freie Presse* on 31 May 1896, 'Das lenkbare Luftschiff', which, in allegorical form, appears to reflect the mocking responses in Vienna to his 'solution of the Jewish question'. Then follows the full text of *Der Judenstaat*. Four articles that were published in Herzl's Zionist newspaper, *Die Welt*, during 1897 and 1898 conclude the anthology. These articles, which examine anti-Semitism and the Jewish response in France during the Dreyfus Affair, the anti-Jewish agitation during the German–Czech nationality conflict in Bohemia, and the pogroms in the summer of 1898 in Austro-Polish Galicia, are among the most politically incisive that Herzl ever wrote, and well worth re-reading. All in all, a very useful anthology for the German-speaking reader, especially in Austria — given the current climate of opinion — though its value for specialists will obviously be smaller.

Norbert Leser's volume, which grew out of a symposium held in Vienna in May 1985, also has a pedagogical value that may not have been intended at the time, in demonstrating the destructive legacy of Austrian anti-Semitism and the degree to which Herzl's Zionism was a response to it. It is, therefore, somewhat unfortunate that the editor, a distinguished Austrian historian of ideas, in a long essay on the intellectual background of the *fin de siècle* goes to such lengths to exculpate Karl Lueger — the turn-of-the-century Mayor of Vienna — from any responsibility for the racial anti-Semitism which brought such disaster to Austria, and above all to its Jewish citizens. Leser denies any intention of rehabilitating Lueger and the Christian Social Party, but, in his anxiety to draw an *absolute* dividing line between popular Catholic and pan-German or Nazi anti-Semitism, he comes close to writing an apologia that obscures more than it illumines. Even more disappointing is the very derivative piece by Ruth Burstyn on Herzl, von Schönerer, and anti-Semitism, which takes one of the most dubious of all Carl Schorske's theses and virtually plagiarises it in a German that singularly lacks the wit and style of the original. Burstyn is not the first, nor will she probably be the last, to be seduced by Schorske's beguilingly simplistic notion of the crisis of Austro-liberalism into explaining Herzl or reducing his Zionism to a functional equivalent of pan-German *völkisch* irrationalism.

Admittedly, there are interesting parallels between German romantic nationalism and Jewish nationalism in East–Central Europe (pointed out, among others, by Julius Schoeps in a previously published essay on the Viennese *Kadimah* reproduced in the Leser volume) which find later echoes in the writings of Nathan Birnbaum, Martin Buber, and Ahad Ha'am. But, significantly in my view, all these ideologists of 'cultural' Zionism became adversaries of Herzl, whose political philosophy and general outlook derived from different sources. This is at least hinted at in the competent contributions by the late Alex Bein (Herzl's first biographer), Jacob Allerhand, and Harry Zohn, though none of them breaks any new ground. Only the concluding article by Nike Wagner, comparing Herzl and Karl Kraus, offers a really distinctive and original viewpoint. Wagner does not analyse either Herzl's *démarche* or his Zionist metamorphosis *per se*, but seeks rather to explain the aesthetic sources of Kraus's aversion to his Viennese contemporary. At the same time she draws some illuminating contrasts between their respective attitudes to journalism, politics, sexuality, and scientific or technical progress. This article, more than any other in the volume, succeeds in placing Herzl in his Viennese context, but it is done, as it were, through a glass darkly, and inadvertently exposes the limitations of this approach. For Herzl, like Freud, Schönberg, and other outstanding figures of *fin de siècle* Vienna, also transcended his time and place. Any account which overlooks just how *un-Viennese* Herzl was in so many ways will not do him justice.

Adolf Gaisbauer's monumental study of Zionism and Jewish nationalism in pre-1914 Austria (based on a doctoral dissertation) is a very different type of book from the two volumes just discussed. Where they are obviously aimed at a popular audience, Gaisbauer rigorously documents everything, reproducing pages upon pages of Austrian Zionist speeches, protocols, organisational statutes, and reports, taken from the press, of even the most obscure provincial Zionist activity; where Dethloff and Leser focus on one individual in the context of his time, Gaisbauer has written an *organisational* history (the first systematic attempt of its kind) which covers the formative years of Zionism not only in Vienna but also in Bohemia, Moravia, Silesia, the Bukovina, and, above all, Galicia under late Habsburg rule. This is an immense undertaking and one can only admire the *Sitzfleisch* and dogged determination of the author to allow no detail to go unrecorded, however insignificant or repetitive it may appear. A careful reading of this book — itself a feat requiring exceptional stamina and conscientiousness — must once and forever put paid to the myth of Austrian *Schlamperei*. This is Germanic *Gründlichkeit* of the highest order.

There are, moreover, some important themes buried beneath the factological assault with which Gaisbauer seeks to overpower the reader. The book does partly make its point that Habsburg Austria was a key laboratory of the Jewish national renaissance; it does demonstrate the variety and complexity of Zionism in the Habsburg lands and also the crucial importance of the distinct but related trend of Jewish national politics (*Landespolitik*); it undoubtedly provides a unique compendium of data about the origin, development, and platforms of provincial Austrian Zionist bodies about which there is no serious literature except for the occasional monograph in Hebrew. Moreover, despite the thinness of its pages on Herzl and Viennese Zionism (among the weakest in the book) and its virtual failure to use any archival sources — particularly those available in Jerusalem — Gaisbauer does offer the first Empire-wide view of early Austrian Zionist history.

But these contributions, though important, do not compensate for the failure to integrate the development of Austrian Zionism into any coherent perspective relating either to modern Jewish history or to the social, cultural, and political history of the late Habsburg Empire. There is, for example, barely any discussion of the impact of the national awakening of the various peoples in the Empire on the Zionist movement, or of the position of Jews caught between rival nationalist movements in Austria–Hungary. The obvious question why Zionism spread more rapidly in Austria than in any other Western country is never really addressed; nor is any balance drawn between the strengths and weaknesses of the Austrian movement as a whole. Also missing is any analysis of the role that Zionism played as a modernising agency in the specific socio-economic and cultural conditions of late nineteenth-century Austria. The more philosophical discussion in the brief Introduction remains far too abstract and detached from the main body of the work to provide an answer to these, and other, fundamental questions.

These serious flaws are the more regrettable because the well-intentioned author has obviously laboured so long and hard to put together an orderly account of his subject. Unfortunately this is not enough. The result, too often, reads like a fetishist throwback to outdated traditions of nineteenth-century positivism. Such history-writing seems to cry out for the therapeutic irony of Nietzsche, Kraus, or Musil. Zionism, after all, whatever one may think of it, has been an exciting and dramatic human adventure. But this is history without colour or tone, sterilised and anaesthetised, like a patient laid out on the operating table.

Freud's Jewish Identity

Sander L. Gilman

Peter Gay, *A Godless Jew: Freud, Atheism, and the Making of Psychoanalysis* (New Haven and London: Yale University Press [in Association with Hebrew Union College Press, Cincinnati], 1987), 182 pp., £10.95.
Peter Gay, *Freud: A Life for Our Time* (London: Dent, 1988), 810 pp., £16.95.

Peter Gay's grand biography of Sigmund Freud is without any doubt the definitive 'Freud for our Times'. It is a major work of scholarship and erudition which presents the reader with a clear and crisp image of the life, works, and times of 'the Father of Psychoanalysis'.[1] Gay's earlier series of lectures on Freud's Jewish identity is, according to the author, but a preface to the larger work, and they are echoed (but in a more subdued and critical manner) in sections of that work. To begin this review at its conclusions, I respect Gay's reading of Freud but I disagree with some of it — just as he dissents from my own work on Freud's Jewish identity.[2] Indeed, Gay's own position is inconsistent, and it is the disparities between the 'Jewish Book' and the biography which fascinate the reader of both volumes.

Gay's Efroymson Memorial Lectures at Hebrew Union College[3] on Freud as a 'godless Jew' are an attempt to refute the claims made by certain scholars about the centrality of the idea of 'Judaism' to Freud and Freud's system. But Gay simplifies the problem by engaging with discredited scholars from the 1950s, such as David Bakan, who argued that Freud was a crypto-mystic or, at least, a hidden Jew. Such scholars also defined 'Jew' in terms of a religious context. Gay quite correctly points out that Freud's Jewish identity had very little to do with religious practice. Even though Freud's parents may have held to traditional beliefs, Freud's own family celebrated Christian holidays. Freud's wife, who had been raised in an Orthodox home, was forbidden by her husband to light the Sabbath candles once she was married, a fact which evidently (according to Gay) marred their relationship from its very beginning. So clearly, Freud was not a religious Jew. He was clearly also not an ethnic Jew. He saw himself as a transplanted Moravian, as an Austrian, as an unhappy

Viennese.[4] Only far down that line did he identify himself as an ethnic Jew. Ethnic Jews lived on the 'Mazzesinsel', the Second District, far from the Berggasse. And he certainly was never a 'political Jew'. His sympathies for Herzl and early Zionism were tempered by his (faulty) sense of political reality, his sense that the European powers would never permit a Jewish state in the Middle East.

Well, what kind of a Jew was Freud? He was a 'godless Jew', according to Gay, who clearly expects the juxtaposition to startle. Jew and atheist — these concepts jowl on jowl in a title must jar! However, such a juxtaposition startles only if the definition of the 'Jew' has anything at all to do with religion. For Freud, of course, the definition of the Jew certainly has nothing to do with religion, politics, or ethnic identity. We must keep in mind Freud's own definition of what a Jew is. In his 1926 speech to the Viennese Lodge of the B'nai Brith (which he had joined in 1895) he states that 'obscure emotional forces', 'a clear consciousness of inner identity', and most importantly, 'the safe privacy of a common mental construction' define the Jew for him.[5] It is the latter which is of interest since it is precisely the definition that Otto Weininger, one of the apostles of Jewish self-hatred, Jew and anti-Semite in one, provided for the Jew at the turn of the century. Jews were not biologically but psychologically distinct from (read: 'inferior to') all other human beings. Freud, who read Weininger's 1903 revised dissertation, *Sex and Character*, in manuscript, internalised Weininger's definition of the Jew and transvalued it, making it into a positive self-definition which avoided any religious, political, or ethnic dimension.

This is, of course, the problem with Gay's idea of Freud's Jewish identity. For Gay it was merely a label which Freud maintained while being a truly Enlightened opponent to the metaphysics of religion, in the great nineteenth-century tradition of Buckle, Nietzsche, and A. D. White. It is no wonder that Gay, whose own major scholarly works both describe and exemplify the Enlightenment ideal of the virtue of rationality, can in the Freud biography evoke Voltaire (the arch-enlightened Jew-hater) as an intellectual parallel to Freud's position on religion. Some of us, following Adorno as well as Foucault, are much more sceptical about the Enlightenment's claim for, and on, rationality. Many see the claims on the rational as a means of avoiding the complex pitfalls of the irrational. Freud does exactly this in claiming the rationality of science for psychoanalysis. He avoids confronting the polluted (and polluting) subterranean world of the racist implications of science by creating a science in which many of the claims against the Jew (such as the special, sexualised nature of the Jew) are sanitised and made into universal claims for human nature.

Gay, in defining Freud's Jewish identity, avoids the (for me) evident model, which is one of internalisation and projection. Inherent in Freud's world, or at least in those aspects of the world to which he early gives great value, are racist models of the Jew. He must deal with these models of the Jew within himself in order to function within his world. And what is this world? It is the world of science which Freud enters as a student and young colleague in the university, within which he formulates the basic structures of psychoanalysis, and out of which he attempts to escape in the 1920s with his advocacy of lay analysis. For the biological scientist (and Freud was a biological scientist) and the physician of the nineteenth century absorbed the ideology of race like mother's milk.[6] It was part of the high culture of science, never questioned, even by Jewish scientists who were seen in this world as being more limited in their mental construction than their Christian compatriots, or so Freud's teacher Theodor Billroth maintained.

The argument about the structure of Freud's sense of self as depicted in Gay's biography also ignores this aspect. Indeed, his primary discussion of the ideology of race comes almost at the very end of the volume (pp. 618–23), evoked by the rise of Nazism in Germany and the threat of the Anschluss. Since 'race' is never mentioned in his book on Freud's Jewish identity, this is the major difference between Gay's two Freuds; and it is an important one. For, in acknowledging the role of race in defining the anxieties for the Jews in the 1930s, Gay points backwards in his biography to his earlier discussion (pp. 15–18) of cultural anti-Semitism, implying that that, too, may well have had something to do with race. But race remains an amorphous category, placed in the streets and not in the classroom; in the graffiti and not in the textbooks. It is precisely the ubiquitousness of race within science that provides the ambivalence which can help one understand Freud's 'Jewish' identity. His is a reaction formation which sees new value in the category of difference that is generated. Thus, it inherently has nothing to do with the categories of religion, ethnicity, or politics. It has to do with psychology — and from this model emerges the sense of self which makes it possible for Freud to see himself both as 'scientist' (creating a new science which transcends all racially polluted sciences of his time) and as a 'Jew', possessing the (now transvalued) 'safe privacy of a common mental construction'.

Peter Gay's biography is extraordinary. It is without a doubt the best single work on Freud to appear within the past decade and it will be mined by future scholars (and teachers) who need a clear and concise presentation of Freud's works and life. My caveat (and it is hardly a major one) is that it is too clear, too clean, too organised. Gay's refusal to see the importance of a broader (non-Sullowayian) definition of science as the cultural matrix and institutional centre of Freud's existence, a science which is inherently anti-Semitic, weakens his argument. It also avoids many ambiguities which would complicate Gay's image of Freud as the great rationalist.

Notes

1. Who is the mother?
2. See my *Jewish Self-Hatred: Anti-Semitism and the Hidden Language of the Jews* (Baltimore, 1986).
3. What an extraordinary place — a reformed Rabbinic Seminary — for a lecture series on such a topic! Was it selected because it was an appropriate location for a lecture on a great atheist or as a comment on the nature of Reformed Judaism?
4. 'Unhappyviennese' should be written as one word. It was an affectation which many Viennese intellectuals shared, a sign that they were suffering under the demands and

weight of living at the centre of the known universe; demands and weights, however, which they were willing to shoulder for the furtherance of human civilisation. See Hofmannsthal, Altenberg, Kraus, *ad infinitum*.

5. Cited from the translation in *The Standard Edition of the Complete Psychological Works of Sigmund Freud*, 24 vols (London, 1953–74), 20, pp. 271-2.
6. There's the mother!

Vienna 1900:
The Need for New Editions

Reinhard Urbach

Those who claim to be familiar with Austrian literature of the turn of the century are deceiving themselves. For the work of many authors is simply not available in reliable German editions, let alone in good translations. The publishing situation is disastrous. What is needed is an *Österreichische Bibliothek der Jahrhundertwende*, a coherent series of new editions of Austrian authors. This series might include: Leopold von Andrian, Raoul Auernheimer, Hermann Bahr, Richard Beer-Hofmann, Franz Blei, Max Burckhard, Jakob Julius David, Felix Dörmann, Leo Ebermann, Karl Emil Franzos, Egon Friedell, Theodor Herzl, Ludwig Hevesi, Ernst Mach, Rosa Mayreder, Robert Michel, Josef Popper-Lynkeus, Felix Salten, Richard von Schaukal, Ludwig Speidel, Daniel Spitzer, Wilhelm Stekel, Otto Stoessl, Bertha von Suttner, Karl von Torresani and Fritz Wittels.

Against this list of authors, most of whose works are unobtainable in reliable modern editions, we may set a second group whose work has frequently been reprinted: Peter Altenberg, Alfred Polgar, Arthur Schnitzler and Stefan Zweig. The problem with these authors, however, is that they are not available in scholarly editions which take account of the full range of texts and variants, let alone the wealth of unpublished manuscripts. Only in a small number of cases are more systematic scholarly editions available or in preparation: Hugo von Hofmannsthal, Karl Kraus and Robert Musil.

The problem may be illustrated by focusing on a single author. In recent years Arthur Schnitzler has received a great deal of critical attention. This does not alter the fact that the basic requirements for scholarly research (reliable editions, documentation, and commentaries) are still lacking. The publication of his diaries, edited by Werner Welzig under the auspices of the *Österreichische*

Akademie der Wissenschaften, represents a decisive step in the right direction. But this only reveals more clearly the inadequacy of existing editions of Schnitzler's other writings.

Works like *Das Wort* and *Der Zug der Schatten* have been issued in a form so lamentable that they cannot be used with a clear conscience. The volume of *Aphorismen und Betrachtungen* requires extensive revision, as the editor omitted to include Schnitzler's notes on the theme of religion. Further editions of his letters are needed, including his correspondence with his publisher, S. Fischer, with Heinrich Mann, Felix Salten, Richard Beer-Hofmann, and Domenique Auclères, with members of his family, and with women friends like Marie Reinhard and Marie Glümer.

There is no adequate bibliography of translations of Schnitzler's writings into other languages (apart from French and English). Thus, the reception of his work in other areas of the Habsburg Empire remains undocumented. More information is needed about his library and the range of his reading (here his diaries constitute an important source). Further investigations are needed into his attitude to literature, music, the theatre, psychoanalysis, and politics, as well as the evolution of his literary style. The manuscript variants of some of his most important writings, transferred to Cambridge University Library after the Nazi occupation of Austria, still await systematic analysis.

The example of Schnitzler raises questions about the wider context of Austrian literature at the turn of the century. How is that cultural situation to be reconstructed on the basis of such inadequate documentation? How are the activities of 'Young Vienna' connected with those of other subcultures, like feminism, socialism, Zionism, or psychoanalysis? We know that Schnitzler visited Franzos and that Hofmannsthal was acquainted with Ferdinand von Saar. The critical reactions of an earlier generation to turn-of-the-century literary developments are also reflected in the diaries of Marie von Ebner-Eschenbach. But the interactions between these groups and generations have not been systematically analysed, indeed they *cannot* be properly analysed in the absence of reliable editions. For the average reader, figures like Hanslick, Kürnberger, Speidel, and Torresani are merely names. How can one possibly assess their significance, or that of Halm, Hamerling, or Bauernfeld, when the texts can be obtained only in libraries or in antiquarian bookshops?

A balanced reassessment of the turn of the century would involve not only new editions and further scholarly research but also a programme of popular education, through exhibitions, school textbooks, and other publications. But popularisation may result in superficiality if it is not supported by careful discrimination. The cult of 'Vienna 1900' has resulted in a one-sided view of that period, based on cultural clichés rather than precise information. There is a fatal temptation to play down the differences among authors or artists of this generation whose work has certain similarities. In fact, there could hardly be a greater contrast than that between Kraus and Altenberg, or Klimt and Schiele. To make the achievements of this generation fully accessible requires a programme not merely of popularisation but of precise differentiation.

Reinhard Urbach

Note

Adapted for publication in English by Edward Timms. An earlier version of this article appeared under the title 'Literatur der Jahrhundertwende in Wien: Desiderata', in Peter Berner, Emil Brix, and Wolfgang Mantl (eds.), *Wien um 1900: Aufbruch in die Moderne* (Vienna, 1986), pp. 101–3.

Part Three
Reviews

Claudio Magris, *Donau - Biographie eines Flusses*, tr. Heinz-Georg Held (Munich: Hanser, 1988), 477pp., DM 49.80.

It befits this story of a great river, first published by Garzanti in 1986, that it should itself be an undertaking of daunting proportions. It is composed of 169 discrete prose pieces, which display to the astonished reader what can only be described as dazzling erudition.

The strategy is convincing. Using the river as a *fil d'Ariane*, Magris takes us through a maze of historical data, cultural phenomena, and associated reflections, and he does this, without any doubt, in a most judicious and elegant manner. Yet I must confess to an occasional sense of weariness as the journey went on. Perhaps because there is so much that is remarkable between Ulm and Tulcea, I registered a distinct feeling of relief when we finally got down to the Delta and to the open sea.

For the reader, the book divides itself into two sections: the stretch from the obscure sources of the river to Budapest, with which one is more or less acquainted; and the reaches beyond Belgrade, where the historical, cultural, ethnic, and political patterns are so strangely kaleidoscopic that only very few can claim to have even a rudimentary grasp of their countless permutations. Whilst it is true that the author is always at pains, when we are at staging posts like Regensburg, Passau, Linz, or Vienna, to show us the less familiar aspects of these places and their inhabitants, it is almost unavoidable that his observations should, at times, come dangerously close to the stuff of which lesser guide books are made. The informed reader will also be left dissatisfied by the passing comments on such figures as Altdorfer, Stifter, Altenberg, or Wittgenstein, to name just a few. Conversely, of course, we wonder, further down the river, whether the author's apparently boundless knowledge amounts to more than an assemblage of re-related and anecdotal materials.

There is reassurance for the doubting reader, though, in the many passages of the book which testify to the guide's outstanding talents – the way in which, in a page or two, he is able to say more than is contained in many a compendious tract. The cameo, for instance, which shows Eichmann in 1934 enjoying a week's retreat in the monastery at Windberg increases our understanding of the 'fascist mentality' by a quantum leap. It seems to me that Magris's strengths as a writer come into their own *en miniature*, when he 'intensifies' the focus on his object of study. There would, therefore, appear to have been from the outset a contradiction between this particular virtue and the sheer size and extensiveness of the Danube project.

A book like *Donau*, sited halfway between academic and creative discourse, needs to rely on the unmistakable presence of its author. It is a pity, therefore, that Magris does not put more trust in his subjective perception, that he tends to surround even that which is before his eyes with all kinds of secondary references. The great river about which Magris writes is the stream of civilisation and hardly ever the Danube itself.

Although Magris must have visited all the places of which he gives us his account, there is, apart from a few scarcely developed pictures, little evidence that he has actually seen the great landscapes alongside the Danube. Nature is marginalised in this biography of a river. Where it is allowed an appearance, it is soon submerged again by the flood of historical and cultural information which Magris is in the business of managing. In other words the picture on the book's cover, Altdorfer's *Donaulandschaft mit Schloß Wörth*, holds a promise which the book fails to fulfil. Though it is an admirable work in many ways, it is lacking in what I would call sensual commitment. Too much in it is made of paper only. Magris himself must have recognised this shortcoming for he thematises the issue in the two sketches 'Im Delta' and 'In t'el mar grando' with which the book concludes. In these dozen or so truly splendid pages it becomes evident to what extent great prose depends upon the ability to see. Nowhere else in the book does Magris achieve a degree of immediacy comparable to that which marks his description of the dissolution of this great river. The effect is overwhelming, and raises doubts in the mind of the reader about the validity of much that went before.

By way of postscript, it should be said that the translation by Heinz-Georg Held is in every respect quite exemplary, and that it will do much to help the book gain the wider readership it deserves.

W. G. SEBALD

Thomas Bauman, *W. A. Mozart*: *Die Entführung aus dem Serail*, Cambridge Opera Handbooks (Cambridge: Cambridge University Press, 1987), xiii + 141 pp., paperback £9.95.

Tim Carter, *W. A. Mozart*: *Le nozze di Figaro*, Cambridge Opera Handbooks (Cambridge: Cambridge University Press, 1987), xii + 180 pp., paperback £9.95.

This valuable series has now grown to more than fifteen volumes, and its aims and achievements are doubtless familiar to many readers. Thomas Bauman, known and respected for his authoritative and illuminating *North German Opera in the Age of Goethe* (Cambridge, 1985), departs from the normal pattern in that the entire slim book is written by the author himself. Its six chapters cover 'Introduction', 'Conception and Creation', 'Oriental Opera', 'Synopsis', 'The Musical Language of the Opera', and 'The Opera in Performance'. The Introduction sets the scene with admirable clarity, and the first of several tables lists the successful operas performed at the National Singspiel in the sixteen months (too short a period?) that led up to the première of Mozart's work. Chapter Two includes a neat tabulation of the musical numbers in Mozart's score alongside those in Johann André's earlier setting of Bretzner's libretto (the comparison is by no means entirely to Mozart's advantage: just a few years later he would surely have set the elopement scene to music, as André did, rather than allow it to be constructed largely in spoken dialogue interspersed with songs). This chapter also contains the *Entstehungsgeschichte*, with due emphasis on the wretched delays to which the work was exposed, and a skilful summary of the librettist Stephanie's achievements and shortcomings. Throughout, Bauman shows not only a sound knowledge of every aspect of the subject but he also consistently brings the familiar to life, and reveals originality and common sense in pleasing combination.

The chapter on oriental opera briefly and clearly sets out the historical situation, paying due attention to Bretzner's wider contribution to the genre as well as to influential works from the stages in Britain, France, Italy and Germany. Especially interesting is the evidence that Grossmann's *Adelheit von Veltheim* and Bretzner's *Belmont und Constanze* were written simultaneously but independently. Here, and in the following synopsis, the author demonstrates with finesse and firm outlines the relationship between Bretzner's libretto and the revision that Stephanie undertook for Mozart, as well as making perceptive comments on Mozart's setting. The use of parallel columns where differences occur allows an economical exposition of the similarities and differences. An unfortunate oversight in the cast list omits to identify Johann Ernst Dauer as the original Pedrillo; instead, Adamberger is named for both tenor parts.

The largest chapter is the one on the musical language of the opera. After initial consideration of the nature of 'Turkish' music in eighteenth-century parlance and practice, and comment on Mozart's unique achievement in the musical creation of Osmin, there follows a section on the architecture of the score and its dialogue scenes. A brief passage on the structure of the solo numbers is followed by a fascinating study of 'Martern aller Arten', with unfamiliar material about the qualities of the Berlin singer of Constanze for whom André wrote his original Singspiel, and then the principal features of Mozart's setting for Caterina Cavalieri of this controversial aria, set at the tonal and structural centre of the score. Pedrillo's Romanze is also analysed deftly, though the trochees are surely in the melody, the iambs in the (metrically quite varied) verse, and not the other way round. Belmonte's 'O wie ängstlich' is also discussed in some detail. The closing section of this chapter, 'Unity and Coherence', finds space for a comparison between André's and Mozart's settings of 'Traurigkeit', but is chiefly concerned to argue for the musical and dramatic consistency of the Singspiel, which it does triumphantly.

The chapter on the opera in performance includes fairly conclusive evidence that the famous response of Bretzner to Mozart's unauthorised use of the libretto ('A certain individual, *Mozart* by name, in Vienna has had the audacity to misuse my drama *Belmonte und Constanze* for an opera text . . .') is itself a much later fabrication. A couple of rare slips in this chapter: Ulbrich's opera is *Der*, not *Das blaue Schmetterling*; and Niemetschek is spelt thus, not Niemtschek.

Tim Carter's study of *Le nozze di Figaro* is a larger book than Bauman's, differing from it superficially in the important respect that Carter, like most of the Cambridge Opera Handbook authors, has invited outside co-operation. Michael F. Robinson's chapter on 'Mozart and the *opera buffa* tradition' is placed second and sets the scene well for the analytical and descriptive chapters that follow. Robinson makes many shrewd points, but (perhaps because of pressure of space) he does make rather sweeping statements ('The dénouement, previously [he is speaking of the 1770s] left till the third act, had always . . . left an impression of anticlimax because it did not coincide with an impressive

185

musical item. From now on it was always incorporated within the second-act finale . . .'). His observations on the formal influence of Paisiello's *Il barbiere di Siviglia* (the most popular opera in Vienna in the 1780s, apart from Sarti's *Fra i due litiganti il terzo gode*) are cogent and revealing, and he neatly sums up the nature of Mozart's superiority to Anfossi on the basis of their settings of *La finta giardiniera*.

After a firmly drawn Introduction (nodding only in having Joseph II still alive in 1792 – it was his brother and successor Leopold II who died in that year), Carter settles to his own principal tasks with the third chapter: 'Beaumarchais, da Ponte and Mozart: From Play to Opera'. This is an excellent exposition of often complex material. The Synopsis serves its purpose very well, though both here and in the study of the music that follows one is reminded how swiftly Mozart scholarship has progressed in recent years: Alan Tyson's name occurs many times in the text and in the copious and detailed endnotes, but Carter hardly had time to come to terms with the implications of Tyson's challenges to accepted beliefs and his new discoveries and identifications (*Journal of the Royal Musical Association*, 112(1), 1987). And Carter has chosen to make rather little of the problems of order in Act III, first set out in 1965 by R. B. Moberly and Christopher Raeburn in their influential article in *Music and Letters*.

The heart of the book is Chapters Five to Seven, in which illuminating discussions of verse and music, and of music and drama, in *Figaro* are separated by a close study of the trio for the Count, Basilio, and Susanna. The first of these gives da Ponte his due for the excellence of his solutions to most of the problems of compression posed by the adaptation, and his prosodic skills. The second, which is actually more than an analysis just of this trio, contains admirable perceptions about Basilio's malicious return to his opening phrase: 'Irony is exploited to make a virtue out of a musical necessity.' The study of 'Music and Drama in *Le nozze di Figaro*' is again full of insights, about such matters as the pacing of the action, the shifts between emotional levels, and the differing responses to dramatic and lyrical situations of librettist and composer, all of which point towards the creative tensions that make *Figaro* an absolute masterpiece. Finally there comes an eminently readable outline of the opera's performance history, providing, in addition to the fascinating material about the work's first decades promised in the Preface, some well-chosen comments about its reception and reputation in our own century, especially since the First World War.

Both these volumes are enrichments to the Cambridge Opera Handbooks. They are sober yet lively, thought-provoking, even taxing, in some of the demands they make on the reader; stylistically they are at times a bit clumsy, yet they are thoroughly rewarding. In both books, notes, bibliography, and discography bring us right up to date; and the reproduction of the pictures and musical examples has a crispness of definition that was lacking in some of the earlier volumes.

PETER BRANSCOMBE

Alice M. Hanson, *Die zensurierte Muse: Musikleben im Wiener Biedermeier*, tr. Lynne L.
   Heller (Vienna, Graz, Cologne: Böhlau, 1987), 264 pp., 380 Sch.

When Alice Hanson's *Musical Life in Biedermeier Vienna* was published in 1985
in the series Cambridge Studies in Music, the scholarly reviews that greeted it
were a curious mixture of severely reserved praise and sharp criticism. Almost
all acknowledged that the author had unearthed some valuable and hitherto
overlooked source material; equally unanimous was the verdict that she had
frequently proved incapable of correctly interpreting its significance. Yet in its
English version the essential merit of the book lay in its ability to convey a sense
of the cultural climate of the Vienna of Beethoven and Schubert, with quotations
from vivid eyewitness accounts and other contemporary material employed as
the main technique in filling in the details of the canvas. That the limitations
of such a documentary approach were not realised by Dr Hanson was one of
the main faults of the book, for many of the passages quoted would undoubtedly
have benefited from more detailed critical appraisal. But it would be churlish
to deny that through her work Dr Hanson placed before a wider readership
material hitherto known only to specialists in the field, and, in so doing, offered
some illumination on a long-neglected area of musicological research.

It is some measure of the inherent significance of this volume that it should
have been translated into German so speedily. And, since translation usually
provides a golden opportunity for the discreet improvement of the mistakes,
oversights, and infelicities of the original, this publication should have been
highly welcome. Regrettably, *Die zensurierte Muse* must be seen as a missed
opportunity.

In fact, the translation follows the original English text with depressing
accuracy – there is not even a new preface – while the endnotes and other
scholarly apparatus have not received the radical overhaul they deserved. The
already inadequate index of the English edition has been reduced to an even
sparser 'Personenregister'. Indeed, the only substantial improvement is that Dr
Hanson has been able to excise from the appendices one of her more
embarrassing mistakes, namely the conflation of a text from Bäuerle's *Aline oder
Wien in einem anderen Weltteile* with the melody of 'Brüderlein fein' from
Raimund and Drechsler's *Das Mädchen aus der Feenwelt*.

Enough has been made by reviewers of the English edition of the sometimes
merely careless, sometimes more culpable mistakes and oversights of the text,
and little purpose will be served merely by adding to that list. But perhaps a
more central question may be addressed, namely the extent to which Hanson's
monograph functions not only as a self-contained study, but also as a starting-
point for further detailed investigation of some of the topics touched on within
its pages. It is here that some of the more worrying omissions are to be found,
for despite the relatively comprehensive listing of contemporary sources, the
bibliography of secondary literature contains surprising lacunae.

Taking but one example, that of the Bänkelgesang. the deficiencies of Dr
Hanson's bibliography become immediately apparent. Although she cites the
important studies by Rebicek (n.d.) and Naumann (1921), the contributions of

Böhme (1920), Koller (1931), Holzer (1943), and Leopold Schmidt (various), all of which have at least an indirect bearing on the subject, are not mentioned. For a book published in Austria, perhaps the most surprising omission of all is that of Maria Glöckler's (1964) doctoral thesis 'Der Bänkelsang als öffentliches Beeinflussungsmittel', which draws heavily on Viennese archival material.

These bibliographical deficiencies demonstrate what is, perhaps, the fundamental problem with Dr Hanson's work in both its English and German versions. Her enthusiasm for the subject has led her to tackle an enormous range of material, albeit drawn from a relatively restricted chronological span. In offering a wide-ranging study, she has not only been forced to move into areas well removed from music history, but has also had to contend with a wide range of musical and cultural phenomena. As a consequence, her laudable efforts to bring unfamiliar source material to a wider public have resulted in a work of considerable unevenness, which, in places, can be used only with extreme caution. It is, indeed, a pity that the opportunities presented by a translation were not taken.

EWAN WEST

Mark G. Ward (ed.), *From Vormärz to Fin de Siècle: Essays in Nineteenth-Century Austrian Literature* (Blairgowrie: Lochee Publications Ltd, 1986), v + 136 pp.

The volume contains seven papers delivered at a joint meeting of the Conference of University Teachers of German in Scotland and the Austrian Institute, London, held at Edinburgh in 1985. The most stimulating of these, in my view, are Wendelin Schmidt-Dengler's 'Französischer Symbolismus und Wiener Dekadenz' and Mark G. Ward's 'The Truth of Tales: Grillparzer's *Der arme Spielmann* and Stifter's *Der arme Wohltäter*'. Schmidt-Dengler takes a new look at the reception by *Jung Wien* ('Young Vienna') of French symbolism. He recalls Emil Rechert's *Baudelaire und die Modernen* and its anticipation of Walter Benjamin's Baudelaire essay. Felix Dörmann's selection of poems for his translations from Baudelaire is appraised, together with the characteristic features which created obstacles for their reception in Vienna. Dörmann's own poetry is skilfully assessed, and the reasons for his being regarded as an 'outsider' persuasively argued.

Mark Ward's comparison of the stories by Grillparzer and Stifter sends one back to them with renewed interest. He compares in an illuminating way their structure and the function of the intercalated first-person story: 'The important point is that the resolution to the various enigmas surrounding the central figure is only achieved at the end of the text, not as the culmination of a growing structure of revelation, but as the result of a clearly signalled change into a different mode of discourse' (p. 34). The effect of this internal *récit* on the frame narrator in Grillparzer's tale ('Jakob . . . is powerless; his narrative, vouchsafed to the narrator, remains without effect') is contrasted with the response of Stifter's narrator, who sustains his sympathetic understanding of the pastor by taking charge of his will, supported by the broader community. One could, of course, add that the more positive attitude of the 'broader community' is in a sense represented in *Der arme Spielmann* by the old gardener, who recalls the central figure's courageous last action for the narrator, and by Barbara, whose stricken face is shown to us in the last sentence. But it is clear that both authors let the central character control the interpretation of his own life, each in a different way, and this is well brought out in the article.

Bruce Thompson and Karlheinz Rossbacher contribute very informative essays; the first on Eduard von Bauernfeld and Anastasius Grün; and the second on Marie von Ebner-Eschenbach. Andrew Barker shows the impact of Peter Altenberg on a number of modern authors, with some especially interesting points on Rilke's and Kafka's responses. W. N. Boyd Mullan is, in my view, shadow-boxing with his argument about guilt and atonement in Grillparzer's *Des Meeres und der Liebe Wellen* and is much more convincing when he looks squarely at the 'romantic' aspects of the drama, interpreting these in the wake of A. W. Schlegel's use of the term. George C. Schoolfield uncovers the influence of Ibsen, Jens Peter Jacobsen, and Paul Bourget on Rilke's early Novelle *Die Letzten*, and discusses its unintentional parodistic effect. Schoolfield claims that, in spite of its efforts to outdo decadent literature, the story bears up under repeated reading 'mainly because of its dramatic structure'. It may be taken, he suggests, as a grotesque preliminary to *Malte Laurids Brigge*.

MARGARET JACOBS

Jean Paul Bled, *Franz Joseph: 'Der letzte Monarch der alten Schule'* (Vienna, Cologne, Graz: Böhlau, 1988), 565 pp., 476 Sch.

When Franz Joseph was told of the assassination of his heir Franz Ferdinand, at Sarajevo, his immediate reaction was to say: 'Terrible! The Almighty does not allow himself to be challenged . . . A higher force has restored that order which I unfortunately could not maintain.' Franz Ferdinand's marriage to someone unworthy of belonging to the Habsburgs (Sophie Chotek was only from one of the grandest families of the Bohemian high aristocracy) had upset the proper order of the world; now God had revenged himself. The event which was to lead to the First World War, and the destruction of the monarchy itself, was thus seen by Franz Joseph, on first confrontation, as an act of divine family discipline. Jean Paul Bled, in this extremely readable and comprehensive account of the emperor's life and times, sees this reaction as symbolising the fact that although Franz Joseph had become used to being a constitutional monarch, when it came to the dynasty, to the Habsburg family of which he remained the absolute head, he continued to think in terms of God's providence. What is remarkable about the Austrian monarch, as he emerges from this book, is how little he really changed over the almost seventy years of his rule. He learnt to adapt himself to changed circumstances, but, as his reaction to Sarajevo shows, his way of thinking remained much the same as it had been when he ascended the throne as an eighteen-year-old in the crisis of 1848. He really was, as he told Theodore Roosevelt in 1910, the 'last monarch of the old school'. Whether that school had taught him what was required from the ruler of a modern state in the first decades of the twentieth century is another question.

Bled has used the opportunity of this biographical study to write what amounts to a general history of Austria-Hungary in the nineteenth century. He does not say much that is new, but he says it concisely and authoritatively, with a certain flair which his translators have done well to preserve in this German version. Curiously, for all the whirl of events in which Franz Joseph took such a central part, and which have the makings of true, world-shaking tragedy, the book is somewhat lacking in drama. This is not, I think, Bled's fault. Ultimately it has to do with the subject himself. Many dramatic things happened to Franz Joseph, his empire was several times on the brink of collapse, his wife and son met untimely and horrible deaths, he presided over a land in the throes of unprecedented change – but it is most difficult to write an exciting book about an unexciting man.

Franz Joseph's character, as put across by Bled, was definitely that of 'the first servant of the state', not in the dramatic manner of Joseph II, but rather in that of a middle-grade bureaucrat who happened to be Emperor of Austria and King of Hungary. One can understand why Empress Elisabeth felt able to spend most of her time away from Vienna. Perhaps it was this lack of a charismatic personality that created the excessive emphasis on ritual at court and public ceremonies which provided the garment of glory in which even a less-than-inspiring individual could become the subject of a cult (as Franz Joseph certainly was by the last years of his reign).

Franz Joseph would have made an ideal constitutional head of state. He knew how to be majestic. The problem was that he had been brought up to rule as well as reign; and rule he would, and did. Even when he was forced to accept the limits of constitutional monarchy, he did not give up the reins of power. His ministers were *his* ministers; their policies *his* policies. What he said counted, and it counted as much in 1914 as it had in 1878, if not more so. In the latter part of his reign, however, many of his views were not suited to modern times. Bled asks whether it would not have been better if Franz Joseph had not reigned quite so long. The real problem, however, was that this should actually have mattered in an age of mass politics. In his wish to rule as well as reign, Franz Joseph showed himself to be, indeed, a monarch of another age. What would have happened if Austria had possessed a more modern and enlightened ruler is a question whose answer would not, I think, redound in Franz Joseph's favour. Decency, diligence, even majesty, are great things, but not always enough.

STEVEN BELLER

Hermann Bahr, *Prophet der Moderne: Tagebücher 1888–1904*, ed. Reinhard Farkas (Vienna, Graz, Cologne: Böhlau, 1987), 228 pp., 380 Sch.

Students of Austrian literature are surely aware that Hermann Bahr has not benefited from the current interest in *fin-de-siècle* Vienna, and is all but forgotten at a time when the period in which he occupied such a central position is enjoying a worldwide renaissance. Carl Schorske's seminal collection of essays on that time and place ignores the dramatist, storyteller, critic, and cultural mediator, the mentor and chief theoretician of the 'Young Vienna' circle of writers. Unlike some of these, notably Schnitzler, Bahr never became fashionable: his numerous works are out of print, and there has been no English translation of any of his writings since 1916. Donald Daviau, Bahr's foremost American champion, blames the prevailing scholarly neglect of Bahr on Karl Kraus's forty-year polemic against him. True, the image of the 'Herr aus Linz' being dragged from the doomed Café Griensteidl kicking and screaming has persisted. But surely there is more substantial evidence for the widespread assessment of Bahr as a literary chameleon, a 'Verwandlungskünstler' and 'Dandy der Moderne', who embraced with equal enthusiasm *Heimatkunst*, freemasonry and Richard Wagner – or, more charitably, as an intellectual seismograph. In a letter to his father (February 1888) Bahr described himself as 'ein haltloser, von tausend sich kreuzenden Ideen zerrissener und gepeinigter Mensch' ('an unstable person, torn and tormented by a thousand clashing ideas').

Attempting a literary rescue operation (a 'Rettung' in Lessing's sense), the young Austrian scholar Reinhard Farkas has set out to reclaim Bahr from literary limbo and anchor at least his early life and work in the burgeoning modernist realm. Concentrating on Bahr's formative years, the time of his greatest public effectiveness and a crucial period in politics, philosophy, art, and morals, Farkas offers excerpts from Bahr's journals selected from a pan-European viewpoint, and is particularly concerned with defining and describing 'die Moderne' and its Viennese variant.

The editor presents Bahr's journal entries in five sections and prefaces each with a brief essay. He admits that many of these autobiographical jottings constitute 'ein Verwirrspiel mit Tatsachen und Tendenzen seines Lebens' ('a game of mystification played with the facts and feelings of his life'). For, after his conversion to Catholicism in 1909 (to marry Anna von Mildenburg), Bahr rewrote his earlier history in an attempt to suggest a unity that never existed. As he tried to describe his epoch ('diese nervöse Zeit') and solve its 'uncanny riddles' ('unheimliche Rätsel'), Bahr strove to transcend the merely theoretical and to exemplify the new intellectual currents as well as an unfettered spirit and life style in his accounts of artistic experiences, theatrical performances, travels (often hiking and biking), and erotic encounters in several cities. In Berlin he hailed Ibsen as a precursor of modernism and pure humanitarianism and affected the 'coarse earthiness' ('kernige Derbheit') that he discerned in the Naturalist M. G. Conrad. Bahr's intellectual and emotional self-absorption often resulted in hypochondria and self-pitying querulousness. A diary entry of 6 August 1903 is very suggestive: 'Mit der Zeit . . . wird man doch merken, dass es ein Glück für Österreich ist, einen solchen Mann zu haben, wie ich bin' ('With the passage of time . . . people will realise that Austria is fortunate to have such a man as myself'). This is reminiscent of Raimund's lament: 'Es ist ewig schad' um mich'.

Bahr's virtual obsession with everything 'modern' led him, in 1889, to characterise 'die Moderne' as 'unerhört brutal und unerhört delikat' ('unspeakably brutal and unspeakably exquisite'). But in German, as Theodor Fontane pointed out, the adjective 'modern' radically changes its meaning if stressed on the first syllable, becoming a verb which means 'to decay'. Today's new mould may become mouldy tomorrow. Although Bahr's writings made him financially secure, we find him, in 1902, bemoaning his dependent existence ('Pensionistenexistenz'). His revulsion at the corrupt state of affairs in Vienna ('Ekel über den Wiener Sumpf') increasingly caused him to turn his back on Austria, which he likened to a backward Asiatic country. And his multifarious unrealised projects included a kind of Austrian Plutarch or *Wiener Spiegel*, a journal devoted to the exposure of the 'Austrian character' ('das österreichische Wesen'). A cultural mediator despite himself, Bahr dreamed of a social regeneration through literature, art, music, and architecture. And he displayed a becoming awareness that he seemed destined to ride 'das ganze Ringelspiel aller Irrtümer der Zeit' ('the merry-go-round of all the errors of the age') before acquiring the detachment and wisdom of old age.

Among Bahr's rather diffuse jottings there are occasional aphoristic nuggets, notes on such works as *Dialog vom Marsyas*, and perceptive vignettes of friends like Hofmannsthal, Beer-Hofmann, Salten, Klimt, Trebitsch, Burckhard, and Herzl. Bahr visited the last-named shortly before his death and found the world-famous Zionist leader worrying whether he was a writer of the first or the second rank. In July 1904 Bahr conceded 'dass aus dem kleinen Kraus einmal durch irgend ein Erlebnis, eine Frau, Bildung, ein anständiger Mann von fünfzig Jahren werden könnte' ('that some experience – a woman, cultural refinement – might eventually make little Kraus into a decent middle-aged man'). But what is one to make of this diary entry of 16 May 1902: 'Mama gestorben. Hugo hat ein Mäderl' ('Mama dead. Hugo has a girl')?

The very competent editor of these diaries has supplied helpful though sparing notes (references to some persons, affairs, duels, and scandals remain cryptic), primary and secondary bibliographies, and well-chosen photos and facsimiles.

HARRY ZOHN

Gustav Mahler, *Briefe*, ed. Herta Blaukopf (Vienna: Zsolnay, 1982), xx + 459 pp.

Gustav Mahler, *Unbekannte Briefe*, ed. Herta Blaukopf (Vienna: Zsolnay, 1983), 257 pp.

Herta Blaukopf and Kurt Blaukopf, *Die Wiener Philharmoniker: Wesen, Werden, Wirken eines großen Orchesters* (Vienna: Zsolnay, 1986), 288 pp.

———

In 1924 Alma Mahler published *Gustav Mahler, Briefe 1879–1911*, an anthology of 420 letters which, despite its inaccuracies and falsifications, remained of central importance as interest in the composer continued to grow. It is upon this collection that Herta Blaukopf's elegant and concisely annotated edition of the *Briefe* is based, though, of necessity, much has had to be changed. In spite of

Mahler's often uncertain grasp on time and his propensity for not dating his correspondence, Blaukopf adopts a chronological approach, and, compared with the earlier format in which letters were grouped according to the recipient, the gain is immeasurable. Previously mutilated letters to Anna von Mildenburg, the great Wagnerian soprano to whom Mahler had probably been engaged, are now quoted in full (she was later to marry Hermann Bahr), and there are some forty-four completely new letters. Neither Mahler's letters to his wife, which Alma later published in *Gustav Mahler, Erinnerungen und Briefe* (Amsterdam, 1940), nor his correspondence with Richard Strauss, which Blaukopf edited in 1980, are included. *Briefe* thus represents a thoroughly competent and scholarly modernisation of Alma's pioneering work, even to the extent of retaining Friedrich Löhr's biographically important annotations of the letters addressed to him. The collection is a pleasure to use, not least because footnotes are provided at the bottom of each letter, rather than consecutively at the end of the volume, and the pen-pictures of the various recipients provide a further useful though occasionally inaccurate guide (Dr Emil Freund was not born in 1959 [p. 428]).

Whereas *Briefe* is a tribute to Alma as well as to Gustav Mahler, in *Unbekannte Briefe* Herta Blaukopf breaks totally new ground with the presentation of 150 new letters to seventeen addressees, ranging from Cosima Wagner to Arnold Schönberg. As in the earlier collection, readers will be struck by Mahler's vast seriousness of purpose, but they will also meet a new Mahler, for example in the playful letters to Wilhelm Zinne which reveal the passion for cycling which he shared with many other artists in the Vienna of the 1890s. As in the *Briefe*, Zsolnay have again produced a book which is easy on the eye. Its appearance is enhanced by visual material such as a facsimile of Mahler's practically illegible note to Oskar Fried of September 1909 which concludes: 'Verzeihen Sie die Schmierage. Bin in wahnsinniger Hetze. Die 9. ist fertig.' This is a fascinating collection, but the editorial principles have undergone a considerable shift. In *Briefe* the editor was unable to inspect many of the now lost originals, with the result that the modernised orthography of the 1924 edition is retained. *Unbekannte Briefe*, however, being based entirely on manuscripts, follows Mahler's original spelling. Perhaps more importantly, the chronological procedure of *Briefe* has been replaced by the old Alma Mahler approach, in which recipients are once again grouped together. The advantage of this, however, becomes apparent in a further new departure: in place of the biographical sketches of *Briefe* we find that each of the seventeen letter groupings is prefaced by an essay from the pen of an active Mahler scholar on the relationship between the composer and the addressee. Some are slight, but others, such as Eduard Reeser's essay, are substantial pieces of scholarship, and of far greater bulk than the actual correspondence which occasioned them. Mahler was the outstanding Wagnerian of his day, and here yet another perspective is opened up on the symbiotic relationship between the anti-Semitic guardians of Bayreuth and their Jewish devotees.

The interplay of Jewish and Gentile musicians was for decades a feature of the orchestra which Mahler conducted with such brilliance and whose very special aura is the subject of a study by Herta Blaukopf and her husband Kurt, author of a major study of Mahler at a time when the composer had still to be rehabilitated fully in Vienna. Although based on thorough research, *Die Wiener Philharmoniker* is a celebration rather than a critical examination of one of Austria's most venerable cultural institutions, and it benefits greatly from the participation of Christian Brandstätter, who is responsible for the layout and the many fine illustrations. Some will feel, however, that the book begs as many questions as it answers. The orchestra's somewhat tenuous links with the twentieth-century repertoire are barely mentioned, while that tradition which Mahler famously castigated as 'Schlamperei' means that in the Vienna Philharmonic it is still exclusively the boys who make up the band.

ANDREW BARKER

Donald P. Spence, *The Freudian Metaphor: Toward Paradigm Change in Psychoanalysis* (New York and London: Norton, 1987), xx + 230 pp., £15.00.

Much recent writing – one thinks of the work of Max Black, Mary Hesse, and Paul Ricoeur, as well as that of Lakoff and Johnson – has highlighted the role of metaphor in the formation of concepts in both the natural and the human sciences. Metaphors are here seen as functioning primarily as models, a kind of extended sensory apparatus which allows us to see certain sorts of phenomena and certain kinds of causal relationships that would otherwise go unnoticed. Donald Spence's *The Freudian Metaphor* is situated within this context, as well as within the narrower context of recent trends in Freud scholarship. With Bettelheim and Ornston, he stresses the way in which Freud's figurative use of language has been largely lost in Strachey's Standard Edition; with Brooks, Schafer and Shepherd, he emphasises that Freud's intentional uses of figurative language allow us to see clinical happenings in a new manner.

Spence begins by noting the double-edged quality of metaphor. Metaphors both emphasise and suppress. Thus, to see a man as a wolf is to *not* see him as a grown child, and to see all events as determined by an actual unconscious is to exclude the view that some events are random happenings. Spence argues – lucidly, persuasively, seriously, if in a somewhat buttoned-up prose – that many of Freud's central metaphors suppress. Freud himself frequently overlooked the distinction between model and observation, and tended to treat his metaphors as if they were confirmed pieces of reality. Partly in consequence of this, the central metaphors of psychoanalysis have tended to take on a life of their own and have come to be treated as something more than figures of speech. In this way, Spence suggests, these metaphors are disabling rather than enabling.

He locates two broad areas in which disabling metaphors are operative; in both cases their pervasive usage has the clear intention of legitimating the psychoanalytic enterprise. In the first, the metaphor of psychoanalysis as science is shown to be seductive because to become a science is automatically to acquire certain rights and privileges and, in this way, to achieve instant respectability.

We automatically assign a certain respectability to words like 'data', 'theory', and 'hypothesis'; the magic word 'data' transforms the description of what we are doing into something that is subject to the normal constraints of the scientific method, and encourages us to believe that concepts at present ambiguous will become refined as more observations are gathered. Above all, the archaeological metaphor – the image of the excavating psychoanalyst who 'reconstitutes', rather than 'constructs', a past – is seen by Spence, as also by Brooks, as one of Freud's master-plots, one of the most convincing story-lines legitimating his enterprise.

The second area of disabling metaphor, on which Spence has a number of illuminating things to say, is what he calls the Sherlock Holmes tradition. By this he means that psychoanalytic casework is frequently compared with detective work: both genres feature a master sleuth (or therapist) who is confronted by a series of bizarre and disconnected events (or symptoms) reported by a somewhat desperate client (or patient); the sleuth listens, watches, reflects, never prejudging, and almost never surprised, confident that when all the facts are available the mystery will disappear and the truth emerge. Spence suggests that the insights of psychoanalysis should here be turned against its own rhetoric; for the temptation to situate itself in the Sherlock Holmes tradition is a form of resistance – it shows an intolerance for ambiguity, a need to get on with the story, a readiness to leave certain questions unanswered. But to persist in this resistance is to forfeit a good deal. The presentation and pseudo-documentation of psychoanalytic work have tended to convey the impression of more clarity and finality than actually exist. Once the case report is published, it is almost impossible to reconstruct 'what actually happened' in the sessions; because of the Sherlock Holmes tradition, the stereotype is given precedence over more unexpected observations, and evidence that does not fit the stereotype is usually not reported. The tendency to report clinical insights without paying attention to precisely how they were arrived at is one of the most grievous examples of this narrative smoothing, which has the effect of turning a hermeneutic adventure into a staid, pseudo-scientific account which gives the impression that all surprise has been accounted for. Conspicuously absent, by contrast, is an insider's account which describes how analysts listen during the hour, which tells us how they go about choosing how to listen and what to say, and how they amend their response in the face of new clinical material. A literature of psychoanalytic case-studies has been built up which says little about the process of discovery.

Spence then turns, more briefly, to consider an enabling metaphor: the possible analogy between psychoanalysis and the law. Both depend on procedures which are rule-governed. Both are influenced as much by the circumstances of a particular happening as by an abstract set of laws. Neither psychoanalysis nor law can be used predictively; that is, neither body of knowledge contains a set of axiomatic statements which can be manipulated and tested, as in science; the rules which make up these bodies of knowledge are always open to interpretation, and precedent is never final. Since the history of law, like psychoanalysis, is nothing less than the archive of cases, the legal metaphor, it is suggested, gives psychoanalysis a way of making the best use of its past history, of making the most considered use of its accumulated wisdom. If psychoanalysis, in common with law, rests both on cases and rules, it becomes important that psychoanalysts should expand their case reports and develop a new genre of informed peer commentary. They should attend to the significance of the fact that they have a concordance to the Standard Edition, but no concordance of creative specimen cases.

The analogy between psychoanalysis and law is suggestive, and it would be good to see Spence take up the subject again and scrutinise it with the fine-grained patience for detail that characterises his earlier book, *Narrative Truth and Historical Truth* (1982). More unsettled, far less worked out – paradoxically so, given the central concern with metaphor – is Spence's position in the relationship between psychoanalysis and what he calls 'literature'. The question is touched on gingerly at the margins. It seems to arise naturally when Spence says that 'the longer psychoanalysis insists on being a science, the more it will play down one of its main attractions – the search for multiple meanings and the search for decision rules to select among them' (p. 155). It appears to surface when he says: 'Rather than ask "What happened?" the more sensitive reader [or analyst] might wonder, "In how many ways can this text be experienced?" much as we might respond to a poem or a work of art' (p. 108). But elsewhere it is crushed peremptorily out of existence with the remark that 'literature is a bad model because it pretends to a kind of narrative smoothness which can never be achieved . . . it pretends to a kind of detective-story mastery of all the details whereas in practice many details are never understood' (p. 199). That 'literature' cannot be conflated with 'detective-stories' seems too obvious an objection to mention here. Perhaps more to the point, and worth thinking about in this context, is the fact that certain stories, achievements of high literary art, derive their power precisely from their multiple meanings. They are the kind of stories that Walter Benjamin prized most highly.

PAUL CONNERTON

Erasmo Leiva-Merikakis, *The Blossoming Thorn: Georg Trakl's Poetry of Atonement* (London and Toronto: Associated University Presses, 1987), 191 pp., £19.95.

In the introduction to this study Leiva-Merikakis draws a rather partial account of Trakl scholarship to date. Only by disregarding the more subtle approaches of recent years can he reduce the literature to a tripartite scheme of Christian apologism (bad), formalism (worse), and crude psychoanalytic case histories (anathema). It is most surprising that the studies by Detsch and Kleefeld go unacknowledged, given that both address themselves to the key question of poetic atonement, operating well clear of the dogmatic triangle. They perceive that to dismiss any of the poetry's essential constituents (such as the Christological, the abstract structural, or, indeed, the psychopathological) is to impoverish it. Trakl's writing will not only sustain a plurality of readings, but, whatever the specific claims of the critic's chosen methodology, it demands a pluralist critical overview.

The stylised survey given in the introduction establishes the critical perspective throughout. The author's central thesis is that Trakl's poetry 'con-forms' to, is 'in-formed' by, the 'Christ-form' as a model of atonement. He stresses that here poetic form is not hermetically but figurally disposed; aesthetic and ethical sense are seen to conjoin. Trakl is related more or less rigorously to the Apocalyptic tradition, ancient and modern, and to Baroque Passion poetry. Rarely does the cross-reference go beyond the level of 'basic similarity', and one has an abiding feeling that more might have been made of it. The same is true of the suggestive correspondence between individual texts and biblical passages. In either case a more meticulous pursuit of idiomatic and structural parallels might have helped to underwrite a reading which tends towards theological abstraction.

The study takes as its premise the famous aphorism whereby the poet styles his work as 'eine unvollkommene Sühne' ('an imperfect atonement'). Given the focal role of this statement, it is curious that there is no mention that Trakl explicitly associated it with Otto Weininger and thus with the problematics of sexuality as the prime ethical question. This omission (and Weininger does not even find a place in the bibliography) is symptomatic. Leiva-Merikakis's response to what he sees as the prurient excesses of psychoanalytic accounts is to treat the pathological desires which rack the poetic corpus by general anaesthetic. This sanitising principle may serve to streamline Leiva-Merikakis's reading, but it ultimately mitigates persuasive lines of argument.

The single-minded reading after the image of Christ excludes too much. This image may, indeed, propose a figural centre for the poetry, but what of the host of secondary personae who embody the counter-forces of disfigurement and decentring? Trakl's distinctive structures of repetition cannot be reduced to the motions of the *imitatio Christi*, for there is also the compulsive return of the Antichrist under various guises: Cain, Lucifer, Bluebeard, Don Juan. This antagonistic role model has forceful claims to make on the identity of the 'Du'. So, too, does the fallen figure of Narcissus; Leiva-Merikakis's 'Mirror of Recognition' is the focus not only of anagnorisis but also of narcissistic desire. In his efforts to dissociate Trakl from the 'Romantic affliction' of egocentrism, the author recurrently reads dialogue into the apostrophic 'Du' and presses self-reflexive structures into the service of his poet's embracing altruism. His interpretation of 'Rosiger Spiegel' is a case in point: where Leiva-Merikakis recognises only the altruistic mirror-image of Christ, the less dogmatic reader would surely also recognize an image of radical self-alterity – 'verstorben und fremd'.

Leiva-Merikakis's work of transfiguration on Trakl's poetry (witness the born-again 'ungebornen Enkel' of 'Grodek') achieves small purchase on the resistant otherness of persona, image, and form. The apodictic tenor – 'Senselessness has yielded to presence' – rings hollow; the poetry will simply not con-form.

ANDREW WEBBER

Reviews

Philip Payne, *Robert Musil's 'The Man Without Qualities': A Critical Study*, Cambridge
   Studies in German (Cambridge: Cambridge University Press, 1988), xiv + 256 pp.,
   £30.00.

Philip Payne, *Robert Musil's Works, 1906-1924: A Critical Introduction*, European
   University Studies, ser. 1, vol. 961 (Frankfurt, Berne, New York, Paris: Peter Lang,
   1987, 236 pp., 52 SwF.

Aldo Venturelli, *Robert Musil und das Projekt der Moderne*, Europäische Hochschulschriften,
   Reihe 1, Band 1039 (Frankfurt, Berne, New York: Peter Lang, 1988), 272 pp., DM
   57.

Michiko Mae, *Motivation und Liebe: Zum Strukturprinzip der Vereinigung bei Robert Musil*,
   Musil-Studien 16 (Munich: Fink, 1988), xii+508 pp.

Of the four books under discussion here, those by Payne are presented as
introductions to Musil's texts for a general audience from a stated position of
an all-absorbing fascination by Musil's work (*'Man Without Qualities'*, p. xiii).
Such introductions are needed, especially for English-language audiences, and
fascination by Musil's work should not be a hindrance. It is a question of the
degree of generality and of the kind of fascination. Both the fact that the books
are published in series intended for the specialised reader and the way in which
the approach to the early texts is described – Payne could be speaking here, too,
about *Man Without Qualities* (preface to *Works*, p. 7) – suggest that Payne wishes
to be seen as going beyond the introductory level:

> In this study I have not taken the paths pointed by recent developments
> in 'Literaturwissenschaft', because I believe that, for all the wealth of
> material on Musil's works, there are still important areas which merit
> investigation by a more traditional literary-critical approach. My primary
> concerns are, first, the placing of the texts in the context of Musil's
> personal life, his views about the individual work and his Weltan-
> schauung, second, close study and evaluation of each text as a literary
> entity.

If Payne's investigation fails to chart new areas, this is not due to its
'traditional' nature. Yet his responsible, and sometimes imaginative readings,
though on the whole most appropriate for the reader who needs an introduction,
can on occasion be useful also to more informed students of Musil's work
precisely for their clear contextuality.

Like Payne, Venturelli and Mae lack the (not necessarily critical) distance
from Musil's texts which would enable them to develop a certain useful distance
from their own texts. Where Payne paraphrases Musil too directly and simply,
Venturelli does so with too much poetic exuberance and conceptual redundancy,
intent on a sort of creative fusion with Musil (see p. 19). Mae, in contrast, builds
around him the most diligently assembled wall of paraphrased secondary
materials, which she penetrates, from the inside, with Musil quotations. Where
Venturelli draws the reader too much into his preoccupation with his own
thought-processes, Mae forces on her the thoughts of a great variety of writers
only remotely related and even more remotely useful to an understanding of
Musil's intention and achievements.

All the pieces collected in Venturelli's volume have been published before and recently, the majority of them in exactly the same form. There are quite a few repetitions in argumentation, since several of the essays deal in a general way with the question of Musil and modernity. The longest, most substantial and most closely argued piece, translated from the Italian, 'Dichtung und Erkenntnis. Zu Musils philosophischen Studien und zu seinem Verhältnis zur Gestaltpsychologie', deals usefully with Musil's attempt to translate certain aspects of scientific into literary discourse. It deserves to be made accessible to the reader who does not know Italian, but has little connection with the other essays and even less with the title.

Mae's study is the most interesting of the four, because it exhibits so very clearly problems which have been central to a great deal of Musil criticism. The book is based on a dissertation and retains all the flaws of a dissertee's credulity about 'literaturwissenschaftlich' thoroughness. Dramatically shortened and carefully edited – precisely because the writer is both laudably dedicated to the subject and understandably inexperienced – it might have become useful to the Musil specialist interested in yet another attempt to decipher that enigmatic Musilian hallmark, the 'second dimension of thought'.

Now, it is, indeed, highly desirable to situate Musil's texts in their intellectual contexts; it has also proved remarkably difficult because these contexts are particularly rich and Musil's translating, transferring, and transforming reactions to them are particularly complex in their conceptual and stylistic strategies. What would be needed is a clearly, yet flexibly organised selecting and structuring presentation of the contextual materials responsive to Musil's usage of natural language as artefact. This does not mean paraphrasing the materials and quoting Musil; it does mean attempting to understand his intentions and integrate such understanding into the presentation.

Mae's book is a quarry of occasionally interesting information about certain cultural connections in Musil's thought. But how Musil came to develop – and did develop – his indeed extraordinary, quite unique, 'mixed' philosophico-poetic discourse, where it works, why it works, why it sometimes does not work, why it sometimes succeeds so stunningly – all these questions need to be, and haven't been, asked.

Mae warns her reader right at the beginning: 'Es ist nicht möglich zu definieren, was mit Motivation bei Musil gemeint ist. Sie ist eine Bewegung, in die man hineinkommt oder hineingebracht wird, und diesem Charakter der Motivation entspricht in gewisser Weise auch der Darstellungsgang unserer Arbeit.' (p. 2). The study's 'motion' is both 'somehow' and pedantic – precisely what Musil's is not. In Part I of her study Mae is concerned with 'eine Bewegung von Begriffen, Konzepten, Prinzipien'. Taking off from a collage of quotes from Roth's indeed very useful 1972 *Ethik und Aesthetik* (Mae, p. 19) in order to establish the connection between 'Motivation' and 'Sinn', 'Bedeutung', 'Wert', Mae goes on, for the next forty pages, to paraphrase arguments as different as those of Fischer-Lichte, Ingarden, Lessing, and Jauss. But she does so without providing conceptual linkage and without relating the passages to Musil's texts.

She relies entirely on Musil's attempts at describing what it is that he is doing (e.g. Novellenform, pp. 77ff); she seems paralysed when confronted with literary texts. A good example is the comparison between Musil and Flaubert, curiously abstract where she ought to have been concerned about narrative praxis, language usage (pp. 11, 51–2); or her discussion (I, 4, a) of the relation between poetry and psychology in Musil's work, where she extensively paraphrases contemporary psychological positions but quotes Musil to articulate the relation. And when she finally arrives at the last chapter of Part I, (6) 'Das Kunsterlebnis: Motivation als das Vermittelnde zwischen Ethik und Aesthetik' (pp. 140ff), she again relies on quoting or paraphrasing Musil and does not draw at all on the more than one hundred pages' worth of accumulated contextual material, probably because she 'somehow' realises that they have little or nothing to do with the problem she has set out to solve, the enigma of Musil's texts.

The literary interpretations in Part II are intended to prepare for Part III, 'Das Reich der Liebe' which, therefore, she thinks, presents a less abstract, less undifferentiated 'anderen Zustand' than that found in all previous Musil criticism. As have other critics, Mae argues against the 'mystical' interpretation of Ulrich's and Agathe's conversations – actually here is the locus of basic disagreements between two camps. But though I tend to agree with her attitude towards this alleged mysticism, it is not helpful simply to assert a 'Dialogizität' as mediating between the 'gegebenen' and the '"anderen" Zustand'.

Throughout these five hundred pages packed with largely useless secondary material, Mae has neglected to examine Musil's discourse of access, in the tradition of Flaubert, to his protagonists' minds. But the questions that she sensed were important, though she never got around to posing them, are located, articulated, and partly answered right here, in these highly complex symbiotic acts of fictional self-articulation.

DAGMAR BARNOUW

Stephen D. Dowden (ed.), *Hermann Broch. Literature, Philosophy, Politics. The Yale Broch Symposium 1986* (Columbia: Camden House, 1988), xv + 357 pp.

Monika Ritzer, *Hermann Broch und die Kulturkrise des frühen 20. Jahrhunderts* (Stuttgart: J.B. Metzler, 1988), 339 pp., DM 68.

Joseph Peter Strelka (ed.), *Flucht und Exil. Geschichten und Berichte aus zwei Jahrhunderten* (Frankfurt: Insel Verlag, 1988), 329 pp., DM 16.

The centenary of Hermann Broch's birth in 1986 was marked by major conferences in a number of countries. The proceedings of the Yale Broch Symposium are remarkable for the diversity of perspectives they bring to bear on Broch's works. The contributors include three philosophers, a theologian, a sociologist, a political scientist, and two historians of ideas, as well as some sixteen literary scholars, among them several internationally acknowledged authorities on Broch. Nearly every contribution is followed by a commentary or 'response' invited from another participant; and if some of these responses are limited to a brief encomium, then that is a just tribute to the generally high quality of the papers. This is certainly not a merely celebratory or summative publication, but a volume which will provide stimulus for much further detailed investigation of Broch's writings.

In so far as the volume has a central focus, this is to be found in the way that the pursuit of philosophical cognition ultimately determines the nature of all Broch's writing, and more particularly in his insistence that a unifying epochal style characterises all aspects of life in a given period. René Wellek, examining Broch's literary criticism, highlights the severely rationalistic criteria by which Broch tended to assess all literary achievement, and shows that for all its virtues and insights, Broch's Hofmannsthal monograph is an unduly rigorous condemnation of turn-of-the-century Viennese culture. The status of architecture as a readily identifiable paradigm of epochal style is examined from complementary directions by the Yale philosopher Karsten Harries and the Princeton Germanist Claudia Brodsky. Harries expounds the implicitly ethical function with which style is invested in Broch's project for overcoming the 'radical evil' of a world divided into a multiplicity of autonomous partial value systems. Brodsky wittily relates Broch's anxiety over the 'disintegration of values' to the cheerful affirmation of plurality in 'postmodern' architecture, and emphasises the importance of 'building' metaphors for both the discussion of (integral) personality and the overall technique of literary composition in *Die Schlafwandler* (*The Sleepwalkers*).

The function of metaphor and symbol has always occupied a central place in Broch scholarship, and it is this area which prompts perhaps the most fruitful and diverse discussion in the Yale volume. Richard Brinkmann, like Wellek, emphasises the dominance of rationalist categories in Broch's writing: his symbols are intended to be read as symptoms of intellectually perceived processes, and this leads to the paradox that he accepts and applies in his literary technique that very abstraction and functionalism that he deplores as a historical phenomenon. Brinkmann's view finds some corroboration from the Salzburg Germanist Walter Weiss, who stresses the sense in which Broch's metaphors are derived deductively from philosophical precepts. But the most sensitive reading of what metaphorical utterance achieves in Broch's novels is provided by the Tübingen theologian Hans-Anton Drewes in his response to Weiss. Drewes develops an analogy with the paradoxical relationship of parable to reality in the works of Kafka as one of both 'fundamental antithesis and complete identity': viewed in this way – as 'Gleichnis' – Broch's literary imagery appears rather to be working towards a (utopian) elimination of the tension that must always exist for the philosopher between metaphor and concept. Symbolism tempts Ernestine Schlant – sadly, in view of her previous services to Broch scholarship – to a catalogue of putative sexual images of the kind that tends to undermine the credibility of psychoanalytical criticism. More interestingly, if again rather single-mindedly, David Suchoff shows how characters in *Die Schlafwandler* come to identify with symbolic objects in ways that reflect not only cultural disintegration but also the assertion of cultural authority, and thus 'procedures of modern social control'.

As Suchoff's contribution implies, there are inherent ambiguities in Broch's writings which make any attempt at 'ideological' criticism a peculiarly delicate task. Paul Michael Lützeler states some of the paradoxes at the heart of Broch's writing with admirable clarity: Broch was constantly wrestling with the tensions between formal innovation and ethical traditionalism; his Virgil novel epitomises the paradox of a literary avant-garde which seeks to transcend aestheticism within an aesthetic medium; and *Die Verzauberung* (The Spell) reflects the inescapable tension between Broch's sense of humanity's need for a new religion, centred in an earthly absolute, and the patent dangers of an irrational religiosity as expressed in mass political movements. Other contributors explore particular dimensions of these ambiguities. Thomas Quinn relates *Die Verzauberung* to the notion of regressive 'Entzauberung' (demystification) as envisaged by Horkheimer and Adorno, and questions the validity of Broch's attempt to overcome myth by a technique of re-mythologising; but Wendelin Schmidt-Dengler, concentrating on the motif of the child as embodiment of hope for the future, shows how Broch varies a stock image of the popular literature of his time and articulates his own hopeful principle in ways which do not lose sight of the despair out of which it is won. Vasily Rudich highlights the inherent ambivalence of mythopoeia in relation to the Virgil novel, while Luciano Zagari illustrates the subtlety of Broch's poetic achievement by relating it to what is known of the historical Virgil and his works. The philosophers Kuno Lorenz and Joseph P. Lawrence dispute on the merits or demerits of Broch's 'eidetic' theory of cognition. And in the political domain, Joseph Strelka puts the case for Broch's conception of 'absolute' human rights as a foundation for democracy; while the cultural historian Dominick La Capra registers general scepticism about Broch's non-literary writings, and the political scientist Hartmut Jäckel suspects him of having, at root, an 'irrational and self-tortured' attitude to politics. A valuable feature of the Yale Symposium is that it provides the English-speaking reader with clear expressions of these controversial aspects of Broch's work, and shows how judgements about his ideological orientation inevitably reflect the methodological assumptions of his interpreters.

Broch's pursuit of philosophical certainty in the form of absolute values is, again, at the heart of Monika Ritzer's monograph. What distinguishes her investigation from previous studies is the thoroughness with which she places Broch's thinking in the context of philosophical inquiry in his time. The influence on Broch of the Marburg school of neo-Kantianism is well known, at least in outline, but Ritzer is able to document the relationship between Broch's cultural philosophy and a wide variety of thinkers, including Nietzsche, Dilthey, Simmel, Husserl, Spengler, and Alfred Adler. In the nature of the subject, much of the discussion is technical and abstract, and is likely to commend itself only to readers who are already fascinated by the intricacies of Broch's intellectual constructs. But Ritzer moves with great facility among the complex arguments involved, and presents her own insights with clarity and assurance. She does not overlook possible objections to the elements of quasi-religious nostalgia and utopianism which are undeniably present in Broch's thought, but by contrast with the disparagement of Karl Menges (*Kritische Studien zur Wertphilosophie Hermann Brochs*, Tübingen, 1970), for example, her patient reconstruction enables the positive aspects of Broch's intellectual achievement to come to the fore.

The avenue by which Broch approached neo-Kantian thinking turns out to be a rather surprising one: it is Weininger, upon whom Broch evidently drew heavily for his 1914 essay 'Ethik'. The connection becomes less surprising when Ritzer shows how Weininger's notorious ideas about sexual polarity are related to his underlying quest for a philosophical subject capable of responsible action. It is Weininger who, as it were, defines the Kantian categories within which Broch subsequently operated; it is he who defines memory as the pursuit of 'intelligible timelessness', and who sees culture as being possible only in relation to transcendental values. Here, it seems, is Broch's decisive turning point towards the single-minded pursuit of a unifying subjectivity as the keystone of any dependable interpretation of reality. He knew it to be a pursuit that ran counter to the spirit of the times: Simmel had despaired of any possibility of mediation between conceptual generality and individual 'authenticity'; and Jaspers had declared the 'prophetic' postulation of values to be inadmissible in an age of proliferating perspectives. Broch responds by asserting the claim of the absolute, ultimately as an article of faith.

It is well known, again, that Broch was stimulated to the development of his philosophical views, and to the composition of *Die Schlafwandler*, by his discomfiting encounter in the 1920s with Viennese Positivism, which emphatically rejected any attempt at a deductive system of values. Ritzer shows, however, that he also developed a critical awareness of neo-Kantianism as typifying the intellectual abstraction (and, thus, the fragmented subjectivism) of the age. Both these philosophical positions become integrated as *historical* phenomena into his theory of the 'disintegration of values', and the tension between them provides an essential dynamic force in his narrative writing: the 'polyhistorical' novel – which the *Schlafwandler* project becomes – presents philosophical absolutism as the counter-construct to the prevailing absolutism of a fragmented cultural reality. As Ritzer presents it, it is the 'tragedy' of the unifying subject that is articulated through the figure of the isolated first-person narrator in the final volume of the trilogy. By illustrating the intellectual resonances in this and many other themes and motifs, her study makes a valuable contribution to an integrated understanding of the literary technique as well as the intellectual content of *Die Schlafwandler*.

Among the many leitmotifs of the *Schlafwandler* trilogy, a miniature of the Statue of Liberty acquires poignant significance as the cliché of a freedom for which Broch's characters may yearn, but which the limitations of their historical existence prevent them from achieving. The Statue of Liberty also provides the cover illustration for Strelka's anthology of writings on the subject of 'flight and exile'. The collection is a pointed departure from what we have come to think of as 'German exile literature': here is no Brecht or Döblin, no Feuchtwanger or Heinrich Mann. Strelka has assembled anecdotes and reminiscences which range from persecuted French aristocrats of the 1790s to disillusioned Communists of the 1970s, taking in several prominent literary figures along the way. In the main, the texts depict the concrete human predicament of exile: the

Reviews

anxiety and bitterness; the humour and resourcefulness. The choice has been guided by the criterion of 'timeless validity' (p. 321) – and by an ideal of 'genuine' freedom, which is not defined except as the implied antithesis to whatever constellation of tyrannical power these refugees have fled. To understand the historical nature of those constellations, the reader will have to look beyond Strelka's anthology.

DAVID MIDGLEY

Elias Canetti, *The Tongue Set Free: Remembrance of a European Childhood*, tr. J. Neugroschel (London: André Deutsch, 1988), 268 pp., £12.95.

It comes as no surprise nowadays to find a translation from German into English, and relatively straightforward German at that, which does less than feasible justice to its source. *The Tongue Set Free* goes some way towards confirming the rule and thus merits particular attention: it is a praiseworthy if patchy exception, a text that by and large 'tells it like it was'. The patches should not, of course, be overlooked. Like literary translators worldwide, Joachim Neugroschel occasionally makes mistakes, misses the mark, settles for second best; it is clear that few if any of these imperfections derive from linguistic incompetence; and it is clear that in exclusively anglophone circles most, if not all, of them will pass unnoticed. Omissions, for example, do not necessarily disturb the flow of Neugroschel's narrative (see 9/5,[1] where a nine-word sentence disappears, or 197/167, where we lose 'und in Reclam'); Canetti's mother, 'entschlossen, mir in kürzester Zeit Deutsch beizubringen', was indeed 'resolved to teach me German' as fast as possible, if not exactly 'in a jiffy' (82/67); and those who don't know Keller's '"The Three Just Kammachers"' may or may not inquire further (199/168). The principal faults of this version of *Die gerettete Zunge*, however, seem to stem as much from its publisher(s) as from its translator. André Deutsch has evidently taken it over holus-bolus from 'The Continuum Publishing Corporation', which copyrighted it a mere two years after the original first appeared. In other words, Continuum and Deutsch and Hanser between them had almost a decade in which to prepare the text for its current market. For reasons which may make sense in commercial life but in no other, the time has not been used to Canetti's or to his English-speaking readers' advantage, and there will now doubtless be a long wait before this intriguing 'Remembrance of a European Childhood' – as the subtitle calls it – is made properly accessible. Neugroschel's English is not at issue: it is American and can capture the flavours of Canetti's German perhaps better than most other target languages. (Presumably the British, too, will one day learn to 'plume themselves' (10/6) and speak of 'residential houses' (11/7), of 'Every lauding word' (80/65), of a business 'which he sovereignly mastered' (104/88), of faces 'warped with rage' (106/90), of 'vehement downpours' (123/104), of 'Latin declinations' (124/105), of 'roomers' (156-7/133), of 'storming her with questions' (191/161), and of 'high-slung eyebrows' (247/210); presumably it is only a matter of time before they, too, find nothing odd about 'the flags took

Reviews

no end' (92/74) and 'but still and all' (116/98) and 'the taunts stopped at one swoop' (250/212) and 'raising my hand immeasurably' [*ibid.*] . . .).

At issue is the apparent indifference of those ultimately responsible for *The Tongue Set Free* towards their target readership. Why, in the absence of any form of introduction, did the London publishers not at least expand the blurb? As it stands, it is not far short of nugatory, a bit of carelessly printed puffery, and the solitary quotation in praise of Canetti (on the back cover) is little more than an advertisement for Iris Murdoch. And what, in the absence of any annotation, is the layman to make of, for example, the exchange between the young Canetti and his mother about 'Schiller's rotten apples' (203/171)? What of 'Kannitverstan' (272/229)? How will Canetti's literary enthusiasms, e.g. for C. F. Meyer (242-4/229-31), be received by the interested but untutored monoglot? Even if this were a flawless translation – as consistent, precise, and felicitous as the original deserves – it would need re-packaging. A well-designed jacket with a nice photograph of the author may help to sell the book; but help to understand it is confined to a few snippets of contextual information that have been kneaded (by the translator?) into the ingredients. *Caveat emptor* – a bronze medal for Neugroschel, the wooden spoon for Deutsch.

Note 1.   References are to *Die gerettete Zunge* (Frankfurt, 1983), and *The Tongue Set Free* (London, 1988), and appear as X/Y, X being the page number of the German, Y that of the English.

GEOFFREY BUTLER

Klaus Amann, *Der Anschluß österreichischer Schriftsteller an das Dritte Reich: institutionelle und bewußtseinsgeschichtliche Aspekte*, Athenäum Monografien Literaturwissenschaft: Literatur in der Geschichte, Geschichte in der Literatur, 16 (Frankfurt: Athenäum, 1988), 253pp., DM 68.

In the last ten years serious investigative research into the Austrian cultural and literary scene during the years of 'Austro-Fascism' and of Nazi rule has been resolutely advanced in a number of distinguished publications. Notable milestones along this road include two pioneering monographs in the series 'Literatur in der Geschichte, Geschichte in der Literatur', originally published by Hain in Königstein/Ts., Friedbert Aspetsberger's *Literarisches Leben im Austrofaschismus: Der Staatspreis* (1980), and Johannes Sachslehner's study of Mirko Jelusich, *Führerwort und Führerblick* (1985). To this same series Klaus Amann has now contributed another important book, which must, indeed, be accounted a classic of its kind – informative, fully documented, and at the same time written with compelling fluency and conviction.

Dr Amann's main theme is the systematic penetration by the National Socialists of the cultural life and institutions of Austria from the late 1920s onwards. Published exactly fifty years after the Anschluss, his investigation is illuminated by a determination to face up to the political facts of the period, a belated 'Bewältigung der Vergangenheit'. His strategy is to explore how the steady growth of Fascism in Austria between 1933 and 1938 was both exemplified and effected in its literary life. He traces how the Nazis exploited pan-German feeling and anti-Semitic prejudice in an efficiently managed infiltration and reshaping of literary and artistic organisations, a cultural offensive overseen from 1934 onwards by Papen, as German ambassador in Vienna, and Karl Megerle, the specialist on Austria in Goebbels's Ministry of Propaganda. The subsequent shifts in the cultural and ideological climate resulted in the very reverse of the traditionalist continuities that have time and again been ascribed to Austrian literature: the systematic corruption of the institutional infrastructure of literary culture underpinned the rise of nationalist writing and the displacement of liberal and left-wing traditions (which had in many cases been in the hands of writers of Jewish descent). Right-wing writers of whatever colour (pan-German nationalists, patriotic Austrian nationalists, clericals) were gradually drawn into the various literary organisations that the Nazis took over or set up, and such feeble resistance as the Nazis' tactics encountered was easily out-manoeuvred, so that the writers honoured with prizes and titles by the Dollfuss and Schuschnigg regimes were largely identical with those extolled in Nazi literary histories. The sense of purpose that the nationalist writers derived from their newly forged identification with the state provided a momentum that Amann compares to the upsurge of jingoist enthusiasm at the outbreak of the First World War.

It is against this organisational background that the individual authors themselves are introduced, whether willing and self-seeking collaborators or naive (and no less self-seeking) dupes, all exempt from other service on account of their cultural and/or propaganda work. Thus Jelusich, the novelist who was briefly to become director of the Burgtheater in 1938, was already deeply implicated by the early 1930s. So, too, was Weinheber, whose poem 'Österreich 1934' (published in *Das Innere Reich* after the Anschluss but not included in any of his collections) provides the starting point of Amann's Preface. The duplicity of Waggerl is trenchantly outlined in an endnote (p. 220, note 693). Max Mell repeatedly functioned as a respectable front-man. To large parts of the reading public of the time the works of those we now recognise as the major writers of the inter-war period (Schnitzler, Kraus, Werfel, Musil) were anything but representative figures: many writers (Stefan Zweig, Joseph Roth, Robert Neumann, and others) were driven into exile as early as 1934, and, indeed, the battle against liberal and left-wing ideas not only robbed the Austrian government of potentially powerful support against National Socialism – a point long recognised by political historians – but actually provided a basic precondition for the success of the Nazis' cultural politics in Austria. The new orthodoxies were reflected also in critical and academic writing (Nadler, Kindermann), as Austrian Germanistik was largely reduced to propaganda for the one ideological line.

It is a sorry tale, but one that needed telling, and it is hard to imagine that it could be better told in the present state of research. Scrupulous about indicating where his argument contains elements of speculative deduction, Dr Amann has provided a sharply focused account, at once factual and riveting – in sum, a masterly survey which will surely establish itself as one of the cornerstones of research into Austrian cultural history of the 1930s.

W. E. YATES

Konrad Lorenz, *The Waning of Humaneness*, tr. Robert Warren Kickert (London: Unwin Hyman, 1988), vi + 250 pp., £12.95.

Konrad Lorenz died on 27 February 1989, after receiving many honours, including the Nobel Prize, for his pioneering work in ethology, the science of animal behaviour. The famous colony of greylag geese at his Institute for Animal Sociology supplied much evidence for his explanation of 'imprinting', in which young animals learn to follow their parents by responding to visual and auditory stimuli: a process made possible, Lorenz suggested, by the prior existence of innate perceptual schemata. In his more popular works, like *On Aggression* (1966; originally *Das sogenannte Böse*, 1963), Professor Lorenz wrote fascinatingly about animals and applied his theories to human behaviour. His 'biological sociology', as he called it in his last book, has been highly influential, not least through its convergence with American theories of 'sociobiology'. In so far as the Lorenz doctrines are addressed to a lay audience, lay people may reply with some sceptical questions.

First, are human behaviour patterns supposed to be genetically programmed or culturally transmitted? Lorenz fudges this question, speaking sometimes of identical processes, sometimes of 'analogies' or 'parallels', sometimes denying that the distinction matters. Next, does Lorenz's doctrine imply biological determinism? He denies this, but it is not clear on what grounds. Thirdly, do his comparisons between animal and human behaviour rest on anything more than dubious analogies? In *On Aggression* he writes of animals practising 'rituals' and 'ceremonies', of geese 'falling in love', of a jackdaw colony as 'an exclusive circle of old friends', of rats being 'models of social virtue'. These are acceptable as metaphors, but, if pressed further, they seem to yield only an anthropomorphism reminiscent of Kipling's *Jungle Books*. Discussing human society, Lorenz appears to link animal behaviour arbitrarily to his own conservatism. He demands that 'we hold sacred the social norms and rites handed down to us by the traditions of our culture'. All of them? Democracy is apparently not such a norm: he describes a leaderless shoal of fish as 'democratic', and as the most primitive form of social organisation.

The Waning of Humaneness (originally *Abbau des Menschlichen*, 1983) is a rambling and repetitive book, much inferior to *On Aggression*. It deplores the destruction of the environment, the irresponsible power of multinational corporations, and young people's disrespect for their elders. To the biologist, Lorenz asserts, it is clear that civilised man is degenerate, just as domestic animals are degenerate by comparison with their wild and noble ancestors. (This sounds like Nietzsche, but the mentors cited here are Spengler and Klages.) Thus, wild greylag geese form monogamous unions after a lengthy courtship ritual, while tame geese have so far lost their inhibitions that 'the human observer cannot help perceiving the frankly open sexual overtures a house goose makes to a partner she hardly knows as something vulgar, something decadent'. Since only one human culture now exists, our degeneracy cannot be counteracted by intra-specific competition. What is to be done? Lorenz recommends close contact between mothers and infants, and encouraging schoolchildren to care for animals. Admirable suggestions, but hardly enough to save the planet.

To find what is missing, we must turn to an article, 'Die angeborenen Formen möglicher Erfahrung' (*Zeitschrift für Tierpsychologie*, 5 [1943], pp. 235–409), written when Lorenz was Professor of Psychology at Königsberg University. In 1973 attention was drawn to this article by Simon Wiesenthal, and Lorenz expressed his regret that some statements in it might have supplied doctrinal assistance to the Nazi regime. It is surprising, therefore, to find that the present book borrows extensively from the more innocuous parts of this unusually personal paper, in which the argument about civilisation, domestication, and degeneracy is fully developed. The innate schemata which govern ethical and aesthetic as well as perceptual judgements are coarsened by civilisation. An elite of 'Vollwertigen' which retains the old norms finds itself isolated amid a majority of inferiors ('Minderwertigen'). Fatalism is unjustified, however, for biology has the answer:

> The phenomenon of domestication appears in man, just as in his domestic animals, and for the same reasons. Since, however, in mankind's case there is no methodical breeder to play Providence, and the consequences of domestication may blindly take their course, all these causes simply *must* have the predictable effect that a cultured people [*Kulturvolk*] perishes soon after reaching the phase of civilization, *unless this development is prevented by a deliberate, scientifically founded racial policy* [Lorenz's emphasis].

Here are the roots of 'biological sociology'. May heaven preserve us from scientists, however distinguished, who want to play Providence.

RITCHIE ROBERTSON

Milo Dor (ed.), *Die Leiche im Keller. Dokumente des Widerstands gegen Dr Kurt Waldheim* (Vienna: Picus Verlag, 1988), 143 pp., DM 19.80.

The discussion about the political process that ultimately made Dr Kurt Waldheim the President of the Republic of Austria in June 1986 has retained its central importance for post-Kreisky Austria to the present day, as regards both the self-identification of modern Austria and the image of Austria in the world. With the condemnation of Waldheim by an international committee of historians and the coming of the fiftieth anniversary of the occupation of Austria in March 1938 by Hitler's armies, a new wave of protest actions by writers, artists, and intellectuals occurred in February–March 1988. Milo Dor, the editor of this anthology, states in his brief Introduction of April 1988 that the book 'generated itself as a multifarious reaction to the attitude of Dr Kurt Waldheim and, primarily, to his . . . statements'. He claims that it neither intends to be a literary anthology nor a complete record but only 'a plain documentation of the resistance against Dr Kurt Waldheim which he triggered off in friend and foe' (p. 5).

The broad spectrum of responses is shown in the format of the book, consisting of over fifty items which, over and above essays, speeches, appeals, and letters arguing for the necessity of Waldheim's resignation, include poems, cabaret songs, and satirical theatre scenes. The booklet is enlivened by ten drawings, some of them evoking the horrors of Nazism (G. Eisler, A. Hrdlicka, A. Frohner) and subliminally linking them with Waldheim's past and the 'forgetfulness' of his present followers. Some grotesque caricatures of the anti-Waldheim campaign are also included (pp. 15, 70, 130). The main line of argument is set by the title of Milo Dor's introductory essay: 'In was für einem Lande leben wir?'('In What Kind of a Country do we Live?' pp. 7–13). It raises the question of the weakness of democratic traditions and the strength of authoritarian attitudes in Austria's past and present. This is further expanded by politically highly conscious writers like P. Turrini (pp. 65–70), E. Fried (pp. 105–8), and G. Nenning (pp. 114–17).

Many of the essays and poems emphasise the ambivalence inherent in a traditional mentality of compromise and the repression of unpleasant memories which have become evident in the handling of the country's past and the persistence of xenophobia and anti-Semitism. Waldheim often emphasised the need for doing one's duty ('Pflichterfüllung') and linked it with a will for survival even at the cost of complicity with acts of inhumanity (pp. 55–7). This position is attacked and satirised by most of the authors; it is brilliantly analysed in G. Roth's article on 'Das doppelköpfige Österreich. Wahrheit ist Lüge, Lüge ist Wahrheit', in which the Waldheim case is seen as a symbol of a paradoxical linking of truth and mendacity in a society still dominated by the heraldic double-headed eagle of the old Austro-Hungarian Empire (pp. 49–54). The Waldheim affair has again opened up the intricate question of the definition of 'patriotism' in Austria interpreted as either 'German' or 'Austrian'. This problem of 'ethnic identification' is seen by G. Sebestyén as more difficult than that of the political self-identification of the country (pp. 121–2). The resulting confusion is parodied by using Waldheim's own words in a 'Mediencollage' by E. Holloway (pp. 45–8) and an unequivocal declaration by the actor F. Muliar of his 'Austrianness' (p. 134).

By adapting Karl Kraus's often quoted phrase of Nazi times to the present situation ('Was mir zu Waldheim einfällt', p. 72; 'Eigentlich fällt mir zu Waldheim nichts ein', p. 79), parallels are drawn by A. Vogel and A. Janetschek between Waldheim and Hitler. It is a recurring motif of the book, however, to identify Waldheim fully with Austria and the Austrians, talking about 'Waldheim in us' (A. Pelinka, pp. 16–18), a 'normal, a true Austrian' (p. 16), a symbol of Austria's Nazi past (G. Botz, p. 23), an 'Austrian symbol' (P. Rosei, p. 51), 'an exact mirror-image of Austria' (G. Nenning, p. 114). Linking Waldheim with the best post-war parodistic satire of the Austrian *petite bourgeoisie*, C. Merz's *Herr Karl* of 1962, K. Kastelliz presents Waldheim in a self-debunking monologue entitled 'Der Herr Dr Kurt' (pp. 38–41). It is fully in keeping with the best traditions of Austrian political writing that in the most successful pieces of this volume social and political criticism fully merge with language criticism; the use of incorrect and confused language is seen as a sign not only of emotional and intellectual muddle but also of political obfuscation and trickery. This is best shown by a textual strategy in which the extensive use of quotation and montage helps to question the speaker's intelligence and integrity in poems by G. Jaschke (pp. 41–4), W. Herbst (pp. 80–2), and P. P. Wiplinger (p. 84), and the juxtaposition of Waldheim's own statements with social reality in W. Pevny's 'Kommentierendes Gedicht' (pp. 97–101).

Although the volume is dominated by the indignation and shame felt by artists and intellectuals about Waldheim's clinging to power, the contributors show some hope that enlightened critical thinking and human decency will ultimately triumph. They emphasise that probably the shock of the Waldheim case will produce such resistance and 'allergy' against the 'Austrian conditions' that it will trigger off a 'learning process' (G. Roth, p. 53). G. Hoffmann-Ostenhof hopes that the President will not only act as a 'great repressive machine' but, though unwittingly, as a tool of enlightenment ('große Aufklärungsmaschine', p. 14). Under the pressure from outside and inside the country, Austrians may learn to 'remember', which, as E. Weinzierl emphasises, is especially important for young people (p. 83). The activation of public opinion through the Waldheim case is seen by B. Frischmuth as an important 'political object lesson' ('politischer Anschauungsunterricht', pp. 85–6). This is the underlying aim of the whole volume, even if contributions appear in the form of a dream vision (Peter Handke, 'Ich hatte einen Traum', pp. 19–20), a whimsical interview with the tower of St Stephen's Cathedral (Michael Scharang, pp. 73–8), or a grotesque Nestroy parody introducing Waldheim as the gruesome South-Sea cannibal chief 'Präsident Abendwind' (E. Jelinek, pp. 109–12).

LESLIE BODI

Part Four
Obituaries

Erich Fried
(1921–1988)

In September 1988, the telephone rang and I heard his deep, Germanic, imperturbable voice. He announced that the doctors had given him about a year, which could be as long as eighteen months but would not be as long as two years. We talked a little; then he gave his blessing and rang off. Erich Fried's time was now limited.

More limited than anyone knew. He had fought and survived every round in the campaign to unseat Kurt Waldheim, and that in a physical state that would have held most people to their beds. Early in November 1988, Erich Fried set off from his north London house for Central Europe, as he had set off dozens of times before, and went to Baden-Baden for a radio interview. There he collapsed, and there, a few days later, he died.

The elegant German phrase to mourn the sacking of a fine city or the death of a great poet was: 'A brilliant light has been put out.' Gerhart Hauptmann used it when Dresden was obliterated. But Erich Fried, the best-known and best-loved poet in the German-speaking world, wasn't a light. He was a sound.

He was a voice in both senses. He was literally a huge voice: a basso which could reach through a hall, pronouncing slowly and almost pedantically, in short, unambiguous words. Erich Fried was a broadcaster for many years, speaking over the BBC as a socialist criticising what passed in East Germany for socialism. Later, he discovered his gift for public performing, a political orator but above all a reader and introducer of his own poetry to mass audiences. And it wasn't simply because Fried wrote so many poems about love that those audiences were usually young. It was because Erich Fried was not only a huge voice, but also a still, small voice.

The post-war generations of Germans and Austrians have been fatherless. Some literally so. Most, though, had living fathers incapable of talking about the past to their children, or capable only in a language so alien and terrifying that even silence was better. These were moral orphans, and I believe that to thousands of young people in those two countries Erich Fried performed the function of a father.

It seemed, at first, a strange piece of transference. What sort of father for the students of Bremen and the sixth-formers of Essen could be provided by this Austrian-Jewish emigrant from Dartmouth Road, Kilburn, with his huge head and thick spectacles and his teasing wit? But it turned out that he was exactly what they needed.

Here was a man with the sort of authority which an 'anti-authoritarian' generation could accept, whose right to condemn the German past was stainless but never abused, whose attacks on Establishments were not protests from below but thunderbolts of reproof thrown down from above. The man who spoke to them was a Leftist, but in the same breath an Old Testament figure for whom there was nothing relative about the difference between right and wrong, decency and vileness. In times when the word was

213

to 'trust nobody over 30', they trusted Fried.

In 1938, when he was 18, almost his last act before leaving Vienna was to bury his father, who died after Gestapo torture. Much later, he wrote a poem about that beautiful and peaceful day in the Jewish cemetery, which had seemed so remote from what was happening on the city's streets. Its last lines, in rough translation, are: 'They beat my father to death for me / So that I might come into the fresh air, and see the spring.'

That's a deeply Viennese pair of lines, its roots in the soil which produced both Fried and Freud. But it can also be read as a parable about those moral orphans for whom the poet became an *Ersatzvater* – a father-substitute. The orphans fancied that only by a sacrifice, by killing and burying all that their real fathers had been, could innocence and spontaneity be won. But Erich Fried knew better. Innocence cannot be regained, by definition, and he warned that without an attempt at imaginative compassion, the past would not rest.

I think the best thing about Erich Fried was that stubborn refusal to pass evil on as if it were some relay-race baton. He had been driven from his own home and, therefore, could never pardon Israel for driving the Palestinians in turn from theirs. His father had been murdered, but he could insist on free speech for a neo-Nazi or write of the hanging of Irma Grese, the SS guard from Belsen, as a wrong and as a human tragedy. That wasn't religion talking: Fried wasn't famous for turning the other cheek. It wasn't even romantic altruism. It was intelligence.

Erich Fried lived for fifty years among the English, who scarcely knew his name. That was a good joke, which he enjoyed. But it was also a pity, because he could have taught the English two things worth learning. One was that intellectual leadership matters. The other was that socialism, as a moral position rather than as a political party, can never be destroyed while the human race remains recognisably human.

In London, we have the view immortalized by the *Sunday Times* that intellectuals are 'erudite moaners' who are 'out of kilter with the aspirations of plain folk'. Unfortunately, opposition intellectuals who call their publications *Samizdat* or even 'Charter 88' play along with that, by miming the weakness of a persecuted fragment. Erich Fried's life, in contrast, shows that intellectuals who take responsibility for society, who go boldly out and use their work as a sermon-text against cruelty and greed, command huge influence. It is from novels, now, that most British young people learn how to live. Yet how many novelists dare to teach the same lessons aloud from a political platform, in the Albert Hall in London, or the Free Trade Hall in Manchester?

As for socialism, it's only a few months ago that Erich Fried, on a BBC programme, said this: 'As long as you have production for profit and not for social necessity, the world will always be again reduced to a shambles.' In that shambles, Stalin as the deformer of socialism was an accomplice. Lately, though, Erich Fried turned towards Mikhail Gorbachov as a redeemer, come at last when hope was almost gone.

Erich Fried's socialism was, in the end, our ancient struggle against stupidity and infamy. I never read Auden's 'Voltaire at Ferney' without thinking of him. This is how it ends:

> So, like a sentinel, he could not sleep. The night was full of wrong,
> Earthquakes and executions. Soon he would be dead,
> And still all over Europe stood the horrible nurses
> Itching to boil their children. Only his verses
> Perhaps could stop them: He must go on working. Overhead
> The uncomplaining stars composed their lucid song.

NEAL ASCHERSON
(reprinted from the *Observer*,
27 November 1988)

Thomas Bernhard
(1931-1989)

There was something peculiarly incongruous about Thomas Bernhard's death. Someone who had for so long been on intimate terms with sickess both physical and metaphysical ought surely to have become immune to the forces which extinguish life. Moreover, in the course of the last ten years Bernhard almost led his readers to believe that in giving full vent to his venom he had found the tonic that allowed him, against all the odds, to keep body and soul together. Increasingly it had become inconceivable that he might one day desert the enemies he had made and cultivated so assiduously. Yet he did take leave and the manner of this leave-taking suggested a degree of premeditation, even of *mise-en-scène*. For Bernhard's final opus, the play *Heldenplatz*, an unreserved indictment of Austria and the Austrians on the occasion of the fiftieth anniversary of the Anschluss, resounds, for those who see or read it now, with distinct echoes of the author's own departure.

Bernhard's breakthrough to his own unmistakable style came in the mid-1960s when, after several epigonal beginnings which harked back to Georg Trakl, he published the prose works *Frost*, *Amras*, and *Verstörung*. The sense of urgency and finality which marked these extraordinarily powerful narratives appeared to be informed by the author's perception that time was running out, that before long all would be undone. The pace Bernhard set himself in those years was maintained over the next two decades, during which he published another ten or so works of fiction, at least a dozen plays, and a four-volume autobiography. It was this autobiographical account of the artist as a child, as an adolescent, and as a young man which revealed that Bernhard's creative energy had to be drawn *ex negativo* from what can only be described as an extremely fraught early life.

Bernhard was born 'illegitimately' in 1931 in Heerlen, Holland and was brought up in his grandparents' house in Upper Bavaria. His father, whom he scarcely knew, died when Bernhard was still a boy. But the crucial blows came in the years 1949–50, which brought the death of Bernhard's grandfather, to whom he was greatly attached, as well as – under the most harrowing circumstances – that of his mother. It was during those same years that Bernhard himself was an inmate of the Lungenheilstätte Grafenhof, a sanatorium for patients suffering from tuberculosis. This was an experience which he remembers as demoralising and debilitating in the extreme. That this kind of *éducation sentimentale* resulted in works truly baroque in their detailed rendering of processes of dissolution is hardly surprising; what is more astonishing is that Bernhard increasingly managed to extract from the apparently unrelieved scenarios of his fictional and dramatic intentions the sort of hilarity which characterises writers of the stature of Cervantes, Swift, Gogol, Kraus, or Beckett. Though some dissenting voices have been heard, there can be little doubt now that Bernhard is one of the most outstanding European writers of the post-war era. His well-nigh monomanic obsession with the Austrian state of affairs is by no means indicative of a parochial mind. A writer of great urbanity, Bernhard, like Karl Kraus, saw Austria as a paradigm: an 'experimental station for the end of the world'.

Though the reception of his works was hesitant to begin with, Bernhard soon established a large and faithful readership which, by virtue of his verbal exploits and the notoriety that surrounded both his works and his person, he had turned into a captive audience. There was a moment a few years ago when it may have seemed as if Bernhard pandered to his public by permitting it, at regular intervals, to share in vicarious fashion his iconoclastic exercises. On the other hand, Bernhard's works, even those of lesser importance, are determined by an uncompromising vigour which keeps those keen to be witnesses of executions decidedly at arm's length. Quite apart from this, Bernhard's last two novels, *Alte Meister* and *Auslöschung*, dispelled any suspicions that this passionate writer had burnt himself out. *Auslöschung*, above all, is a work of great complexity; it is a moralist's tale like most of Bernhard's writings and it is as relentless as it is beautiful.

Thomas Bernhard's stature has long been recognised in countries like Italy, Spain and France, where his death was front-page news. In the English-speaking world he still passes for a stranger, although 'England' for Bernhard was a metaphor that held a special resonance. The most important texts and plays have remained untranslated, and what has been rendered in English (or American) is hardly accessible. It is now time to take note of a uniquely consistent and forceful *oeuvre*, which may well come to be seen as the *summa* and completion of the canon of Austrian literature.

W. G. SEBALD

Austrian Studies

Acknowledgements: The Editors gratefully acknowledge the support of the Austrian Institute in London. Thanks are also due to Otto Zundritsch (Director of the Institute), Bernhard Stillfried (Austrian Ministry of Foreign Affairs) and Martin Spencer (Edinburgh University Press) for their encouragement; and to the colleagues listed below for their willingness to serve on the Advisory Board.

Books for review should be sent to Ritchie Robertson, St John's College, Oxford OX1 3JP, England.

Manuscripts for publication should be submitted in duplicate to Edward Timms, Gonville and Caius College, Cambridge CB2 1TA, England.

Guidelines: Articles should be written in English and should not exceed 7 500 words. They should be typed double-spaced, using endnotes (not a numbered bibliography) to identify the source of quotations. Quotations should normally be given in the original language, followed by an English translation. A detailed style sheet is available from either of the Editors, on request.

Austrian Studies may be ordered through any bookshop. Since it is designed as an annual publication, it may also be obtained by subscription direct from the publishers, Edinburgh University Press, 22 George Square, Edinburgh EH8 9LF, Scotland.